quest for the
HEXHAM HEADS

PAUL SCREETON

Edited by Jonathan Downes
Typeset by Jonathan Downes
Cover and Internal Layout by Jon Downes for CFZ Communications
Using Microsoft Word 2000, Microsoft Publisher 2000, Adobe Photoshop.

First edition published 2010 by CFZ Publications

FORTEAN WORDS
Myrtle Cottage
Woolfardisworthy
Bideford
North Devon
EX39 5QR

ISBN: 978-1-905723-94-2

Human heads have an enduring fascination. Believed to be Celtic, the carved Hexham Heads have cast a spell over all who have come into contact with them. Others have made examples in their image and those held by the author on this book cover are two such. On the left a replica created by the man who claimed to have made them in the 1950s. The other being made just ahead of a boy and his brother unearthing the subjects of this book. Since learning of the Hexham Heads and acquiring these 'archaic' facsimiles, Paul Screeton has spent forty years following what has been a

QUEST FOR THE HEXHAM HEADS

CONTENTS

A break during a re-enactment for the film *Heads!* In the garden of 3 Rede Avenue, Hexham. The motley crew are (left to right), Ethan Hurrell, Stu Ferrol, brothers Matthew and Jamie Rankcom holding specially-crafted replica heads, Olly Lewis and Graham Williamson. (Paul Screeton)

INTRODUCTION

This is a multi-layered mystery which has become a modern-day myth of epic proportions. It is living folklore which in its strong narrative, rich with characterisation, plenty of drama and built around 'Mrs Indiana Jones meets Geordie Carlos Castaneda' – except this is fact, though overlaid with themes from legend. If ever a tale just tells itself, this is it. Consequently, I will be brief here. I was intrigued when the story broke in the Press forty years ago and have since recorded its development into full-blown mythology. I am passionate about the conundrums within the case and have here attempted a forensic examination for the reader (and myself). As a reporter I have tried to remain detached although my personal involvement has made this almost impossible. As a folklorist myself I have committed the cardinal sin in the eyes of purists of becoming personally involved rather than acting purely as a spectator; such action if casual goes by the term reactivity and when it is deliberate it becomes reflexivity. Esoteric terminology aside, it simply amounts to going native.

For my previous dozen or so published books I worked alone, but for this one I gathered around myself – basically through an ad hoc serendipity – a small band of fellow seekers, a true Fellowship of the Quest. First a nascent film-maker and his friend made contact, a Stanley Kubrick & Tony Frewin style duo with its director a Louis Theroux lookalike who speaks like Jon '*Men Who Stare at Goats*' Ronson with his sidekick a cheerful Frodo Baggins for the 21st Century. That's ex-university graduates Graham Williamson and Oliver 'Olly' Lewis. Then came a swaggering, bearded Geordie freelance journalist, *Fortean Times* contributor and part-time actor conveniently living in Hexham and with essential local knowledge. This was Stuart 'Stu' Ferrol. Although the documentary film *Heads!* was a totally separate enterprise from my book, the four of us pooled our resources, with Stu and I both acting as 'talking heads' and providing contributions as interviewers. Also I separately acknowledge the contribution of a great many people without whose assistance this book would be poorer for facts, detail and analysis.

My initial investigation in 1977 led to a number of magazine and newspaper articles and in 1980 a 16-page monograph, *Tales of the Hexham Heads*. Since then the contradictions from early media coverage have multiplied exponentially with confusion caused by garbled retellings in a multitude of scissors 'n' paste articles and books and the internet has allowed the mythical aspects to multiply alarmingly. The saddest part of this farrago has been the reluctance to tackle primary research. To this end and to rectify the paucity of new information and insight, you have in your hands an account by an author/journalist who has spent countless hours interviewing those protagonists still living and delving into aspects however peripheral to bring a rounded and true picture through a meticulous Quest for the Hexham Heads.
Acknowledgements: I wish to express my gratitude to the many people who shared their knowledge,

experiences and scholarship; gave encouragement and were generous with time and hospitality. I have been awed and humbled by the way my cold case inquiry has enthused so many friends and total strangers from all walks of life. In no particular order, I thank: Colin Robson, Nigel Craigie, Richard Charles Feachem, Judith Coldfield, Sylvia Ritson, Brian Dodd, Dr David Clarke (particularly permission to quote from the Anne Ross interview transcript and a draft of his doctoral thesis), Andy Roberts, John Billingsley, Dr Lindsay Allason-Jones, Roger Miket, Professor Frank Hodson, Dr Bob Curran, Dave Taylor, Dr Simon Crook, Elizabeth Smith, Keith Hardiman, Steve 'Pagan' Jones, Nick Redfern, Dr Steven Cartwright, Kathy Stranks, Dr Jill Eyers, Paul Devereux, Bob Trubshaw, Jon Downes, Dr Peter MCue, Bill Porter, Mike Amos, Myles Hodnett, Peter Moth, Jez Gale, Sonia Smith, Judi Alston, Lawrence May, Derick Tiffin, Colin Dallison, Mark Newton, Carla Rowley, Sonia Welsh, Austin Winstanley, Cliff Eels, Keith Alexander, John Whitfield, Mark Payne, Norman Darwen, David Puglia (US), Robert Schnek (US), Ken Ramos (US), Taras Young, Nick Higham, Sturart McHardy, Dr Oliver Douglas, Betty Gibson,

Style: When you see 'H' capitalised in 'Hexham Heads' and 'Heads' this indicates the original artefacts found in Rede Avenue, Hexham. Note I use no apostrophe with either at any time; an object can't logically be possessive. Another grammatical point which may be deemed controversial is the lower case for 'fortean': following *Fortean Times* founder Bob Rickard's dictum that it denotes a generic description of a philosophy rather than one man's singular beliefs. Double quotation marks denote persons speaking; single, reported speech or quoted material.

Copyright: While every effort has been made to ascertain copyright permission in either text or photographic images, should anyone feel their rights may have been infringed, the author and publisher apologise in advance and promise to rectify any such transgression in future editions of this work.

The (*New*) Dave Clarke Five:
(left to right), Graham Williamson, Paul Screeton, Dr David Clarke,
Stu Ferrol and Olly Lewis.

PART ONE

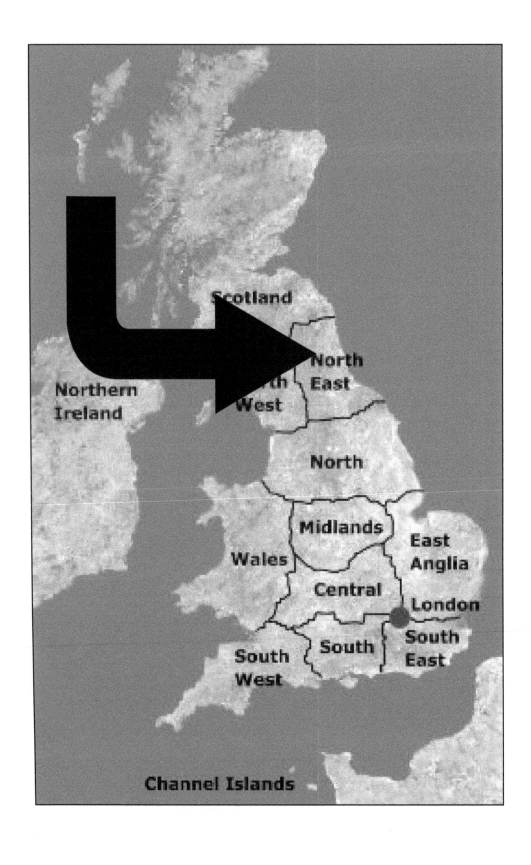

Scotland

North East

Northern Ireland

North West

North

Midlands

East Anglia

Wales

Central

London

South

South East

South West

Channel Islands

CHAPTER ONE
The Finders

One hot morning in the summer of 1977 I was alone, rooting about in a stranger's garden in Northumberland, when I was confronted by the householder's sons. I don't know who was most surprised. Certainly, I was initially embarrassed. Of course, there was a vague method in this seeming madness. I don't know what I was expecting to find, but the two lads surprising this intruder was not what I expected. I had at least knocked at the door and got no reply, but I did have some explaining to do. And justify myself I did, satisfactorily. Also my purpose in the first part of this book is to also explain how these boys' role set in motion a sequence of events which have reverberated for decades and have yet to reach finality.

The boys who found a stranger on a stranger's land on 6 July 1977 were Colin Robson, then aged 17, and his brother Leslie, aged 14. Their place as minor yet pivotal players in this procession of the damned had been assured five or six years previously (versions differ) when they discovered two archaic stone artefacts at the exact spot where I had been poking around. These were what became known as the Hexham Heads, whose history, controversy and ramifications have echoed throughout popular culture and myth ever since. Humble objects, nondescript site, unremarkable finders who had a brief 15 minutes in the spotlight of media attention until macabre events engulfed the whole saga and pushed their role to the sidelines of fortean history. Well, here's another few seconds in the metaphorical Warholian spotlight for the Robson siblings.

The encounter had been sheer luck as my prime purpose for being in Hexham that day was to catch a bus to nearby Wall to meet a famous exorcist in the nearby hamlet of Wall (see Chapter Thirteen). Even the name Hexham is redolent of magic, mystery, danger, cursing in the old-fashioned sense of putting a hex on someone or some object. That name had gone through many changes since being known as Hagustaldes Ham in Saxon times. With a few hours to kill and having read about the Hexham Heads mystery, firstly in *The Journal* of 3 March 1972, and collected a slim file of cuttings on the topic, it seemed too good an opportunity to miss to find out more. I had been intrigued by what I had read and being a long-time fortean with journalistic skills, I thought I would see if I could find out more and iron out the hobgoblins of inconsistency I had spotted which bedevilled media accounts. This conundrum required probing by a phenomenologist who had the time and the patience to do the inquiry justice. Employed as a sub-editor at that stage, it recalled my days as a hack when the chief reporter would - as his morning's first duty - allocate each of us our allotted tasks for the day, often amounting to half-a-dozen assignments to be completed, which meant there was often not the time to get more than a broad but superficial outline of a story before the accompanying photographer took his snap and it was off to do the next job on the list. Under no such restraint from Father Time or news desk that day, I could take it easy as I would have plenty of time to speak to anyone I met concerned with the saga, and in this instance that included chatting to the Robson boys and winning their confidence after so embarrassing and suspicious an initial encounter. We had a genial, mature conversation where I took notes as it was at the back of my mind to write about the Hexham Heads, either for *Fortean Times* or *The Ley Hunter* magazines, so I wanted to be thorough and elicit what details I could, particularly as the mystery was already tainted by discrepancies. I was also aware through journalistic experience that interviewees can be mistaken in what they say, either involuntarily or deliberately; memory plays tricks and some people are given to fabrication or sheer falsehood. Whatever, in all my writings I have endeavoured to signify where I feel there may be false memory, obfuscation or downright deceit and the information I impart here, from works of reference, contacts or witnesses, is to the best of my knowledge and ability as near the truth as possible.

As for the discovery site, Rede Avenue is one of a number of streets of council or former council houses on an estate high above the market place to the south-east and on land sloping less steeply to the west. That unexceptional garden was at No. 3, a semi-detached house having a solid, brick-built, nondescript standard appearance which for its sheer utilitarian purpose would win no architectural awards. Nor would the state of the garden win it any prizes in 1971 or 1972, when Colin was reported to be 11

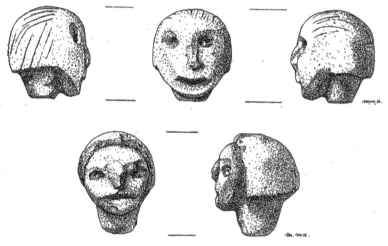

Fig. 5. Stone heads from Hexham

Line drawings of the Hexham Heads by Mary Hurrell, then Archaeological Illustrator for the Museum of Antiquities, from magazine Archaeolgia Aeliana, 5th Series, Volume 1 MCMLXXIII. (Reproduced by kind permission)

and his brother Leslie nine. From what the brothers told me, at the time of the discovery their family had only been residents for two weeks, which might explain Colin's effort at clearing weeds and finding the first Head on the surface. Yet the period of tenancy and whether the Heads were on or near the surface or buried far deeper are all aspects which have proved contentious.

While Colin went about the tidying, Leslie watched distractedly from an upstairs bedroom window.

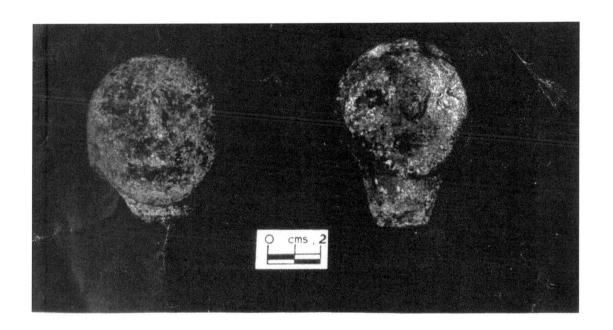

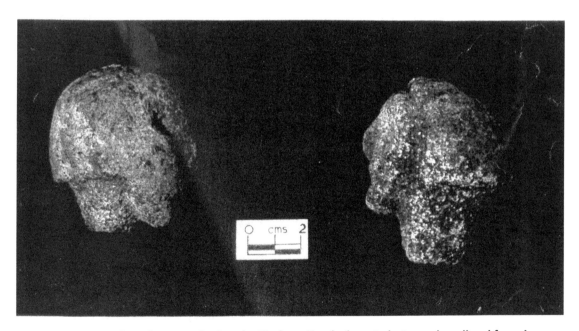

Many comments have been made that the Hexham Heads do not photograph well and few pictures of them exist. This comparison of the two – facing and sideways – is of unknown provenance.

Colin picked what appeared to be a lump of stone about the size of a tennis ball but with a conical protrusion. Clearing the soil from the object, he found that it was crudely carved with human features and the conical part was a tapered neck. Excited by the find, Colin called to Leslie and he joined him. He, too, found a similar artefact. They were heading for brief celebrity.

The carvings, which became known in the media as the Hexham Heads, had subtle differences. One was described as having a skull-like face and was pronounced to be masculine by all who saw or examined it, leading to its becoming known as the 'boy'. Greenish-grey in colour and glistening with crystals of quartz, it was said to be uncommonly heavy. It appeared to have hair modelled in stripes, running from front to back. The other head – the 'girl' or 'hag' – was claimed to resemble a popular expectation of a witch, with wildly-bulging eyes and hair that was combed backwards off the forehead in what was almost a bun. There appeared to still be remaining traces of a yellow or red pigment in her hair.

"I don't fancy yours..."

Having never seen, touched nor examined the original Hexham Heads (yes, as I will explain as we go along, there are and have been more), I am relying on others' descriptions of the pair. One of those in a long line of 'custodians' is Dr Don Robins, a materials chemist, who will feature prominently later in this account and had borrowed the Heads for analysis, but let him describe the artefacts:

> "When cleaned, both heads were seen to be about the size of a small tangerine. Both were very dense and heavy, but each had a very distinct appearance. The first head had a vaguely skull-like appearance with the carved lines and pits of features only faint and vestigial. Nevertheless, its features were vaguely masculine, if gaunt and bony, and were crowned by a typically Celtic hairstyle with faint stripes running from front to back on the crown. The carved stone itself was greenish grey and glistened with quartz crystals. The second head was more rounded and infinitely more expressive. The features were those of a formidable old wall-eyed woman with a strong beaked nose with hair combed severely backwards off the forehead into a bun. Unlike the skull-head the old woman, or hag, showed traces of red or yellow pigment on the hair'. [1]

Meanwhile, earlier back in Hexham, the Heads took pride of place inside the Robsons' new home. The family of seven comprised the two aforementioned sons, Colin and Leslie, an elder brother Philip, sisters Judith and Wendy, then aged 18 and 23 respectively, and parents Jenny and Albert, the father being known locally by the nickname 'Lugs'. At the time of the discovery, Wendy was on honeymoon – this being the last week in May and first in June 1971 - and Philip may have also left home. Naturally, the find was something of a local talking point and according to reports the curios were shown to various friends and neighbours, many of whom must have handled them.

Inspired from another dimension?

It has been said that great historical events cast their shadow before them and in this instance it's certainly true. Perhaps, like ripples when a stone is thrown in a pool, its waves go on forever. Whatever, at the critical point Colin Robson was aged 11 and a pupil at junior school. It was there he made a plaster of Paris head in class roughly similar to those which were subsequently to reappear in Rede Avenue. On my visit in 1977, Colin told me:

> "It was for a competition. I'd never made anything like it before. The master said it was ugly and commented that it should have had a proper neck".

THE JOURNAL Friday March 3 1972

Eerie tale of the two idol heads

By Journal Reporter

SOMETHING that happened 1,800 years ago may force a mother of six to quit her council house.

The Hexham mother says she is terrified of staying there after an eerie night time experience which followed the discovery of two stone heads in her next door neighbour's back garden.

The heads were probably used for worship by a Celtic tribe 1,800 years ago.

Yesterday one of the country's top Celtic experts, Dr. Ann Ross, said the claim by 42-year-old Mrs. Ellen Dodd that she saw a half-human, half - sheep - like figure which touched her as she lay in bed, could not be ruled out.

Dr. Ross, a Celtic linguist and archaeologist, is to see Mrs. Dodd and the boys who found the heads, Colin Robson, aged 11, and his brother, Leslie, aged eight, at their homes in Rede Avenue, Hexham, in May.

Dr. Ross is waiting for a report on the heads by geologists at Southampton University. She said she would be unable to give a final opinion until she gets the report and has made her on-the-spot investigation.

It was more than likely that the heads, two-and-a-half inches high, were

Family fear another night of terror

made by Celtic tribesmen whose main cult was to worship heads as gods. Quite often they worshipped human heads taken from their enemies.

Dr. Ross said she would have to examine the site, near a privet hedge, where the heads were found before she could determine whether the

Robsons' garden and house are over a shrine or burial ground.

Shrines

On Mrs. Dodds' claim, she said: "There is no doubt that if there was a Celtic shrine there — and this has yet to be proved — one would not be

surprised to hear of a supernatural manifestation. There are other examples of this on the Continent and in Britain where shrines have been found and where there have been hauntings."

Mrs. Dodd said: "I have asked the council for a move because I am too nervous to stay here now.

"I had gone into the children's bedroom to sleep with one of them who was unwell and my 10-year-old son, Brian, kept telling me that he felt something touching him. I told him not to be silly.

"Then I saw this shape. It came towards me and I

definitely felt it touch me on the legs. Then, on all fours, it moved out of the room. I was absolutely terrified and screamed for my husband."

The boys' mother, Mrs. Jenny Robson, said: "The unusual thing about this is that before the heads were found Colin made a clay head at school.

"It is remarkable in its likeness to the heads found in the garden. Colin said the idea of making this head just came to him."

Mrs. Robson added that neither she or her family had experienced anything similar to what had happened to Mrs. Dodd.

LESLIE, aged eight, and Colin Robson, aged 11, with the model Colin made before the Celtic heads were dug up.

How the story broke in the media. First off the mark was Newcastle-based regional paper *The Journal* **on 3 March 1972.**

This may not be without significance as 'typical' Celtic heads have a tenon neck to hold them in place as guardians or trophies. Colin's mother had told a reporter:

> "The unusual thing about this is that before the heads were found Colin made a clay head at school. It is remarkable in its likeness to the heads found in the garden. Colin said the idea of making the head just came to him." [2]

In other words, it just came into his head!?

Sister paper on Tyneside, *The Evening Chronicle*, reported it, too, with a picture of Colin proudly holding his handiwork with the erroneous claim that it was he who found both the Hexham Heads. [3]

While telling me about this piece of crude craftsmanship, Colin volunteered to give me his handiwork. I was, to say the least, flabbergasted. Oh, lucky man!

He went into the house and brought his artwork outside. I gratefully accepted this unexpected bonus. I would have asked to see it, but never have expected to own it. I was most grateful, though I recall that my hand trembled immediately upon touching it. Well, certainly it's not a pretty sight. In fact, it is downright repulsive-looking, almost scary. Painted black, brown, red and blue, and with two broken fangs, it was, however, judge second best in the school competition. So thanks again Colin.

Rescue team finds boy

A BOY, aged four, missing for 14 hours in lonely countryside, was found fit and well early today crouching among bramble bushes.

Paul Patchett, of Cowley, Middlesex, was found by the RAF rescue team from St. Athan, Glamorgan, two miles from the spot where he disappeared.

He vanished shortly after arriving at a farmhouse at Llansawel, used by Mr. and Mrs. Gordon Porter, of Hayes, Middlesex, as a holiday home for their six children and 14 foster children.

He walked away from other children while playing and said he was going home.

A full-scale police search was launched, with villagers taking part.

It was only when the wind dropped that searchers heard Paul shouting for help.

A spokesman for the RAF said the rescue team had called off the hunt at one o'clock this morning with the intention of resuming at first light. But as they settled down in their sleeping bags the wind dropped, and one of them heard a faint cry.

Children die after blaze

Two children died and a third is seriously ill in hospital after a fire in a Birmingham house today.

Their parents, Mr. Arno Robert West, and his wife Brenda, both aged 25, awoke to find their house in Kings Heath full of smoke.

Firemen brought out the couple's three children, who had been sleeping in another bedroom. They were taken to hospital.

But Richard, aged five, and his 18-month-old sister, Sarah, both died, apparently from the effects of smoke. Their three-year-old brother, Wayne, was detained at the hospital.

Talks fixed on diving problem

Terror from the Celtic mists . . .

ONE of Britain's top Celtic experts is to excavate in a Hexham back garden.

She believes it is possible that a mother of six who is terrified of staying in her council house there, is experiencing supernatural manifestations because it is on the site of an old Celtic shrine or burial ground.

Dr. Ann Ross, a Celtic linguist and archaeologist, has identified two stone heads dug up from a garden in Rede Avenue, Hexham, as probably idols which the Celts worshipped there some 1,800 years ago. Quite often they worshipped human heads taken from their enemies," she says.

She is interested in the experiences of Mrs. Ellen Dodds, of Rede Avenue, and says that the supernatural cannot be ruled out. Mrs. Dodds has reported a "half-human, half sheeplike" figure which touched her on the legs as she lay in bed with her 10-year-old son Brian, who was ill.

"It moved out of the room on all fours. I was absolutely terrified and screamed out for my husband," she says. The family have now asked the council for a move.

Another strange aspect of the case is that 11-year-old Colin Robson (pictured) who dug up the heads in his garden, had previously made a clay head at school which bore an uncanny likeness to the two-and-a-half-inch stone carvings.

Dr. Ross, who plans to see the Dodds and Robson families in May, says: "There is no doubt that if there was a Celtic shrine there—and this has yet to be proved—one would not be surprised to hear of a supernatural manifestation.

"There are other examples of this on the Continent, and in Britain where shrines have been found and where there have been hauntings."

Judge orders Ali's arrest

A JUDGE has ordered the arrest of former world heavyweight boxing champion Muhammad Ali (Cassius Clay).

The warrant arises from Ali's problems over a financial settlement awarded to his first wife, Sonji.

She has asked for a court order in Chicago requiring him to place £16,920 on deposit in a Chicago bank as surety for alimony payments. She obtained a divorce from the boxer in 1966.

Ali was held in contempt of court three weeks ago for failing to appear for a hearing on his ex-wife's claim. The court wanted to know why he had not deposited the surety for his £470 a month alimony payments.

Judge Norman Eiger, issuing the arrest order, said: "I'm not going to send him to jail without a full hearing.

"I'm just asking the sheriff to bring him into court to explain why he has not complied with this court's order."

The arrest warrant cannot be served outside Illinois. Ali now lives in New Jersey and his lawyer said last night that he did not know Ali's present whereabouts.

Dame Irene raps police re-shuffle

HOME OFFICE plans to reorganise Northumberland's police force were attacked in the Commons by Dame Irene Ward.

"I hope they will be defeated," declared the Tory M.P. for Tynemouth, in demand for a debate on the proposals.

Northumberland's Chief Constable has described the plan as "impractical", she told the Government.

Mr. William Whitelaw, Leader of the Commons, and Tory M.P. for Penrith and the Border, promised to call the Home Secretary's attention to Dame Irene's protest.

But he added that he could not find time for a debate on the issue.

Colin proudly displays his handiwork in the *Evening Chronicle,* 3 March 1972

Not a pretty sight! Up close: Colin's handiwork forty years on. (Paul Screeton)

But there has been one sour note with regard to Colin's craftsmanship which has frankly irked me as it suggests I behaved dishonourably. Colin's mother was phoned by TV production company researcher Sadie Holland in 1994 and I was made privy to her notes and they are scattered liberally at relevant points throughout this narrative where applicable. Littered with minor errors, they have nevertheless proved a goldmine of information. How I obtained them is irrelevant (not from Sadie herself), but seeing as I, too, co-operated with Sadie way back then and the documentary on 'cursed heads' never seems to have materialised, I have felt unconstrained to use this treasure trove, discrepancies and tittle-tattle freely. In her defence, Ms Holland was introduced into a bizarre subject and immersed herself to the point of contagion and awe. The girl done good!

I was, however, a little miffed to have Jenny Robson cast a slur upon my character (taking regard one should not speak ill of the dead). This is what Sadie reported:

> "One day when she was out, Paul Screeton came and took away the head which Colin had made. He said he would bring it back and bring them a copy of his book, but he never did".

Jenny then went on to fire the other barrel at fellow journalist Peter Moth, who worked for Tyne Tees Television, whom she blamed for taking the Heads away and not fulfilling a promise to return them. Colin handed me his head without restrictions, nor do I recall at that stage having maybe anything more than the vaguest notion of a possible booklet.

Things that go crash in the night

The first inkling that the Hexham Heads were anything more than harmless curiosities, but harboured innate malevolence, came with a steady series of strange happenings within 3 Rede Avenue. This I had read about in newspaper reports in Tyneside newspapers delivered to my place of work, the *Hartlepool Mail*, where regional papers were scoured for stories which might pertain to our neck of the woods. Once the newshounds had scanned them, in quiet moments I would clip offbeat titbits for my friend Bob Rickard's *Fortean Times*, while certain selected items would be squirreled away in my vast but disorganised filing system for future possible use. Hence I had amassed a small collection of clippings featuring the Hexham Heads. Thus I knew that in the aftermath of the Heads discovery there had been strange goings on at No. 3 (and an even more dramatic event next door, but that's for the next chapter. Just to whet your appetite, dear reader, it involved a manimal, a chimera, in fact, a were-sheep!). From notes I took 35 years ago, the Robson boys confirmed the basic sequence of events reported in the media.

The Robson family certainly found the events which occurred on a scale of mildly odd and mischievous to downright dangerous and traumatic. The Hexham Heads had been brought inside the house and wherever it was they were being displayed it was claimed they would turn themselves of their own volition to face towards the place of their discovery and original resting place. Press reports at the time in 1972, also reported that a whiplash sound had been heard behind the television set and a mirror was found shattered in a frying pan; glass was also found shattered across a mattress. The boys told me the poltergeist, or whatever, was most active around 2.30 in the night. Those pesky Hexham Heads were certainly proving a troublesome duo and catalyst to bizarre happenings.

The nonogenarian guide's tale

So, for an information busting appeal who do you turn to? – the *Hexham Courant*. Weeklies serving rural communities have solid bases with loyal readers, covering the sort of trivia I reported on as a junior reporter on the *Billingham and Stockton Express* on Teesside. In this case, the *Courant* serves Tynedale and operates as a secular parish magazine writ large. I'd already dealt with the editor of its sister quarterly glossy magazine *Tynedale Life*, Myles Hodnett, so I had high hopes for a good response for my appeal in 2011 for additional information on the matter of the Hexham Heads. I was not disappointed. I received three phone calls and one email (the ratio being a giveaway that new technology has not yet caught on in rural Northumberland).

One of these three telephone callers was a chatty lady, Betty Gibson, who, when she called on 11 March 2011 was aged 94. Like me she was born in Hartlepool, living initially in Thornhill Gardens and then at Ainderby Lodge, The Green, Seaton Carew, before moving to Middlesbrough. Her husband died in 2002 and when I spoke to her she was living in an annexe of her daughter's home in Hexham. Her connection with this story relates to her having served as a guide at Hexham Abbey for 30 years. She became custodian of the Hexham Heads in a long and convoluted succession of people to briefly be guardians of these objects before they finally disappeared into that fortean Bermuda triangle of damned artefacts. She recalled that in the early 1970s two children – she was under the misapprehension, until I explained the circumstances, that they had been girls – had taken them to Hexham Abbey for advice on what they were and what to do with them. This was obviously Colin and Leslie Robson, but let Betty be the narrator:

> "They said they had dug them up and didn't know what to do with them. They gave them to the verger and he gave them to me as I was an archaeology student. I was studying at night classes in a small group tutored by Professor Richard Bailey. He said they were Anglo-Saxon. (I queried this and Betty said she was probably mistaken and that he more likely said they were Celtic). "I had them in my home for a week or two before passing them on to Professor Bailey. I put them on top of the dresser."

In response to the obvious query as to any possible paranormal activity in the home, Betty simply assured me:

> "There was no disturbance in my house from them. They were sent to Southampton University and I haven't heard anything more. I don't know why you're so interested in them". {END INDENT}

Well, to get to the truth, ma'am, the whole truth.

Nationwide exposure for the Heads

Folllowing their discovery in 1971 and regional press interest in the Hexham Heads in 1972, also when the artefacts had migrated to Hampshire, where a manimal distressed their custodians (see Chapter Three), the Hexham Heads featured in a 1973 folklore compendium and in 1974 more Tyneside newspaper columns. However, in 1976, the story burst out of sleepy Hexham and burned its image into national consciousness via a popular television news magazine. The more lurid aspect of a werewolf attributed to the Hexham Heads presence is examined in detail later in this work, but here I'm recording how Jenny Robson found herself the focus of attention for the several million viewers tuned in to the BBC's flagship evening current affairs programme *Nationwide* on 20 February 1976.

The show's reporter in this instance was the inestimable Luke Casey, who provided a sensational purple introduction. But what would you expect from a Celtic expatriate living in a London hotel, but whose home was on the outskirts of Stockon-on-Tees? As a junior reporter with the *Stockton and Billingham*

Express on Teesside, I was a contemporary of Luke's when he was a journalist with the regional *Northern Echo*, working from the Stockton branch office, but whose potential, flair and charisma were already obvious. We shared many drinking sessions together, most memorably a lock-in during Sedgefield Ball Game (it has been suggested there was a connection to the Celtic head cult) after which he propped me up against a bus stop in Stockton High Street and told me to catch the next bus, which I duly did and awoke in the garage at Hartlepool bus station. But to the point … Ignoring the fact that the Hexham events had happened five years previously and the 'house' was, in fact, two adjoining semis, Luke Casey was filmed outside 1 and 3 Rede Avenue telling viewers:

This is what Luke Casey was referring to. 'Unmagical' maybe, but few houses can tell tales as extraordinary as the happenings at Nos. 1 (right in picture) & 3 Rede Avenue, Hexham. (Paul Screeton)

"Well, just recently something very strange happened in this most unmagical-looking council house, at Hexham, Northumberland. Two stone heads were dug up in the garden, in what may very well have been an ancient Celtic shrine. Understandably they caused a bit of curiosity, and Mrs Jenny Robson showed them to people around the estate, including the lady next door".

But to go off on a pertinent tangent, the programme then featured Jenny Robson talking about what happened next door and then moved to Dr Anne Ross. Of course, I will return to the *Nationwide* highlights subsequently, but Mrs Robson's contribution had not gone unnoticed …

The author's tale

Following the *Nationwide* broadcast, author Nerys Dee contacted Jenny Robson for comments to use in an article on the Celtic head cult which was published in the popular astrological magazine *Prediction*. In the piece, Jenny recalled:

> "My two sons found these in our garden in Hexham in 1971 and from that moment we had some very odd happenings in our home. Mirrors and pictures jumped off the walls and a pelmet which was screwed to the wall fell down. Even stranger, doors that were locked at night were found to be open in the morning. My next door neighbour also had disturbances and one night she was aroused by one of her children, so she went to sleep with the child. But she wasn't asleep when the 'thing' came into the room. This she described as half-man half-beast. Her screams even woke my family next door! " [4]

Curiously, Nerys Dee twice referred to Jenny mistakenly as 'Mrs Robsay', but we shall meet Ms Dee again shortly …

The researcher's tale

In 1994, I along with several others connected to the Hexham Heads saga were contacted for information and an opportunity to appear in a televised documentary on the subject of cursed stones. The proposed film was to be made by Granite Productions, an outfit whose figurehead was writer, journalist and film-maker Simon Welfare, perhaps best known for his work on *Arthur C Clarke's Mysterious World*. It seems that after initial inquiries nothing came of the project, but I have been privy to notes made by a researcher, Sadie Holland, whose probing is spread across several chapters. Jenny Robson certainly captivated Ms Holland:

> 'Mrs Robson is an amazing woman. I asked her one question about the heads and she must have talked non-stop for twenty minutes. She has a terrific west Geordie accent and had the most lovely turn of phrase. I thought she was fantastic. This is her story: in about 1970, it was the summer holidays and her boys Colin, aged about ten, and Les, nine, were fed up and fighting in the garden where there was some sandy soil, and he came back with a head made of stone. Les then had a tantrum and said he wanted one, so she gave him a plastic spade and he went and dug one up in the garden himself. They are horrible things. Really gruesome but made with real care. They were told to take them to the abbey to ask the priests there what they thought they were'.

And so, obediently, they did so and that's how they passed to a verger, to guide Betty Gibson and on to Professor Bailey. Pass the parcel without music, chairs nor a prize at the end.

The glossy magazine editor's tale

As alluded to earlier, I had been in touch with Myles Hodnett, editor of *Tynedale Life*, a glossy quarterly publication given away with the *Hexham Courant*. He also carried out a retrospective investigation and Myles helpfully emailed me the text of two articles he wrote on the subject in hand. The first piece made the point few facts had been established and I suspect journalistic licence on his behalf

HIS tale of ripe eerieness emerged from Hexham 36 years ago, raising a whole coven of paranormal experts who swooped in to investigate. From the Fortean Times to Bizarre Magazine and the TV reporters of Nationwide, they all lapped up the eyewitness accounts from Hexham residents who had come into contact with the Heads.

It is one of the few agreed facts that the two roughly round carvings were unearthed by 11-year-old Colin Robson and his brother in February 1972. But whether the boys found them while weeding the garden at home in Rede Avenue, Hexham, or while playing near Hadrian's Wall, the jury is still out.
Having dug up these trophies, described as both about the size of a tangerine or tennis ball, they showed them to their mother, Jenny Robson.

Here the story diverges again. Some say Jenny's neighbour Ellen Dodd was first to see the spirit of the Heads, others assert it was Nelly Graham. But the evidence from both Nelly and Ellen was remarkably similar. Both were sitting up late with a poorly child when a strange creature entered the bedroom.

"It had a body like a sheep and the head of a dark haired man, and stood upright like a man," said Nelly.

"It was a half-man, half-beast. It went padding down the stairs as if on its hind legs," said Ellen.

The Robsons soon had their own share in the spookiness. Glass smashed down on to a bed. Shadowy, shaggy figures were seen about the house. And those little, grinning Heads took to moving about by themselves...

The Robsons had no truck with rational explanations. They knew they were being haunted by the Heads. They handed the wicked little jujus over to a museum, and moved house.

The next to feel the power of the Hexham Heads was a prime "reliable witness", the celebrated archaeologist and author Dr Anne Ross.

Dr Ross was one of England's leading experts on the Celts and their Head cult. If anyone could get to the bottom of the Hexham Heads it was Dr Ross. But those little Heads from Hexham soon got the better of the boffin.

Dr Ross had taken the mystery carvings home to study them more closely. In the small hours she awoke feeling a surge of cold dread. In the doorway stood a figure – taller than her husband Richard – with a wild mane of hair and what looked like a lupine snout. The doctor rose and followed the figure into the corridor, but it disappeared. She woke her husband and they searched the house but found nothing. They agreed to keep the matter quiet, but the wolfman reared his head again a few days later.
This time Dr Ross's teenage daughter Berenice had seen the figure, leaping over the banisters and landing with a thud of its heavy, padded paws.

A few inquiries soon revealed that the discoverers of the Hexham Heads had experienced similar hauntings. Dr Ross packed the two little crania off to the British Museum where they were put on public display. But their fame was brief, owing to reports of "eerie occurrences". No-one knows where the Hexham Heads are now.
The final bizarre twist of the tale was the evidence from Desmond Craigie who had lived at the house in Rede Avenue, Hexham before the Robson family. "Celtic heads? Rubbish!" said Desmond. "I used to work in a concrete ornaments factory and I made the heads as toys for my kids, in about 1956!"

Wow, clincher? But contemporary descriptions of the Heads say they were "weighty, grey-green and glistening with quartz crystals," not cement. One head was gaunt, crowned with a Celtic hairstyle of backward stripes. The other looked female – hair in a bun, beaky nose, squint eyes, and traces of red or yellow pigment. And is it likely a couple of concrete balls could have fooled the country's top archaeologists?

Maybe one day the Heads will be re-discovered, in an unlabelled box at the back of the umpteenth shelf in megavault 666 of the National Archive? Then the truth about Hexham's wolfman may at last be revealed?

hardly helps later researchers such as myself. Take this proposition:

> 'It is one of the few agreed facts that the two roughly round carvings were unearthed by 11-year-old Colin Robson and his brother in February 1972.' [5]

Actually, I suspect Myles found that in my 1980 booklet (Hexham library has a copy) and I believe I have misled researchers since and that they were certainly discovered end of May / early June 1971. This critical fact is 'enshrined' in a message-board posting to the Fortean Times readers' forum by Wendy Davison:

> 'I'd just like to clarify a few points regarding the Hexham Heads. I am one of the daughters of the Robson family and it was my two younger brothers who unearthed the heads. They actually discovered them in late May/early June of 1971. I know this as factual as I was on my honeymoon in Scotland when the boys found them and took them to Hexham Abbey to see if the priest could identify them. Initially they were thought to be Roman and ended up at the Newcastle Museum of Antiquities. It was early 1972 when we were paid a visit from someone from the museum but I can't recall his name. We were told then that they were assumed to be of Celtic origin from about 200BC and that the human head had been worshipped by the Celts and that they would place decapitated heads brought back from battles and place them on posts around the settlement as protection. They apparently also carved heads from stone and placed them on pillars in their temples. The half man half wolf apparition had been reported from other Celtic sites and according to the guy from the museum there apparently was a site in Germany where the locals would not go near because of similar sightings'. [6]

As for *Tynedale Life*, the account continued:

> 'But whether the boys found them while weeding the garden at home in Rede Avenue, Hexham, or while playing near Hadrian's Wall, the jury is still out.'

This is just plain silly, surely? Also, discussing disturbances in the Robsons' house, Myles refers to 'shadowy, shaggy figures were seen about the house'! Maybe in his imagination, but these scenes have no corroborative evidence. Also 'the Robson family handed the wicked little jujus over to a museum, and moved house'. African juju! Yes, they did go to a museum. But it was the Dodds next door who asked for resettlement. Members of the Robson family contacted Myles after reading the article in the autumn 2008 issue of *Tynedale Life*, giving the journalist an opportunity to indulge in more lurid speculation.

He noted that it's a mystery that has never been resolved and observed that it 'could have come from a book of ghost stories by M R James'.

Stirred by the resurrection of the Hexham Heads story, Jenny Robson and children Colin and Judith were in 2008 all living separately near Hexham in the village of Ovington and agreed to recount their

OPPOSITE PAGE: In 2008, *Tynedale Life* editor Myles Hodnett reprised the events which put Hexham on the mysteries map. (Reproduced with permission of *Hexham Courant*)

experiences. Myles reported:

> 'Jenny, now 82, remembers the day as if it were yesterday. She said there was a patch of ground in her garden at Rede Avenue where nothing ever grew. And it was there that he son Colin began digging, on that fateful day 36 years [it was in 1971] ago. About two and a half feet down, he unearthed an object with carvings on it. It was a stone head. Further digging by his younger brother Les produced the second head. "One was a man and one was a woman and they had this yellow stuff in their eyes," said Jenny. "The eyes were really menacing." Later research revealed that the eyes were made from a type of quartz not usually found in this country. We took them round to our next door neighbour, Nellie Dodd, and then to the Abbey and they thought they might be Roman corbels," said Jenny. The Abbey then sent them to the Museum of Antiquities in Newcastle to see if they could shed any light on them'.

What is most significant about this account is the depth at which the Hexham Heads were found. Colin Robson had told me they were on the surface. As for the yellow quartz eyes and the suggestion of foreign material, I have a whole chapter on the disputed analyses of the Heads constitution. As for the abbey reference, it suggests the mother accompanied the boys. Roman corbels sounds a wild guess, but whatever, the Hexham Heads did travel to Newcastle for examination.

One of the perennial problems for all fortean investigators is chronology problems, either from faulty memory, sloppy reporting by media or deliberate falsification. Also time lapsing since an event can warp any true chronology. With that in mind, Myles also recorded that:

> 'Three days later though, there was a knock at Jenny's door and standing there with the two heads was a professor from the Museum of Antiquities. They were Celtic, he explained, not Roman and when Jenny mentioned the incident next door (see next chapter), he produced a book showing a creature from Celtic mythology which perfectly matched the description. And once the heads were back in Jenny's house strange things started to happen'.

So, three days? Another version has the Heads passing from a verger to a guide and on to an archaeologist. Three days seems a ridiculously short time, was the 'professor' Richard Bailey and how could a petrological analysis be done in so short a time? As I keep mentioning, chronology here is wayward. Anyway, the account in *Tynedale Life* continued:

> '[Jenny] placed them on a shelf facing the room [?], high up where her children couldn't reach them. The next morning, the heads had moved and were facing towards the spot in the garden where they were found.'

Daughter Wendy, in her account to the *Fortean Times* forum, elaborated:

> 'When the heads were in the possession of my family we placed them on a shelf and every morning we noticed that they had moved position to face the spot where they had been found. To ensure no one had tampered with them through the night I decided I would place them under my bed where no one could access them, but the next morning they had moved from the top right of the bed to the bottom left - as near as possible to the spot where they had been discovered. Crazy but this is all true'.

While Hodnett continued:

> 'And in that same spot, where nothing had grown before, a white flower grew and stayed in bloom for a long time. Then came the more disturbing incidents: taps turning on by themselves, a mirror flying across the room, glass jumping out of photo frames and smashing, the sound of a baby crying in the garden …The Robsons never saw any apparition though'.

No 'apparition'! So much for the previous article's 'shadowy, shaggy figures' in 3 Rede Avenue. However, Colin and Leslie had referred to the white flower when I spoke to them in 1977. In fact, Colin, who lived next door to Judith in Ovington at this time, told Myles:

> "There was an atmosphere in the house ever since I found them. I was eleven in 1972 [1971?] and it was quite frightening. It was nerve-wracking – the lights going out all the time. I think they were possessed by an evil spirit. It makes me believe there is something more out there than what we see. I have seen things jump off walls and that will live with me for the rest of my life, no matter what anyone says'.

A separate reality (Judith's tale)

I, too, travelled to Ovington and spoke to the Robson family's daughter Judith, now Mrs Coldfield. My reception on a gloomy 15 February 2011 was unexpected as she seemed freaked out that I had arrived unannounced and accompanied by Graham Williamson and Oliver Lewis carrying filming equipment and Stuart Ferrol bring up the rear. After assessing the situation through the curtains my persistent knocking persuaded her eventually to open the door a few inches. After I ushered away my companions and with a great deal of special pleading and seemingly having my mojo working, I was allowed inside. We sat on a settee; she white-haired and looking old beyond her years made herself comfortable at one end while a man I presume was her husband went to make me coffee while a younger man sat in a corner searching the internet. Her's was not the spirited, friendly reception I had received over the phone two years previously, after being put in touch by Myles Hodnett, when I was planning an updated Hexham Heads book. Then she had promised to take me to meet her mother (but not on a Tuesday, Jenny's bingo day), but her mother had died during the interim and anyway my quest had been sidetracked by the unfortunate death of my friend and fortean philosopher John Michell, about whom I shelved the project to write an appraisal of his life, books and influence, *John Michell: From Atlantis to Avalon*. Also, following my meeting with Judith, it came as no surprise to learn from one of my many new informants in the close-knit community of Tynedale that Judith had suffered a serious stroke during the intervening period and that as a child she had been struck with polio. The stroke may – or may –or may not have relevance.

Judith's comments told quite a contrary version of events to those I had thus far collected. Among the salient facts to emerge was a contradiction to an early report that the sisters' in plural mattress was covered with shattered glass during the poltergeist-style manifestation. Judith, then 18, was the only daughter still at home as Wendy was then 23, "married and lived away at the time". As for the mirror falling and shattering, Judith said it was inexplicable that the hook and chain remained attached to the wall. Both their television set and lights would turn on and off of their own volition. Judith corroborated Colin's statement to me that the scariest events occurred around 2.30am and that the heads would "move so they were facing each other", whereas other accounts claimed they would both face in the same direction towards the spot where they were discovered. Other disparate elements were that the notion the Robsons had only moved in two weeks previous to the Heads discovery was stated by Judith to be "at least two years" and even more contradictory that unlike Colin and Leslie Robson stating to me categorically that the artefacts were found on the ground, Judith gave the discovery as being at a depth of "four feet at least, if not more". She continued:

> "Colin was digging a hole. He was bored. When he found the head, Leslie was like, 'I want one, too', so he found another one."

Of the Heads subsequent history, she told me:

> "The lads took the heads to the abbey, where someone told them they thought the area was an old place. It had a history. They thought it was Celtic. There was a story at the time that there was a Celtic burial ground, but we never looked into it".

Aspects of the saga where Judith supplied supplementary information of great value are dealt with in more specialised chapters in this book, including exorcism, strangeness outside the house and the Heads ownership and possible whereabouts. She also told me that subsequently the house had been bought by the eldest brother, Philip, and had been rented out.

When visiting Rede Avenue on a regular basis throughout 2011, No. 3 was always empty and neglected although in private ownership, but gained a new tenant, Sonia Welsh, during the summer. The present owner and Sonia were agreeable to us filming a re-enactment of the Heads discovery, which took place in October 2011, when I took the opportunity to test the theory that the Robson boys had dug a deep hole at the exact spot Judith had indicated to me on a map of the garden, I hit concrete at one foot deep. Earlier, council tenant at No. 1, Mark Newton, voiced his opinion: "People are probably put off by its reputation". This seemed rich coming from a man living at a house with a **real** reputation. But more of Mark anon.

CHAPTER TWO
THE NEIGHBOURS

Whereas conventional semi-detached houses are traditionally side-by-side, Nos. 1 and 3 Rede Avenue are back-to-back, consequently there is more likelihood of any disturbance – be it loud music or a domestic row – being heard. When all hell broke out next door, Jenny Robson assumed there was marital or familial friction among her neighbours' family; even in the middle of the night. She told her version of events several times to the media, but it should be borne in mind that a wall – and surmises – divided her version and recollection from those to whom it occurred and what was or was not witnessed. It became Jenny Robson's, rather than Nellie Dodd's first-hand account, which in 1976 *Nationwide* viewers saw. Jenny told reporter Luke Casey:

"Well, it was a few nights later [after the Heads discovery], there was such an awful crash [?] next door – the screams ... it was terrible ... we were all awake. Next morning I asked her what had happened, and she said this horrible thing had come into her bedroom. One of the children was ill with toothache and she's been in the bedroom with her, and this thing came in the bedroom. It was half-man, half-beast. Of course we laughed, but ... it sounds so horrible, y'know ... Something like a werewolf [!] ... and her husband came running in to see what it was, but this thing had gone padding down the stairs, and she could hear it, y'know ... padding down the stairs ... as if ... on its hind legs ... and when he went downstairs the front door was open ... so evidently it had gone out the front door". (1)

And that's how Luke Casey (right) presented the terrifying incident to a shocked and bemused viewing public. Maybe his finest hour! Many remember *Nationwide* for nothing else! That brief segment had such impact. Charming, experienced and almost charismatic, it seems, however, Luke didn't quite fit the *Nationwide* template and they parted company. Latterly, Luke found a cosy niche presenting a folksy half-hour magazine programme of tales from rural Northern England, *The Dales Diary*. The 1976 classic also gave national exposure to Jenny Robson and Nellie Dodd, who were subsequently interviewed on at least one local TV station, the details of which I have not been able to ascertain.

Jenny Robson was still speaking on behalf of her neighbours in 2008 when Myles Hodnett, penning a retrospective of the Heads saga, wrote:

> 'But the next day, Nellie told her what had happened. Her two sons, Brian and Trevor were in bunk beds and one accused the other of pulling his hair. To settle them, Nellie got in one of the bunk beds and began to fall asleep. But as she was dozing off, she felt a malevolent presence in the room and then something started to pull at her. Opening her eyes, she saw what looked like a half-man half-beast creature lurking in the bedroom. It then bounded down the stairs before disappearing. "I was laughing, thinking the story was funny at the time," recalled Jenny'. [2]

Jenny Robson and children Colin and Judith recounted their experiences for *Tynedale Life*. (Reproduced with permission of *Hexham Courant*)

Of course, previous to the *Nationwide* broadcast there had been the reference in a 1973 Reader's Digest book, but the earliest local media interest I have been able to trace comes from March 1972. How the regional media was most likely alerted is dealt with in the next chapter, but publicity to strengthen a claim for council house relocation had doubtless been whispered. The first news story's introduction even suggested this:

> 'Something that happened 1,800 years ago may force a mother of six to quit a council house. The Hexham mother said she is terrified of being there after an eerie night time experience which followed the discovery of two stone heads in her next door neighbour's back garden'. [3]

However, in a 2011 interview with the Dodds' eldest daughter Sylvia, now Ritson, she told me with great conviction the council had been very sympathetic, agreeing the house was too small for eight people and there was a more suitable one in Bondgate Crescent. Sylvia added that the size of the family was only partially of concern. "There was a dual reason," Sylvia told me. "Marie wouldn't go into that bedroom afterwards".

The rebuttal and explanation followed what may not have been the most politic question to ask, but one I couldn't ignore as when members of the public approach journalists with claims of a too-good-to-be-true but eminently circulation-boosting 'ghost story' it is often council house tenants manipulating the media for a chance of acquiring a bigger/better home in a more salubrious neighbourhood. Sylvia was adamant the publicity was "not used as a reason to move house," and added realistically, "as the family kept growing we kept moving".

The 1972 *Journal* piece continued with Nellie Dodd, then 42, telling its reporter:

> "I have asked the council for a move because I am too nervous to stay here now. I had gone into the children's bedroom to sleep with one of them who was unwell [Marie, with earache] and my ten-year-old son, Brian, kept telling me that he felt something touching him. I told him not to be silly. Then I saw this shape. It came towards me and I definitely felt it touch me on the legs. Then, on all fours it moved out of the room. I was absolutely terrified and screamed for my husband".

Soot used as smokescreen

Yet another fuller account is a recollection by Nellie Dodd from 22 February 1994 to TV researcher Sadie Holland. At the time Sadie telephoned, Nellie was by then living at 62 Peth Head, Hexham. According to the notes Sadie made at the time, they read:

> 'Spoke to Mrs Dodd 22:2[:94]. She told me that she and Jenny Robson were neighbours and friends and they were talking over the garden fence when little Colin found the first head. Mrs Dodd brought them into the house. At night, her girls used to say that they could hear pitter-patter in the bedroom, and she told them not to be silly as it was only the soot falling down the chimney. But then one night the smallest child, Marie, was crying. Mrs Dodd went into her room, where Trevor and Brian were also sleeping. Mrs D asked Marie if she wanted her mammy to get into bed with her, and just as she was getting in, she felt a "thing" trip over her foot. She looked up and saw a sheep-

thing with a man's head – very big and black. It was walking on four legs out of the room and Mrs D screamed. Her husband (now dead) came running in, and he must have crossed paths with the sheep, but he didn't see it. Mrs D thought it was because only she had held the heads in her hands. She could hear the thing going down the stairs with its hoofs clicking. Brian said that he had felt something stroke his cheek, and Mrs D thought it might have been the head. I asked her why it would have happened. She said that she had never seen a ghost or anything before that incident, or indeed since. She thought that it might have been because the houses were built on an ancient burial ground. They were so frightened by all of this business that they moved away'. [4]

Later on, when Myles Hodnett resurrected the saga he stressed the disparities in the accounts, but muddied the waters further with this observation:

'Here the story diverges again. Some say Jenny's neighbour Ellen Dodd was first to see the spirit of the Heads, others assert it was Nelly Graham. But the evidence from both Nelly and Ellen was remarkably similar. Both were sitting up late with a poorly child when a strange creature entered the bedroom. It had a body like a sheep and the head of a dark-haired man, and stood upright like a man," said Nelly. "It was a half-man, half-beast. It went padding down the stairs as if on its hind legs", said Ellen.'

Surely, I surmised, these must be one and the same person. Journalists are human and make mistakes. Perhaps 'Graham' was Mrs Dodd's maiden name. [5]

Sylvia's Mother says …

Of the four people to answer my appeal for information which was published in the *Hexham Courant*, I was particularly pleased to be in contact with members of the Dodd family. An email from the already mentioned Sylvia Ritson dated 13 March 2011 intimated her willingness to help and an offer to meet me, which I duly did.

It was by this stage that I had recently met a fellow fortean with local knowledge, Stuart Ferrol, who had originally written me regarding the Heads way back in 2002. It seemed a good idea to involve him in the quest now I had teamed up with film-maker Graham and his assistant Olly, so I contacted him again and he replied very fully and affirmatively on 16 January 2011.

As a lifelong resident of Hexham he'd lived nearby and played as a child in Rede Avenue and as a writer specialising in fortean and local history topics had an obvious interest in the Hexham Heads saga. He also had local information and knowledge of neighbourhood phenomena which he felt possibly connected either directly or as a context.

One piece of information he alerted me to in his initial letter was, to his mind, the often overlooked fact that opposite the two houses in Rede Avenue stood an imposing and noxious slaughterhouse which gave off a constant stream of plaintive doomed animal cries and the sickening smell of offal and he suspected may have had a bearing on what Nellie Dodd (who was coincidentally an acquaintance of both Stuart's parents, the first of many connections we were subsequently to find out) had seen. He also made me aware that Rede Avenue and part of the nearby school stood on what used to be a farm and recounted examples of dogs, one of them his parent's and the other belonging to a previous caretaker, acting strangely in a corridor of the school which led out to or even replaced part of the old farm.

Stuart had written for a local paranormal periodical, and would later for *Fortean Times*, about the suspected wolf depredations that occurred around the Hexham area in 1904/05 and how some commentators, including Charles Fort, had questioned whether the wolf seen by so many people had actually existed. In his articles he'd drawn another connection with the case of the Hexham Heads, feeling that a possibly spectral wolf-like apparition seen in the area where artefacts were found that gave rise to the appearance of weresheep and werewolf-like entities must be more than a coincidence.

As for his own heritage he can count a dame (not the pantomine kind, a militant suffragette no less, whom I would have doubtless disapproved of as she tried to blow up Esh Winning railway station), a mayor of Hexham (twice) and famous Pinkerton detectives amongst his family tree.

Back with Sylvia Ritson, I had arranged for her to pick up Stu and myself outside *The Forum* pub just off Hexham's market place on 18 March 2011. During the short journey to the picturesque village of Acomb, she told us she was a registered general nurse and currently employed as a senior lecturer in nursing at Northumbria University. I also established that the family name was Dodd (and not Dodds as

Sylvia Ritson. No one can say "You should get out more" to her as she was just back from Egypt and Iraq, lecturing on nursing practice and her globe-trotting makes Marco Polo sound like a hermit. (Paul Screeton)

had been often reported) and that her mother signed her name Nellie (and not Nelly, as some journalists guessed). Our trip was to the Sun Inn, owned by brother Brian. We took our drinks into the smart dining-room area for privacy and Sylvia proved to be by far the more articulate and opinionated. Brian was friendly enough, but seemed reticent to take the lead in answering questions, I must admit I had around 30 questions and the marathon meeting lasted three hours, throughout which the atmosphere was relaxed, without any stress, even after such a lengthy 'interrogation'. Stu had the advantage (shorthand having defeated me) of recording the whole conversation, and during one of several excursions to the bar by Stu and I, Brian unwittingly committed to tape the comment, "there's nothing in it" – I assume meaning it was a non-story rather than financially.

Admittedly, some of the following may seem dull to those who want cracking yarns, but true forteana proceeds slowly by way of information gathering, collating, confirmation and treble checking discrepancies. So, the interview with Sylvia and Brian began with my asking about the controversial period when Colin and Leslie Robson discovered the contentious Heads. Well, they lived next door and their opinions should carry some weight. Sylvia assured Stu and I that the Heads were found on the surface, which would suggest a modern rather than ancient origin. Sylvia told us, "Our family was close friends with the Robsons. Jenny brought them to show my mother. She said they looked awful and couldn't imagine why someone would want to make something so gruesome. I held one and it felt very heavy". Brian agreed, saying, "Colin showed them to me later. They were really heavy. Really weird".

The weirdness next door at No. 3 had all the hallmarks of the familiar poltergeist. Brian told us he was present when a picture jumped off the wall and also when a bottle of dye exploded. Both he and Sylvia confirmed the whiplash sound behind the Robsons' TV set. Sylvia summed up the situation, saying:

"Jenny was a down-to-earth woman; a pragmatic, balanced person and she'd err on the side of caution. There were no flights of fantasy. She was very honest".

The macabre bedroom man-beast
As a prelude to the manimal's manifestation, Sylvia related how she and her sisters would hear the aforementioned 'soot'. She recalled:

"There was a pitter-patter akin to a cat or dog walking on a laminated floor. It terrified me that it was birds nesting and I heard soot falling, but the grate was empty. There was always a horrible feeling in the house. I would think something was behind me".

But something very real **was** present on the night of Nellie Dodd's encounter. Our conversation focussed on the fateful events. Everyone was in bed. The Dodd parents were strict about bedtime. Nellie, then 42, and her husband Isaac, 43, had a separate room. The children slept in two other bedrooms. Trevor, eleven, and Brian, ten, slept in bunk beds, while the youngest, seven-year-old Marie had a single bed. In the third bedroom were the other three girls, the eldest being Sylvia at 15, Ellen aged 13, and Carol, aged nine. A cramped household for the 20th Century: the house has since been modernised with a bathroom replacing one of the bedrooms.

Back in 1971, Sylvia said the creature chose to make its presence felt at the "dead of night", somewhere between midnight and 4am. Although the regional media had reported that the sick child being nursed was Brian and with toothache, Sylvia, and Brian himself, were insistent that it was Marie who was unwell and with a painful ear infection. What happened next is précised here:

Brian Dodd. Owner of two pubs in Tynedale, pictured outside one of these, *The Sun Inn*, Acomb. (Paul Screeton)

Brian: Tell you why I was awake - it was because me dog downstairs was literally howling, big style. And I wanted to go down, see to her. And I got to the top of the landing, and by this time, mind – honestly, I'm not joking – I was petrified. And I was too scared to go any further. And the landing window was smashing about. And so I rushed back.

Paul: And you hid under the bedclothes?

Brian: Aye, I hid under the sheet, I was too... I was sweating with fear at that point. Believe you and me!

Sylvia: You were soaking!

Brian: I hadn't peed the bed.   [*All laugh*]

Sylvia: 'Cause you ran to bed, and that's when - you said - you pulled the sheet over your head, and that's when it pulled your head

Brian: Something pulling me hair. Whatever it was.

Sylvia: And what me mam's version there was, she'd obviously opened her eyes when this happened to Brian, saw this... thing, she didn't know...

Brian: She said it was half-man, half-sheep.

Sylvia: And she was adamant... Definitely, definitely half man, half sheep, is what she always said it looked like. Up on two legs, with the cloved - you know, the cloved feet. We said, "Aw, get away", but she said it was definitely half-man, half-sheep. But she thought she was dreaming. But then it appeared to trip or stumble.

Stu: Probably after you pushed it back.

Brian: Yeah. I'm wondering if she'd seen it after it stumbled, or... It went near her legs

 Sylvia: ...that's when she realised it wasn't just what she was seeing, because she had her legs, and she was near the bottom of the bed, and it went like that - it actually touched her. On top of her clothes. And she knew by the weight of the touch that she wasn't dreaming.

Brian: What amazed us at the time was that this had been going on in my bedroom for – I would say it seemed like hours, but it had been quite a while - and nobody else seemed to hear anything.

Before meeting Sylvia and Brian I was hoping the creature might be described as a more lurid and bloodthirsty werewolf rather than a less threatening sheep-human hybrid, particularly as Jenny Robson had told Luke Casey it was "something like a werewolf". However, Brian confirmed that "our mother was adamant it was half-human, half-sheep". And Sylvia went on to totally spike my guns, vehemently insisting he mother "never said it was a werewolf. It had cloven hooves. She said that 'til the day she died". But those **claws** touching Nellie? Anyway, Brian had the final word:

> "I didn't see the creature as I was under the bed covers. One thing I can tell you,
> I've never ever experienced fear like it. And I don't think I'll ever experience it

again. Nothing fazes me now!"

The weresheep has left the building

Sylvia then recalled what happened next, according to her mother:

> "It was running and on hind legs, after tripping. There was heavy padding. It could definitely steady itself. It had a human-type bottom half and a sheep's head. It walked like a human".

But cloven hooves and claws for hands? And what of the remainder? Here we have an ovine head and human lower parts, whereas Nellie had told Sadie Holland it was very big, black, sheeplike and had a man's head.

Yet when I asked Sylvia and Brian if their mother ever described the colour of the manimal, I was told "no colour was ever mentioned". To add to the conundrum, Dr Don Robins, who we will meet later and who was another person through whose hands the Hexham Heads passed, described it as 'black'. How did he know or was he just being fanciful? [6] Robins, in another account, had a simplistic version of the event:

> 'She had been putting her child to bed when a terrifying creature – which she described as half man-half animal – came into the room from the corridor then turned and ran away'. [7]

Whatever the man/beast was, it seems to have left through the front door, which was secured by a Yale lock and kept locked at night-time. It was apparently a particularly windy night and the landing window was open despite having two catches and Sylvia, then the eldest of the six children, commented that, "the kids were all in bed early and couldn't have done it". But to open a Yale lock with claws!?

Pictures of Anne Ross have proved almost as elusive as the Heads themselves. A series of three is taken from her appearance in TV broadcast *The Celts*.

CHAPTER THREE
THE ARCHAEOLOGIST

The story took on an element of gravitas when a renowned Celtic scholar showed an interest in the Rede Avenue site and its former decapitated stony incumbents. In what may be the initial media representation of the Hexham Heads mystery, as we journalists say, you need to have a local angle upon which to 'hang' a story, and *The Journal*, based in Newcastle upon Tyne, had a 'peg' in Anne Ross. The regional morning newspaper recorded that Dr Ross, described as a Celtic linguist and archaeologist, had given her opinion that Nellie Dodd's were-sheep experience 'could not be ruled out'. [1] It was also revealed that Dr Ross planned to meet Mrs Dodd and also the boys who discovered the Heads. She also hoped to make an on-the-spot examination of where the artefacts had been found. This was to be two months hence, but there was no reference that this was to coincide with a talk she as to give in Newcastle. A lecture which would give the audience more than it paid – or bargained – for!

My hunch is that an astute publicist wanting to liven up interest in what might have sounded a deadly dull as ditch-water talk by Dr Ross, discovered a lurid local connection to brighten up a lecture on an esoteric subject by mailing 'sexed-up' publicity releases to local papers with the Hexham Heads connection. Whatever, *The Journal* (stating she was 'Newcastle born') went on to say the academic desired to probe the discovery site before she could determine whether the garden at 3 Rede Avenue and Nos. 1 & 3 overlaid a burial ground or shrine. The newspaper quoted Dr Ross on Nellie Dodd's claim:

> "There is no doubt that if there was a Celtic shrine there – and this has yet to be proved – one would not be surprised to hear of a supernatural manifestation. There are other examples of this on the Continent and in Britain where shrines have been found and where there have been a haunting".

The news report also noted that Dr Ross was awaiting a report on the heads from geologists at Southampton University (where she was a research fellow). She added that until she had seen the petrological analysis and visited Hexham she would not be able to come to a conclusion, but it was more than likely they had been made by a Celtic tribesman.

In the same day's Newcastle *Evening Chronicle*, Anne Ross was quoted as saying that, "quite often they worshipped human heads taken from their enemies", and that Nellie Dodd's supernatural manifestation was possibly associated with being above a Celtic site of sanctity. The article's introduction even dramatised the story with 'one of Britain's top Celtic experts is to excavate in a Hexham back garden'. [2]

Later in the eight-paragraph story (standard length, as according to journalistic legend that's an average reader's attention span) is an identical quote from Dr Ross, suggesting a rewrite from its sister paper or more likely transcription from publicity material.

Dark shadow of the werewolf

But Dr Ross had been keeping a dark secret. Previous to her speculations on Hexham there had been dramatic events in a leafy suburb of Southampton. A wholly unexpected and fearful experience was recounted by Anne Ross. Perhaps for the first time ever. As a major contributor to *Folklore, Myths and Legends of Britain*, a lavish compendium compiled for Reader's Digest, Dr Ross revealed to an anonymous writer of the introduction [in fact, freelance Kenneth Rayner Johnson] her scary encounter with a werewolf standing in the doorway of her bedroom.

At the time, she carried out research work for various museums and in this capacity was asked to examine the two carved heads which had been found in Hexham. The book states that this consultancy was carried out 'late in 1971'. Anne Ross gave readers this personal reaction to the Hexham Heads:

> 'Though there was nothing unpleasant about the appearance of the heads, I took an immediate, instinctive dislike to them. I left them in the box they had been sent in and put it in my study. I planned to have them geologically analysed and then to return them as soon as possible to the North". [3]

Dr Ross went on to relate the subsequent events which were associated with the presence at the detached house at 6 Rose Road, Bevis Mount, Southampton:

> "A night or two after they arrived – I didn't connect this experience with the heads until later – I woke up suddenly at about 2am, deeply frightened and very cold. I looked towards the door and by the corridor light glimpsed a tall figure slipping out of the room. My impression was that the figure was dark like a shadow, and that it was part animal and part man. I felt compelled to follow it, as if by some irresistible force. I heard it, whatever it was, going downstairs, and then I saw it again, moving along the corridor that leads to the kitchen; but now I was too terrified to go on".

At this point Anne Ross returned upstairs to the bedroom and woke her husband, Dick, who searched the house, but found nothing. There was no sign whatsoever of any disturbance nor any evidence that it had ever been there physically. She continued:

> "We thought I must have had a nightmare, though I could hardly believe that a nightmare could be so real, and decided to say nothing about it".

But a subsequent event was to prove that a nightmare would have been preferable to the reality and that what Dr Ross saw was only too real and substantial. She then related the next disturbing development:

> "A few days later, when the house was empty, my teenage daughter Berenice came home from school at about 4pm, two hours before Dick and I returned from London. When we arrived home she was deathly pale and clearly in a state of shock. She said that something horrible had happened, but at first would not tell us what. But eventually the story came out".

Berenice, too, had witnessed the werewolf:

> "When she had come in from school, the first thing she had seen was something huge, dark and inhuman on the stairs. It had rushed down towards her, vaulted over the banisters and landed in the corridor with a soft thud that made her think its feet were padded like those of an animal. It had run towards her room, and though terrified, she had felt that she had to follow it. At the door, it had vanished, leaving her in the state in which we found her. We calmed her down as best we could, and feeling puzzled and disturbed ourselves, searched the house. Again there was no sign of any intruder, nor, in fact, did we expect to find any".

The haunting, or whatever it was being played out, shared a transient interface with daimonic reality; an intrusion from elsewhere on the outer edge which continued. Dr Ross revealed further domestic confrontations with paranormal activity:

> "Since then I have often felt a cold presence in the house and more than once have heard the same soft thud of an animal's pads near the staircase. Several times my study door has burst open and there has been no-one there and no wind to account for it. And on one occasion, when Berenice and I were coming downstairs together, we both thought we saw a dark figure ahead of us, and heard it land in the corridor after vaulting over the banisters".

Anne Ross then explained how she came to link the presence disturbing the household with the Hexham Heads:

> "Later, I learnt that on the night when the heads had first been discovered, the North-country woman who lived next door to the garden where they had been unearthed was putting her child to bed when a horrifying creature – she described it as half-man and half-animal – came into the room. She began screaming and only stopped when her neighbours arrived. She was convinced that the creature had touched her, but what happened to it, she did not know. There was no sign that anyone had broken into the house, and the incident, like the incidents which have taken place in our house, is quite without any rational explanation. The strange thing is, the heads have gone now, back to the museum. But this thing doesn't seem to have gone with them".

As the writer of the book's introduction observed, the tale is 'tantalisingly inconclusive' and 'almost too extraordinary and frightening to believe'. And naturally 'Dr Ross believes it, and so do the others who were personally involved' plus the far from final, 'All that remains is a chilling question mark'. One that may remain forever....

Those who read the account in the superb Reader's Digest compendium are more likely to be the general public or persons interested at whatever level of seriousness in folklore, rather than the committed paranormalists or specialists deeply immersed in the supernatural or fortean realms who formed the core readership of the short-lived but excellent *Alpha* magazine. Here in 1980, the Reader's Digest account was précised in a barely-disguised version of events which formed part of the beginning of Dr G. V. 'Don' Robins's investigation into what is commonly known as the stone-tape theory. Perhaps carried away with an urge to dramatise events even more, Don repeated Anne Ross's "dark like a shadow" description, but later in the piece rephrased it as 'the appearance of the huge black creature'. [4] Don – I was in cordial correspondence with him at this time – was to play a pivotal role in this affair, but we'll come to the fortuitous, or perhaps otherwise, circumstances in which he came to acquire temporary custodianship of the Hexham Heads.

Peter Underwood's account

A more narrative-based account of the events at 6 Rose Road, Southampton, was given by Peter Underwood in his 1983 memoir, *No Common Task: The Autobiography of a Ghost Hunter*. [5] Born 16 May 1923, his maternal grandparents lived in a haunted house, from where his childhood interest in ghosts and psychic phenomena grew into an abiding interest. Apprenticed to a publishing firm, he went on to write fifty books on haunting, exorcism, vampires and the occult in general, plus several biographies including Boris Karloff and even Danny La Rue.

The following account is the result of a friendship struck up between himself and his wife Joyce and Anne Ross and her husband Dick. Despite visiting the Feachems at home in Southampton and subsequently their visiting the Underwoods' home, plus his having 'her remarkable story on tape', his fascinating account is seriously flawed, as I will point out as I analyse it.

Underwood begins by telling how the Heads were sent from Newcastle to Southampton and Dr Ross for her to give an expert opinion. Underwood perhaps exaggerated and put a sinister spin on the parcel in which they arrived by describing the Heads as being 'enclosed in a coffin-like box'. Anne Ross told the spook sleuth 'she felt immediately a sudden and intense coldness, and she took immediate dislike, intense and powerful and lasting, to the heads (which were in appearance little different from hundreds that she had handled over the years)'. He adds that Dr Ross made an immediate cursory examination of the Heads and concluded that on balance they were probably genuine Celtic artefacts. He then described the werewolf's first physical manifestation as happening on the night of the Heads arrival, describing how 'at two or perhaps three o'clock in the morning' Anne Ross found herself suddenly fully awake and alert. Underwood revealed that the bedroom was normally warm, but to Dr Ross it felt extremely cold. As her gaze took in the whole of the room, her gift of second sight made her aware that there was 'a presence of some kind in the room with her'. From lying facing the window she raised herself up from the bed and looked towards the door. There, she saw a 'great black form' measuring six feet in height and which gave the impression of being a hybrid creature – half man, half wolf.

He records that the hallway light outside the bedroom had been left on as a comfort for her son, Richard Charles. Only a small matter, but Underwood gives the boy's age as five years, which is probably more accurate that the eight/nine years estimate the now adult son gave to me in 2011. The 'form', as the author described it, departed the bedroom and moved on to the well-lit landing. Anne Ross felt the urge to follow the nightmarish 'wolfmanifestation'. Passing through the bedroom door, she saw the beast padding down the stairs at speed. When it reached the halfway point (perhaps significant if you take liminality into account – author Kingsley Amis had characters express themselves at this midway point and, of course, most memorably of all it's where that humanised fabrication Kermit and Cousin Robin sang the song *Half Way Up The Stairs* ...), the intruder vaulted over the banister and landed with a soft plop in the downstairs hall. It then disappeared towards the back of the house.

The account continues by describing Dr Ross's husband, 'a burly, no-nonsense, practical commercial artist' (certainly a talented artist and cartographer, but commercial artist? Certainly best known for archaeological books) appearing at the top of the stairs wanting to know what the devil was going on.

OPPOSITE: Peter Underwood and his wife became friends with Dr Anne Ross and her husband Dick.

From

DR. ANNE ROSS

6, ROSE ROAD, SOUTHAMPTON, SO2 1AE

SOUTHAMPTON (0703) 24410

March 1st, 1976.

Dear Mr Underwood,

Thank you for your letter of February 23rd, and enclosures. The Nationwide programme only told the story in a very aetiolated form, and to tell you the whole experience in detail (as well as many other experiences I have had with inanimate objects from antiquity which seem to emanate or pick up powers, usually of an unpleasant kind.) The odd thing was that I did not know of Mrs Robson's experienc in Hexham when I had my own. And the heads have disappeared. But it is a long story and perhaps we could meet sometime and I can tell you about it properly.

I shall look forward to getting and reading your books.

With kind wishes,

Yours sincerely,

Anne Ross.

One of a number of letters sent by Anne Ross to Peter Underwood; this one mentioning the *Nationwide* broadcast and having a reference to the period when the Heads were first presumed lost.

This contradicts her version in the Reader's Digest where she woke him in bed to search the house. Together they searched every room in the house in Underwood's version, but only after she explained the circumstances. No trace whatsoever being found or anything disturbed. In view of the high strangeness, according to Underwood the couple thought it prescient not to mention her encounter to anyone else. Hence at this stage neither child was aware of their mother's disturbing sighting. So, Berenice was totally unprepared for own encounter.

Apparently the parents arrived back home around 6pm and Underwood states there was a prearranged signal to indicate who was at the door. When fifteen-year-old Berenice opened it, she was trembling with shock. According to this version she had returned from school only an hour before her parents. Upon opening the front door, Berenice was confronted by the same monstrosity which had menaced her mother. The book describes it as 'a black form, half-man and half-wolf, crouching on the stairs'. Likely it was again halfway up the stairs as it again leapt over the banister with a loud plop on the hallway floor. It then 'scarpered' away towards the back of the house and entered the music-room. Underwood located this distressing experience four days after Anne Ross's own bedroom visitation, and as with her mother's instinct and bravery, Berenice also felt impelled to ascertain where the hairy monster had gone. She cautiously opened the door of the music-room and, lo and behold, the phantom had disappeared.

Underwood then reprises the scenario whereby the presence was both sensed and heard in the house. He also adds the detail that Jason, the family cat 'was seen suddenly to freeze for no apparent reason and stand with his hackles up, staring, terrified, at something invisible to his human companions'. Well, this is hardly unique in paranormal investigations, but nevertheless confirmatory evidence the felid knew more about the presence than its adoptive family. Underwood also reports what sounds like typical poltergeist behaviour of doors opening and slamming shut of their own volition.

It is now critical – as will become apparent – to quote verbatim from the autobiography:

> 'All three children saw the form; the husband never saw it but he heard it, was aware of its presence and could not disbelieve the rest of the family. A few days later the family were at dinner in the dining-room when the thing – whatever it was – jumped over the banister again and everyone heard the sound as it landed in the hall. An immediate search of the whole house revealed nothing to account for the noise but the hall was noticed to be abnormally cold'.

After a four-day gap, Richard Feachem Snr – who normally enjoyed robust health – was so ill he had spent the day in bed and had his dinner there at seven o'clock.

> 'Afterwards the older daughter picked up a couple of things to take downstairs and the younger daughter carried the tray, a little ahead of her sister. The older girl reached the top of the stairs and was about to walk down when she heard a terrific crash seemingly ahead and then, following almost immediately, the "plop" sound that they all associated with the creature jumping over the banister. Thinking that her younger sister must have dropped the tray – although she was in fact only just ahead of her – the older girl hurried down the stairs to find her equally puzzled sister trying to discover the cause or reason for the loud sounds; and then they were joined by their father, who had already heard the noises and came hurrying from his bedroom'.

There is only one problem here. The family numbered four – not five; one daughter –not two. How did a respected investigator make such a fundamental error, particularly as he seemed well familiar with the family and had taped Anne relating the events? Knowing my friend Dave Taylor was on familiar terms with Underwood, I asked if he would act as a go-between to sort out daughters conundrum. In an undated letter in response to Dave's inquiry of 5 July 2011, Underwood replied:

> 'Re: the Hexham Heads. At this distance of time I cannot be sure about the Ross children but I seem to recall the name Bernice [sic] as that of the daughter who figures in the story. Perhaps the two children were a son and a daughter (the son would know!!). Yes, my wife and I visited the family at Southampton and they visited us, as you will see from the enclosed photocopy letters. ... As I recall I contacted Dr Ross after hearing something of the story of the relics; subsequently we met several times and I have a tape somewhere I took of her at my home relating the whole story. .... Didn't I hear a story that years after the story erupted someone appeared who claimed to have made the heads?'

Underwood then focussed on the archaic heads present in the house, around ten in total awaiting analysis. I'm not sure by which authority he contended 'all seemed to be harmless, and benevolent rather than malevolent'. The following passage refers to an anonymous scientist friend of Dr Ross who often took discoveries for analysis, but he took a particular dislike to the Hexham pair, refused to have anything to do with them or the others, saying he had encountered too many accidents while ferrying Celtic heads by car. The paragraph concludes with Underwood claiming 'eventually the heads were sent to Dr Don Robins' – whereas Don's account has them handed to him in 1977 at Southampton University - as we shall see and which came as a bombshell.

Underwood mentions the role played by Hexham man Des Craigie (see Chapter Four) and the fact that scientific analysis had so far been unable to determine the age of the Hexham Heads (see Chapter Five). The author correctly concludes, 'it is very difficult not to be impressed by this sombre, careful scientist and her story of strange happenings, a story that is confirmed by other people'.

A Hexham Pandora's box ...

Interviews with Anne Ross are rare, although as a public speaker and university lecturer she could never have been described as reclusive in her heyday. A tape-recorded chat she had with author and award-winning South Yorkshire journalist David Clarke on 2 July 1994 at her home in the village of Bow Street , near Aberystwyth, Wales, is extremely interesting. He was there researching material for a book which subsequently appeared as *Twilight of the Celtic Gods*, co-authored with Andy Roberts. It would doubtless have been even more a classic piece of rare documentation had it not been for the malfunctioning of Clarke's tape-recorder, causing gaps to have been left in the transcript, of which I have a copy and which covers such matters relevant to the narrative here as the man who is the subject of the next chapter, members of the Ross/Feachem family, petrological analysis, other stone heads and related weirdnesses she had encountered, continuous archaic Celtic survival practice in Perthshire, Scotland, personal psychism, exorcism, 'deck of cards' theory and werewolves' role in her life, and beginning actually where the story seemingly ends with the Hexham Heads whereabouts (each aspect being dealt with separately as it pertains to spice up my narrative). Unless the recording/transcription is to blame, Anne Ross's pattern of speech seems extraordinarily disjointed for a literate scholar and experienced speaker, so please bear with the text wherever it appears. So, referring to the Hexham Heads, Anne Ross told Clarke:

> "All I do know, these were the nastiest things I've ever encountered. Dick was very

> level-headed and not given to seeing ghosts and having psychic experiences, and
> the two children, and every one of us, and Charles [the son] was very interested
> …. The most awful moment was when the cats became terrified, and they would
> see it on the stairs and their hackles would rise and they would back absolutely
> rigid, and then I thought this is getting dangerous. And we all heard it, you see, on
> the landing. It was a ghastly thing and it went on for a long time and finally I had
> to get rid of all the stone heads I had in the house. There were seven".

After some tangents, relevant as they were, and worse the breaks in the conversation denoted in the transcript by leader dots, she commented:

> " …. And each of us had our own experience …. When we began to see it, on that
> awful night it walked or loped across in front of the wardrobe …. "

So it was not just in Anne Ross's bedroom doorway. It was at some point in the room. How close to the sleeping/waking Anne might it have come? A full inquiry being hampered by the missing gaps and episodes through machine malfunction or dodgy tape. Yet the discussion, as transcribed, is disjointed but intriguing, but Dr Ross seemed to keep wandering throughout into other interesting areas in mid-sentence, whereby putting it into some coherent order has been quite a task. Nevertheless, here are more comments central to the creature's presence and the Heads influence, starting with the Heads arrival:

> "But as soon as I opened the box …. But when I opened the box, I opened it in an
> objective way not knowing about the Hexham thing and before I had even
> touched them I was filled with horror and I have never been like that. They were-
> n't grotesques. If they had been horrible grimacing things that wouldn't have
> bothered me normally, but there was something about them staring up balefully
> out of that box and they were so small, and I just covered them over quickly. I just
> couldn't bear them. And it was only, well I think it was obvious really from a very
> early stage that there was something attached to them; that they hadn't come
> alone as it were. I have had heads before that I have not particularly liked and
> which I haven't particularly wanted to have in the study, very few but there have
> been heads, but if they have been used for sacrifices or something and maybe if
> stone does retain something, but there is no significant way of recording it. It's
> like sound. They say every sound that is made goes on forever and that every
> ripple in the pool in which you throw a stone, those ripples go on and on indefi-
> nitely. So whether there is something else connected with stone, I don't know. I
> mean, Don Robins has done some work on that …."

Yes, Dr Robins, the organic chemist of The Dragon Project fame, collaborator with Dr Ross on the co-authored book *The Life and Death of a Druid Prince*. (see Chapter Seven)

Freudian repression

Also in 1994, author Ian Wilson, who specialised in books on paranormal subjects, contacted Anne Ross to verify points in Peter Underwood's investigation in his book *No Common Task*, whose account she had not previously seen. She pointed to certain inaccuracies in the ghost-hunter's account and Wilson duly rectified these in his retelling of events in Southampton. In her reply, Dr Ross stated candidly that, 'The whole subject was so traumatic that I have done a very deliberate "Freudian" forgetting, and never refer to it or think about it if I can possibly help it'. She added that she was convinced the Heads 'possessed a strange and disturbing evil power' linked with the wolfman and tellingly Wilson suggests she was totally sure because of their crude fashioning that the artefacts were of pagan Celtic origin, but the presence locally of a seeming head cult around Hexham made this more than likely. [6] In the same paragraph, Wilson alludes to 'three attempts to bury them provoked fresh disturbances'- a departure from the general script!

Crossbow savage maims kitten

As Anne Ross was well aware, carved heads often carry a malevolence about them – whether real or imaginary – and if the household had become cursed, one particular incident persuaded Anne and Dick to move. The family had lived in Rose Road for many years, but when a kitten, which had been shot with an 18-inch piece of sharpened bamboo which protruded from either side of its body, painfully dragged its dying body up the infamous staircase to lie on the landing screaming in agony, it was too tragic to bear. Dr Ross told the local paper:

> "This is the last straw so far as I am concerned. I think I shall never get over this terrible, terrible thing. I heard the dreadful screaming and followed the trail of blood up our stairs. It was a terrible sight. This poor little terrified creature. I am haunted by it. This is the last straw so far as we are concerned. When we moved to Rose Road 20 years ago it was a pleasant area with other families like ours. Nowadays the neighbourhood is quite different. There are lots of young people, strangers from all over the place, living in bedsits. I keep thinking that the arrow could have come through our kitchen window into my husband. I am afraid now and cannot let our other cats out, apart from anything else. Today my husband has been to the estate agents and put our house up for sale". [7]

Insp Bill Stocking, appealing for the public's help in tracking down the vile perpetrator, commented:

> "Not only was this a terribly callous thing for anyone to do, but next time it could be a child that is shot. The force with which the arrow penetrated the kitten's body, passing right through, indicates that a crossbow must have been used".

No longer employed at the university, this may be the time Anne and Dick moved to mid-Wales. Where No. 6 Rose Road stood is now a block of flats named Chandler Court. As to whether the kitten's ordeal was chance or the house still carried a jinx, I'm sure they made the right decision to leave, but maybe she had already dabbled too deeply into dark realms.

Haunting horror of animal's death drives couple from their home

CROSSBOW FIEND KILLS KITTEN

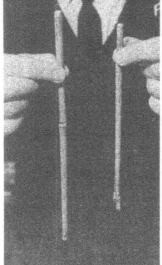

HORRIFYING: The remains of the homemade crossbow bolt that killed the kitten.

THE haunting horror of a kitten impaled by an arrow and screaming in agony is driving a Southampton couple from their home.

Inch by inch the dying animal dragged itself up the stairs at a house in Rose Road, Bevois Mount. It then lay on a landing, shrieking, with an 18-inch piece of sharpened bamboo protruding from either side of its body.

"I think I shall never get over this terrible, terrible thing," said authoress Dr. Anne Ross.

"I heard the dreadful screaming and followed the trail of blood up our stairs. It was a terrible sight. This poor little terrified creature. I am haunted by it."

Today Portswood police appealed for help from the public in tracking down the person who shot Dr. Ross's kitten with a crossbow yesterday.

"Not only was this a terribly callous thing

Mary Ackroyd reports

for anyone to do, but next time it could be a child that is shot," said Inspector Bill Stocking.

"The force with which the arrow penetrated the kitten's body, passing right through, indicates that a crossbow must have been used."

The horror for the police and the vet who tried but failed to save the life of the shot kitten is paled by the effect of yesterday's incident on Dr. Ross and her family.

"This is the last straw, so far as we are concerned," the former Southampton University lecturer said.

"When we moved to Rose Road nearly 20 years ago, it was a pleasant area with other families like ours.

"Nowadays the neighbourhood is quite different. There are lots of young people, strangers from all over the place, living in bedsits.

"I keep thinking that the arrow could have come through our kitchen window into my husband. I am afraid now, and cannot let our other cats out, apart from anything else.

"Today my husband has been to the estate agents, and put our house up for sale."

The incident which persuaded Anne Ross to quit her home of 20 years. (Cutting courtesy of *Jez Gale, Southern Daily Echo* and efforts of Dr Simon Crook).

MARCH 20th 1974

New twist in head puzzle

L¹

By Journal Reporter

THE CONTROVERSY over who made two carved stone heads has taken a fresh twist.

For Mr. Desmond Craigie, the Hexham lorry driver who claims to have made the Celtic idols now lying in Newcastle University's Museum of Antiquities, has made three more.

The heads, almost exactly the same as the originals, are sitting at the bottom of his garden in Prior Terrace.

And now one of the country's top archaeologists, Newcastle-born Dr. Anne Ross, has promised to visit Mr. Craigie.

Haunt

Dr. Ross said last night: "If Mr. Craigie really did make the original heads, it is even more interesting. I would say it is a very remarkable thing for a person to do."

The original heads were discovered two years ago in a garden in Rede Avenue, Hexham, by two brothers, Colin Robson, now aged 13, and Leslie, now aged 10.

The heads, at first thought to be Celtic idols at least 1,800 years old, began to haunt a neighbour, Mrs. Ellen Dodd, and her family.

The heads were sent to Dr. Ross, a freelance archaeologist living in Southampton, who said they were probably Celtic religious symbols. And while she had them in her home, Dr. Ross, too, began to feel haunted.

The same figure, half-human and half-beast, that Mrs. Dodd saw, was again seen in Dr. Ross's room.

But 53 - year - old Mr. Craigie said: "No one dares to admit they were wrong."

Mr. Craigie, who claims he made the originals for his five-year-old daughter, Nancy, to play with in about 1956, says the heads were made from a mixture of different cements and sand.

Dr. Ross said: "I have got a perfectly open mind about these idols. I never did say they were definitely Celtic or put a date on them, though I thought they were old.

"As soon as I get the chance I will willingly come to see Mr. Craigie."

CHAPTER FOUR
THE CLAIMANT

As a scene-setter, I related how the Robson boys made a second surprising discovery in their back garden – me. But before I made the lads' acquaintance that sunny summer morning, I had called at Hexham building suppliers' Newmans' yard to track down another key figure in the Hexham Heads mystery, Desmond Craigie.

At the point where the mystery had taken on a veneer of scholarly respectability and acceptance of the supernatural, plus an explanation based on a Celtic heritage 1,800 years old, along came a black swan moment. To everyone involved's surprise – and no little consternation – came the wicked messenger. So many times when something is in the news, there comes someone to deliver an uncomfortable blow to its credibility and particularly its provenance – be it book plot, song tune, invention, recipe ... or archaic heads. You don't have to be a fortean to know this; any time a lot of money is being made you can bet there's likely to be a challenge. It doesn't even need 'great claims require...' - this is Hexham – not quite Royston Vasey – but local heads for/from local people. And for the uninitiated a 'black swan' represents something regarded as unexpected occurring, but which on due reflection might have been anticipated. Here the black swan became transformed in the form of a local lorry-driver. Knight in shining armour representing commonsense and truth, archaeological adversary, legendary mischief-maker, Desmond, Dessie or Des (I'll refer to him as Des as this is how his wife called him) Craigie was then aged 53 and he claimed to have manufactured the Hexham Heads. So, artisan, iconoclast, trickster and pantomime villain rolled into one.

Des chose to unveil his bombshell in the regional *Evening Chronicle*, which awarded it 13 paragraphs spread across two columns on an inside page, beginning with Des "laughing his head off" about his claim as 'idols' maker. The interview went on:

> "I made them – 16 years ago. I lived in the Robsons' house for about 30 years and my father was still the tenant until a year ago. I made the heads from bits of stone and mortar simply to amuse my daughter, Nancy, when she was a little girl. I actually made three but one appears to have got lost. They were out in the garden for years. Nancy and I recognised them when we saw a drawing of the heads in the papers [*The Journal* and *Evening Chronicle*, 3 March, 1972]. I definitely made them. I have been laughing my head off about these heads and I cannot understand why all this attention is being paid to them". [1]

OPPOSITE: How the *Evening Chronicle* told how Des Craigie was "laughing his head off".

Heading into 'grave error'

By Journal Reporter

TWO stone heads discovered in a Hexham garden and believed to have been made by a tribe of Celtic head-hunters 1,800 years ago, may not be so ancient after all, a lorry driver claimed yesterday.

"In fact I made them," said 53-year-old Mr. Desmond Cragie, of Prior's Terrace, Hexham.

The heads which have been studied by geologists at Southampton University, were discovered in the back garden of a house in Rede Avenue — the same house in which Mr. Cragie lived for 30 years and which, until last year, was occupied by his father.

"I made these heads from local stone, sand and water 16 years ago for my daughter to play with," said Mr. Cragie.

"It's really funny to think about all the fuss that is being made about them."

Report

But Dr. Ann Ross, of Southampton, is still waiting for a final report from the geologists.

The heads, she said yesterday, were "highly sophisticated."

"Stylistically they have every appearance of being very old."

Dr. Ross said Mr. Cragie's claim was "very interesting" and she hopes to investigate it further when she comes to Hexham in May to inspect the garden where the heads were found by 11-year-old Colin Robson and his brother Leslie, aged eight.

The *Chronicle* contacted Dr Anne Ross for her expert opinion of this extraordinary declaration:

> "Mr Craigie's claim is an interesting story and I will have to investigate. Unless Mr Craigie was familiar with genuine Celtic stone heads it would be extraordinary for him to make them like this. They are not crude by any means".

Next day's sister newspaper *The Journal* gave the story single-column status and nine paragraphs. Des told readers:

> "In fact, I made them. I made these heads from local stone, sand and water 16 years ago for my daughter to play with. It's really funny to think about all the fuss that is being made about them". [2]

Putting on a brave face, Anne Ross defended her reputation by proclaiming that the Hexham Heads were "highly sophisticated" and "stylistically they have every appearance of being very old". She added that she found Des Craigie's claim "very interesting" and hoped to investigate further. The next development in the saga came when legendary North-East journalist Sydney Foxcroft came across the account in the Reader's Digest, which he misleadingly described as a 'children's educational book', though Ross herself so categorised it. The veteran hack, well versed in tabloidese, summed up the complex mystery without subtlety or favour in the *Sunday People*:

> 'Who knows best about the two mysterious ornamental heads dug up in a Tyneside garden? The eminent Celtic scholar and archaeologist? Or the bluff Geordie building site worker?' [3]

Des Craigie was interviewed at his new home at 20 Prior Terrace, Hexham, where he told Foxcroft:

> "The lady got it wrong. I made the heads for my daughter 18 years ago to show her what sort of work I did. I simply scooped up two handfuls of stuff as if I were making a snowball. I moulded the mixture into two balls and with a knife I carved eyes, ears, a nose and a mouth. Then I shaped rough necks so that the finished heads could stand on a shelf. It only took a few minutes.

How morning regional newspaper *The Journal* announced Des Craigie's claim.

MYTH OF THE 'EVIL' HEADS

Ancient or modern? The two heads that have caused all the controversy.

It's a Wild, Wild World

Parents sue for naughty Ina

Mannheim, West Germany: *Saturday.*

THE PARENTS of a quiet blonde girl who turned into a sexy pin-up are suing the local tourist board —because their daughter is no longer a virgin.

Ina Kruse won a contest to publicise the beauties of the Rhine Valley city.

Her topless figure adorned 50,000 posters, after the tourist board had suggested she "should try to be a little more sexy."

Modelling contracts and TV commercials followed— and 18-year-old Ina found a new boy-friend.

Then her parents — she was no longer a virgin — decided to sue the board for £200,000.

They claim that if she had not won the contest her virginity would still be ----act.

Gulp!

VIENNA: To win a bet of 15p, which he needed to enter a big-money national competition, Johann Luggi, 16, an Austrian farmhand, swallowed three live frogs. He now faces a court charge of cruelty towards animals.

WHO knows best about the two mysterious ornamental heads dug up in a Tyneside garden?

The eminent Celtic scholar and archaeologist? Or the bluff Geordie building site worker?

The archaeologist, Dr. Anne Ross, says they were "carved from local Northumbrian stone, perhaps during the Roman British period, about 1,800 years ago."

But the labourer, Desmond Craigie, claims they are made of sand and that he turned them out in his lunch-break a mere 18 years ago.

Dr. Ross, of Southampton University, tells of her findings in a children's educational book called "Folklore, Myths and Legends."

And she describes mysterious spirits and apparitions that appeared while the heads, sent to her by a Newcastle museum for examination, were in her house.

Blocks

At his home in Prior Terrace, Hexham, 20 miles from Newcastle, Desmond Craigie told me: "The lady has got it wrong. I made the heads for my daughter 18 years ago to show her what sort of work I did."

Mr. Craigie said he was working for a firm that made artificial stone blocks.

"I simply scooped up two handfuls of the stuff as if I were making a snowball.

"I moulded the mixture into two balls and with a knife I carved eyes, ears, a nose and a mouth.

"Then I shaped rough necks so that the finished heads could stand on a shelf. It took only a few minutes. The next day the heads hardened and I took them home."

The Craigies displayed

— By —
SYDNEY FOXCROFT

the heads in the window of their old home in Redeare, Hexham.

At no time, the family say, did anything mysterious happen in the home— although Mrs. Nelly Dodd, who once lived near by, tells of a mysterious creature touching both her and her son Brian one night in their own home.

When the Craigies moved to their present address the heads were left behind. Later the two heads sent to Dr. Ross were dug up in the Craigies's old garden.

At her home in Rose Road, Southampton, Dr. Ross, 46, admitted: "I may well have made a mistake in dating these heads—that's why I haven't dated them in the new book I am working on.

"But a special tetrological examination method showed they couldn't have been moulded.

"These heads are extremely evil. Whatever age they are they have attracted some medieval power. Perhaps they were buried on the site of a Celtic memorial.

"As soon as they left my house the creatures I described in the children's book disappeared.

"I would like to meet Mr. Craigie and see him make another head."

Journalist Sydney Foxcroft saw Dr Ross and Des Craigie as some female Goliath versus a puny labourer.

The next day the heads hardened and I took them home".

This was in his lunch-break when Des worked at a company called Alco making concrete posts and the account went on to say the Craigies displayed the heads in the window of their old home in Rede Avenue and revealed that 'at no time, the family say, did anything mysterious happen'.

Anne Ross defends herself

Syd Foxcroft contacted Dr Ross for her expert opinion and she admitted:

> "I may well have made a mistake in dating these heads. That's why I haven't dated them in the new book I am working on. But a special tetralogical examination showed they could have been moulded. These heads are extremely evil. Whatever age they are they have attracted some mediaeval ('evil' is the more likely word and I suspect a copytaker's error when Foxcroft phone his story in, particularly as elsewhere Rede Avenue appears in print as 'Redeare') power. Perhaps they were buried on the site of a Celtic memorial. As soon as they left my house the creatures I described in the children's book disappeared. I would like to meet Mr Craigie and see him make another head".

On the subject of a reporter's copy being mangled, not only copytakers can make errors and I suspect eithr Foxcroft or a sub-editor gave a simplified version of events when after Des claimed he originally made three heads in 1956 and one ended up in the dustbin, he supposedly told journalist Syd Foxcroft he 'scooped up two handfuls' for the Heads creation – not three. I suspect the story was tailored to match the two extant Heads for simplicity's sake as the loss of the third seemed both immaterial and could confuse a *People* reader!

Someone on *The Journal* newsdesk must have spotted Foxcroft's effort among the sex and titillation with its quotable material from Anne Ross, but Des got a mention:

> "I made them for my daughter. I was working at an artificial stone firm and simply moulded the mixture and roughly carved the face".

And after discussing the petrological analysis, Dr Ross affirmed that she intended, ''to come North and see Mr Craigie and examine the area where the find was made". But what she Dr Ross did not tell *The Journal* reporter was that she had returned the Hexham Heads to Newcastle, which was revealed the next day. (see Chapter Three) Also, Des Craigie rose to the challenge and created a further three archaic heads, which were reported as being 'almost exactly the same as the originals, are sitting at the bottom of his garden in Prior Terrace. Des was back in the news and Anne Ross again promised to meet him, commenting:

> "If Mr Craigie really did make the original heads, it is even more interesting. I would say it is very remarkable for a person to do. I have got a perfectly open mind about these idols. I never did say they were definitely Celtic or put a date on them, though I thought they were old. As soon as I get the chance I will willingly come to see Mr Craigie". [4]

Des's rejoinder to this was, "No one dares to admit they were wrong", and stated again he made them for daughter Nancy as a five-year-old in 1956.

As good as his word, Des made three more archaic heads to demonstrate his capabilities.

Without a date nor venue it is, however, established that Anne Ross gave a lecture in Newcastle upon Tyne some time in 1974 (this not being the 1972 public talk which triggered media attention upon the Heads). Des Craigie was in the audience, accompanied by an unidentified journalist. Dr Ross referred to the Hexham Heads in the talk entitled 'New Thoughts on Old Heads' and told the audience the claimant was present. At this point Des stood up and asked her to acknowledge the genuineness of his claim. In our chat at his home, Des claimed Anne Ross promised to rectify the impression that the Heads were ancient, adding, "To say they were old would be conning people". Yet in 1972 she had retorted that:

> "Mr Craigie's claim is an interesting story and I will have to investigate. Unless Mr Craigie was familiar with genuine Celtic stone heads it would be extraordinary for him to make them like this. They are not crude by any means".

Although Anne Ross continued to doubt that Des made the Heads, she went on record as noting that "the so-called typical Celtic head is, in fact, a myth", although there is a unifying "common, elusive, but indisputable quality of non-humanness".

Meetings with Des Craigie

When I first contacted Des at the yard in Hexham he was about to set off on his day's deliveries with a loaded lorry. He said he would be finished work around 4pm and I was welcome to call at his home after that time. I arrived sweating after a four-mile walk across fields from the village of Wall (see Chapter Thirteen) and was offered a cup of coffee by Des's wife Jean. Fortunately, I made some notes of our conversation, but it was certainly a light-hearted natter rather than a serious interrogation.

When I mentioned the three heads he had made in response to Anne Ross's challenge, Des revealed a box with the gruesome trio laid out. I handled each and, having already showed him the head made by Colin Robson, asked if he, too, would be willing to part with one? From affability, he became hesitant, there was a silence, a reluctance, perhaps some frantic surge of brain activity seeking a reason to refuse my request. But if Des saw himself as a knight in shining armour defending truth and upholding his honour he had let his visor slip and luckily for me his wife rode to my rescue as a housewifely Jeanne d'Arc.

> "Oh for God's sake give him one of the heads, Des. They're nothing but trouble for you. When he goes down to the club his mates take the mickey out of him about this whole business. He'll come back from the bar with a pint and they'll point at the froth on the beer and say 'Nice head you've got there, Des'."

So, through a mixture of pluck and luck, I became the owner of a genuine Desmond Craigie sculpture – two pseudo-primitive works of art in one day. **Thus I began in earnest my quest for the Hexham Heads.** Would I ever find the elusive original artefacts? What chance of adding them to my so far nascent collection? If so, would they prove to be ancient or modern? Did it really matter? They already had achieved notoriety! And at one end of the timescale were the warlike Celts with their severed head cult and at the other a peaceable yet irascible modern-day head-hunter – me.

Well, my mojo was working that sweltering sunny day, so could there be another red-letter day and I become possessor of the enigmatic, elusive true Hexham Heads?

But dreaming aside and back to harsh 1977 reality, as we chatted Des recalled the original Heads:

> "Nancy played with them as dolls. She would use the silver paper from Penguin
> chocolate biscuits as eyes. One got broken and I threw it in the bin. The others just
> got kicked around and must have landed where the lads found them".

At this point I bid adieu to Des and Jean and headed home with my day's unexpected trophies, memories of a meeting with a leading exorcist and little realising how many subsequent pilgrimages I would make to Hexham.

Once the Hexham Heads reached the media spotlight it touched upon the Craigie family and Des recalled how his daughter Nancy ran excitedly from her home one evening to tell her father the Heads had been featured by Peter Moth on a Tyne Tees Television news feature programme. In 2011 his son Nigel showed me a photograph of himself, Nancy and father looking at a copy of the Reader's Digest book and I noted that when I first made Des's acquaintance the same book was in the lorry cab. It had been bought for Nigel by an uncle and Des commented to me that when his son read it his reaction was:

> "Dad, have you been here before? One thousand eight hundred years ago!"

Reincarnation theory is a tangent too far and so suffice it to say that Des reacquainted me with the entry and depictions of Celtic heads in the Reader's Digest book, pointing out that had he modelled his (presumably replica) heads on the real thing, he would have been the last person to volunteer anything which might suggest any untoward influence. He also told me he had requested the entry in the book be amended in future editions to include his claim of creating them, but the publishers declined.

Heads return to Geordieland

As already emphasised, chronology has been a vexed aspect, not helped by dodgy memories, possible deliberate motivation and even maybe fortean fragmentation of the time continuum! There is, however, documentary evidence that the Heads were returned to Newcastle's Museum of Antiquities as a Newcastle newspaper carried a report early in 1974. Using a journalistic convention, it announced that 'those allegedly "evil" stone heads were back in a Newcastle museum last night', which could mean a newshound had just found out and that they could have been there for weeks, even months, without having come to notice. The piece was a single column story, but illustrated across three columns with technician Roger Miket displaying a Head in each hand. Roger commented:

> "I don't regard them as being sinister at all. They are just archaeological material
> to me. We are interested only in establishing whether they are genuine Celtic
> carvings or not. But I suppose the public would be far more interested in the
> supernatural side of it. Anyway, they don't worry me". [5]

The report stated that their future was undecided, but they were currently in that notorious twilight zone of any museum, the reserve collection, and not on display to the public. At this point, through a journalist's involvement, Des paid a visit and astounded a custodian (so security conscious that she would not allow them to be viewed until another official was present) by announcing that they were his handiwork

---

OPPOSITE: The author holds two 'archaic' heads: one made by Des Craigie (left) and the other by Colin Robson. The picture dates from 1982, during his pseudo-werewolf phase.

---

and he wished to have a look at them to refresh his memory.

This is where a mysterious photograph enters the picture! Des Craigie is holding what I can only assume to be the original Hexham Heads – with tenons. The brick wall behind could be Rede Avenue – or anywhere. No one, his son Nigel included, can identify the photo's provenance. But the tenons suggest a pre-1971 date.

Mystery photograph! Candid camera shot of Des and what the author suspects are the original Hexham Heads, but the snap remains shrouded in mystery. Where? When? Why?

Heads return to Hexhamshire

During 1975 the Heads were returned to where they originated and an undated cutting in my possession (the typeface suggests *The Journal*) suggested intriguingly that the whole saga was about 'to end exactly where it began – deep beneath the soil of a Hexham garden'. The reporter cannot have given the cuttings file even a cursory glance when he continued that the Heads, 'have been sent back to the family which found them after being in Newcastle University's Museum of Antiquities ever since'. No reference to Southampton and the werewolf whatsoever! Nor any inkling that not only the Robsons

After seeming keen to be reunited with the Heads, Jenny Robson threatened to bury the "horrible things"!

'Celtic' idols will be buried

A FOUR-YEAR contro-
versy over two "Celtic"
idols is to end exactly
where it began — deep
beneath the soil of a
Hexham garden.

The two idols, at first
thought to be Celtic, have
been sent back to the family
which found them after
being at Newcastle University's Museum of Antiquities
since 1971.

But last night, Mrs. Jenny
Robson, of Rede Avenue,
Hexham, said she was con-
vinced that the idols were
genuine.

"I want them out of this
house. We are going to bury
them back in the garden
where they belong. They
caused so much distress
after my two sons found
them that I don't want a
repeat."

When the carved stone
heads were first found it
was the start of strange
goings-on in the Robson
house.

Pictures fell off walls,
a curtain pelmet crashed to
the floor and a mirror fell
off the kitchen wall.

A neighbour became so
frightened after seeing a
half-man half-beast apparition that she pleaded with
the local council to move her
to another home.

The heads were taken over
by the university, but after
Mr. Desmond Craigie, a lorry
driver, of Prior Terrace,
Hexham, claimed he made
the heads from a concrete
mix in 1956 the controversy
began.

Now most academics are
convinced that Mr. Craigie
was telling the truth. Even
so, Dr. Ann Ross, a leading
expert on Celtic archaeology,
said she had been haunted
by the heads.

Dr. Ross, like the Robsons'
neighbour, claimed she had
seen the weird beast-man
when the head was in her
house.

Mrs. Robson and her
family are convinced that
the heads are genuine.

She gave the heads to her
cousin, Mr. George Watson,
of Allen Drive, Hexham, a
few days ago. Then his wife,
Doreen, smelled incense in
the bedroom.

Said Mrs. Robson: "She
said she would not have
them in the house any
longer and insisted that my
cousin should give the heads
back to me.

"I don't like them at all
and I don't like the children
playing with them. They
have caused too much
unhappiness.

"I am going to bury them
in exactly the same spot
where they were found and
just hope that that will be
the end of them. They are
horrible things," said Mrs.
Robson.

wanted them back, but that Des Craigie had also made a claim on their owner-ship. However, the piece mentioned a further short journey before their threat-ened reincarceration, revealing that Jenny Robson 'gave the heads to her cousin, Mr George Watson, of Allen Drive, Hexham, a few days ago. Then his wife, Doreen smelled incense in the bedroom'. Unfortunately, both George and Doreen have since died; their daughter, also called Doreen, still lives in Allen Drive, which leads up the hill directly to 1 & 3 Rede Avenue, but now at a dif-ferent house and has not answered my letter requesting information and seems to have an aversion to Stuart Ferrol. Win some, lose some. But I would love to know more of whatever strangeness the Heads created for the Watsons. In the piece, Jenny Robson cast a little more light on the Heads brief transfer and reit-erated her threat to see them reburied:

> "She [Doreen] said she would not have them in the house any longer and insisted that my cousin should give the heads back to me. I don't like them at all and I don't like the children playing with them. They have caused too much unhappiness. I am going to bury them in exactly the same spot where they were found and just hope that that will be the end of them. They are horrible things". [6]

So, why did she want them back? Did she carry out her threat to rebury them? I rather think not.

Kitchen sink drama

> "He was good with his hands, such as gardening, but I'm not aware of any craftsmanship, though he helped me make model aeroplanes. That day he was in the kitchen with cement and sand, using the washing-up bowl. My mum went ballistic!"

That's Des's son Nigel describing the day his father picked up the gauntlet thrown down by Anne Ross and set about recreating three more 'Celtic' heads. The subject came up after Nigel responded to my appeal for information in the *Hexham Courant*. He telephoned me the evening after publication to share memories of his father. Born in 1962, he now works in Hexham JobCentre Plus, proved easy to talk to and seemed both willing to confront anomalous phenomena and magnanimous and unflinchingly unretributive in the face of those who doubted his father's credibility. He has retained the cache of Hex-ham Heads 'memorabilia' which his father showed me back in 1977, to which has been added later cuttings, and even my correspondence with his Des and a copy of my booklet *Tales of the Hexham Heads*. Nigel added that the fascina-tion had passed on to a third generation with his ten-year-old son having devel-oped a strong interest in the Heads.

OPPOSITE: Chip off the old block, so to speak! Nigel Craigie pictured in the cinema above Hexham's J D Wetherspoon pub, The Forum. (Paul Screeton)

FIlming of Nigel was undertaken appropriately in the cinema above Hexham's The Forum pub on 15 March 2011, where he proved chatty with Graham and Stuart during the filmed mild inquisition. Afterwards I asked for clarification on a couple of points, including whether Des had any knowledge of ancient history and he told me he doubted he knew anything of the Celtic era, though conceding that the Heads looked "similar to the genuine ones". Of the demonstration trio, I pointed out that I reckoned the one in my possession looked more ordinary than the other two, perhaps why it was the one he chose to offer me. The others bear stronger features, yet Nigel and I had difficulty identifying which was each from an old cutting. The one Nigel now has which most resemble 'a hag' also proved somewhat recalcitrant to being photographed that day. Nigel being more polite and politically correct than me referred to the Heads as "one lady, one male".

I left until last the vexed question of whether Des was an opportunist or the genuine creator of the Hexham Heads. Nigel's robust defence of his father "was as honest as the day is long. All he was doing was putting the record straight".

As it turned out, the quality of visual and sound reproduction from that 'shoot' proved unsatisfactory and I arranged for a repeat filming on 30 September 2011, which turned out to be a glorious 30 degrees C Indian Summer lunchtime interview, this time conducted by me in the sylvan setting of Hexham House Gardens. The interview covered familiar ground and some of his comments appear in later chapters. For the camera, I asked Nigel to reprise what he told me of the kitchen sink incident and he obliged with a fuller description:

> "We lived in a small flat and had a small kitchen, so there wasn't a lot of room for him to work. Sometimes he borrowed our mum's washing-up bowl, much to our sort of disgust a little bit, to work in, and to mix his materials and so forth. I think the dishes were probably left at the side when he did it! But he fashioned the three. Obviously he was doing it from memory, so they're not an exact replica of the originals, but they look as though they're pretty close to my mind".

He didn't mention his mother's anger at Des misusing the bowl, but at one point Nigel conceded that, "I think she was head of the house". Maybe, but she lacked Des's notoriety and the spotlight. As Nigel told me earlier:

> "If he was alive today he would have been fascinated by all this attention. He would have been on the internet to see what people were saying."

Doubting Thomas, Dick, Harry and ... well, just about everyone
Well, people didn't need the internet when they either rang me or I went out and interviewed them. If Nigel Craigie is unswerving in his belief that the Hexham Heads were his father's handiwork, it is a pity that daughter Nancy has not come forward to corroborate his legacy. Detractors are many, from Celtic scholar Dr Anne Ross to his close mates in the RAFA Club, with members of the Robson and Dodd families and 94-year-old Betty Gibson in between. In the next chapter I will examine what the geologists thought – and this is where professionals argue and get their rocks off, gentlemen behaving badly and dirty tricks! However, later in 2011 when I interviewed the Dodd family's Brian and Sylvia, I

As with the Hexham Heads themselves, the duo now residing in Prudhoe with son Nigel and family, from the trio Des Craigie made to demonstrate his ability to Dr Anne Ross, were reluctant photographic subjects. Very similar to one another, yet rather different to mine from the same batch, in that both have larger eye sockets, wider mouths, more pointed noses and grooves to denote swept back hair. And even more different to the originals. (Paul Screeon)

asked each to assess whether they thought the Hexham Heads were ancient or modern they appeared undecided so I asked for an approximation, whereby Sylvia reckoned, "I'd err on the side of ancient" and when pressed, "70/30", whereas Brian also plumped for "The Celtic side, 80/20".

Another person who doubted Des Craigie's claim was the nonagenarian one-time brief custodian of the Heads, Betty Gibson. When in 2011 I asked if she had known Des, she told me, rather witheringly:

> "Dessie Craigie claimed to have made them. Said he had made them for his daughter. We had a shoe shop in Hexham and he went in. I didn't know him well. My husband played football with him. When he announced he had made the Heads all the ordinary folk treated it as a joke"

An even more strident opinion came from Robson family's daughter Judith Coldfield when I broached the disputed origin of the Heads:

> "His claim is, pardon me, a load of crap. You won't be able to print that! Who

would make something like that for a child? Anyway she'd be too old. There's
no way she was using silver paper for eyes. [and Des's motive?] He thought
there was money involved".

For an expert opinion I asked Dr Steven Cartwright, who pronounced, 'most likely ancient'.

For an amateur but informed opinion, Graham Williamson travelled to Hebden Bridge, West Yorkshire, and filmed author of *Stony Gaze* John Billingsley, who commented:

> "That's the reason for the choice of the term; that 'archaic' gets us off the [Celtic]
> time hook, the dating hook. Now, the dating hook is one reason why a lot of
> archaeologists like to keep away from carved heads. It's because it's so hard to
> date them, and you don't want to say, 'Oh, yes, this is a Celtic head', for some-
> body to come back and say, 'Oh, I carved it in 1957', for instance! Yeah, that is a
> famous case, but it's not by any means an isolated case".

Graham brought up the topic of the Hexham Heads more directly later in the discussion and John praised Anne Ross's pioneering work in Celtic studies and how her book *Pagan Celtic Britain* "put the whole idea of the head in its proper place". More specifically, John commented:

> "For the Hexham heads, it was a situation which many an archaeologist has faced,
> where you've got these objects that are undateable. But somebody's standing
> there asking you for a date. And sometimes you don't always get it right. But
> Anne Ross's work is absolutely crucial in the context of Celtic studies, particularly
> at that time. She really changed the drift of Celtic studies to what it is today; a
> much more widely nuanced field. And, er, the Hexham heads, I have to say, was
> an unfortunate incident in that. Shouldn't be held against her".

Mmm. Many of her colleagues believed she was deluded to hang on to the Celtic option, but if she had asked for support in Hexham, the term landslide comes to mind – in her favour.

CHAPTER FIVE
THE BROADCASTER

I could have entitled this chapter as 'The Mothman Memories' as a cultural/fortean nod in the direction of John A Keel and New Jersey's Point Pleasant, but certainly broadcaster Peter Moth played a small, but key role in the early development of the Hexham Heads myth. A somewhat shadowy figure so far in the narrative, nevertheless then a household name, he met the Robson family and took the Heads away from them, also filming Des Craigie on location with his unexpected claim and Anne Ross in the studio for the Tyne Tees Television early evening regional news magazine programme *Today at Six*. Archive gold for researchers, but again despite our efforts it is more documentary evidence seemingly consigned to oblivion.

As for my memories, I well remember the *Nationwide* broadcast on this topic, but not the Dr Ross 1972 TTT one. In 1977, Colin Robson recalled Peter Moth visiting the Robsons's home and taking away the Heads to pass them on to Anne Ross. Similarly, Nigel Craigie recalls visits to their house by Moth to record Des's contribution to the programme. As for Moth himself. His C.V. or credentials are only peripherally relevant, so briefly, The Rev Peter Cecil Moth trained and was ordained as a United Reform Church minister, moving to a parish in Kenton, Newcastle, before a career change to Tyne Tees Television, where he became a reporter and presenter on Today at Six in 1969. He retired as director of programmes in 1996 and returned to the ministry. He told Graham Willliamson, "I got my mortgage out of broadcasting and my insurance out of the church" and also, "I think I'm quite proud of myself for remembering so much!" Indeed! But there are a few inconsistencies, but in this investigation it is just not memory playing tricks, and for a 75-year-old I think he did a grand job.

I had contacted Peter Moth by email to set up a filmed interview for Graham, but through circumstance was not present when this was undertaken on a cold evening in December 2011 in the austere environs of Trinity Church, Whitley Bay, though while chatting had asked a few pertinent questions myself. The flavor of the interview between Peter Moth and Graham is best given in transcript form:

Peter: The reason for setting about the story was having seen that Dr Ross was coming up to give her lecture – and I think she was publishing a new book about the same time... and I picked up the story and was interested in it, and we went to see if we could find the family. It turned out we could; the heads were in a cupboard in their front-room. The family found them rather creepy, to put it mildly, and they had a significant issue with the misfortune following them. So we did some filming with the family and the story – Des's story of finding them [*sic*]. Er... and then we did a studio interview with Dr Ross. And my memory is that probably we recorded that in the afternoon. I couldn't go to her lecture, if I recall, because in fact while she was lecturing I was on air on the news programme that night. So we recorded

OPPOSITE: The Rev Peter Moth in a cold church interviewed by Graham Williamson for his film *Heads!* (Graham Williamson)

a piece with her in the studio, and she had also met... I think it was Des, certainly some of the family... and was quite willing to take the heads back with her to see if it was possible to get some sort of dating of them. She was, if I recall, from the University of Southampton, and her expertise was Celtic history with particular reference to witches. And she wanted the geology people... I think it was something to do with the petrochemical [sic] people, who are obviously to do with geology, to have a look at the heads and try and identify the kind of stone or rock they were from, and from that to work out whether they were likely to be genuine or not, whether they matched the era and so on. And the last I saw of them was Dr Ross putting them in her bag.

Graham: Right. And you borrowed them from Jenny Robson, didn't you? Am I right in thinking that?

Peter: I saw them in the house and they gave them to me. In the house in Hexham. Er... With, as I recall, one of them saying the words "We don't really want these back." My view was that I asked them if they were happy for Dr Ross to take them to do some work with them, and they were certainly entirely happy about that. I contacted Dr Ross, or I tried to contact Dr Ross afterwards. The first time I contacted her I don't think she'd actually got them to the geologist, the second time I think she had and the third time she was ill. And I really lost contact with her after that. She said she'd contact me subsequently. Now I gather Dr. Ross is extremely ill, and I'm not sure whether she's still alive.

Graham: She has dementia at the moment – she is still alive, but apparently can remember nothing of her academic career, sadly.

Peter: That's it, yes. It does seem as if the curse of the heads follows people rather. But that was, as I say, the last time I saw the heads was with Dr. Ross. Have you ever seen them yourself?

Graham: Not the originals, no. Other than in photos and the like.

Peter: Yes. They're about – I would say about the size of a billiard ball. Slightly smaller than a tennis ball. And they are rather... malign-looking things, really, I have to say. Although perhaps you expect that because you've heard the stories about them.

Graham: Were the heads shown on the TV broadcast you did?

Peter: Yes, we had them in the studio as I recall.

Graham: And then they were taken by Anne Ross?

Peter: Well, Anne took them along with her to her lecture, I think. But as I say I can't be absolutely certain of that. If that was not the case, then we sent them on to her.

Graham: Now that lecture, I believe I'm right in saying, was the one where Des Craigie met Anne Ross.

Peter: Yes – yes, I think he'd made arrangements that he could.

Graham: I was just wondering why Des Craigie wasn't invited into the TV studio with Anne.

Peter: Well, we'd already done a piece with him which we'd filmed. So we'd got Des Craigie's story on film and we wanted Anne's view on it in the studio.

Graham: So the whole Des Craigie thing was recorded before Anne Ross was contacted?

Peter: Yes. Well, she'd been contacted because she was the... the spark of the whole story, if you like, so we made sure she was coming up and we could talk to her, and then we went and did the preparatory pieces as a standard news feature. You film some of the background and you talk to some of the people who are directly concerned – in this case, talking about the Hexham Heads.

Graham: Do you know if the tape still exists?

Peter: I'd be very surprised! As I say, it was a news feature story and they did at that stage tend to get discarded. I doubt that the film – and it was a film interview we did with Des. We were still using film on news at that stage, before tape came into the interview – but again I would be very surprised if that piece survived at all. If it was anywhere, it would be in Teesside University.

Graham: Oh, right. Okay. I might check out the archives. How many times did you meet Des?

Peter: Just the once, I think.

Graham: What was your opinion of him?

Peter: He seemed nice. Pleasant enough, straightforward bloke, actually. I never made my mind up on the story. That's why I was quite keen to find out what Dr Ross's findings were on the subject. I thought she was partly skeptical, but she was sufficiently interested to want to take it further.

Graham: What were your opinions of Anne Ross when you met her?

Peter:I thought she was a, a clever, um... obviously educated, very pleasant lady. In many ways a typical don, but with considerable charm. In fact, I recall we had dinner after her lecture. [1]

Being an ordained priest as well as a journalist, Peter was asked by Graham for his opinions on paranormal phenomena surrounding the Hexham Heads phenomena:

Peter: I've never been greatly sold on the supernatural. It did seem to me that it was not unlike a lot of other stories of that kind, where people think of creepy things and they get slightly out of control. But I have to say the heads were creepy, and certainly their record of bringing trouble to the people who had them was considerable. And it seemed to me that the family were not keen about them... as I recall, Jenny was telling me about plates falling off the wall, and that kind of thing.

Earlier, when I contacted Peter Moth myself, he said he was neither present when Des Craigie subsequently visited the Museum of Antiquities nor as made plain that by broadcasting at the same time was he with Des at Anne Ross's lecture. [2] A subsequent email from Graham to Peter established (?) no petrological examination had been undertaken at the time of the TV report.

CHAPTER SIX
THE GEOLOGISTS

As Charles Fort wisely observed, 'For each and every expert there is an equal and opposite expert'. Unsurprisingly, this maxim applies with regard to the analyses of the composition of the Hexham Heads, a debate into their age and provenance which has seen some caustic comments followed by a petulant rebuke. Then add to this the reactions and divisions in the populist camps, either supporting Anne Ross's swords 'n' sorcery ethereal Celtic golden era or Des Craigie's bricks 'n' mortar dystopian post-war austerity period. Essentially at stake was the warring geologists' reputations and in their respective corners an experienced archaeologist and an amateur sculptor. But there could be no victor and neither combatant came out of the bout unscathed with both's integrity tarnished. In my opinion there was no prizewinner whatsoever and as for the ancient or modern dating, the jury's still out.

In a North v South contest, two well-qualified 'experts' were asked their opinions and their petrological reports were diametrically opposed – one believing the Heads to be centuries old, the other of very recent age. Frank Hodson, Professor of Geology and Dean of the Faculty of Science at Southampton University, made his report merely upon microscope evidence, but Dr Douglas Robson, Senior Lecturer in Geology at Newcastle University, took the more radical approach of removing parts of the Heads, maybe gaining an unfair advantage and certainly behaving without any authority or permission. I also have been informed that Dr Robson withheld his initial report when Des Craigie dropped his bombshell claim. Professor Hodson did not have this strategic advantage as Craigie's claim was first made in a Newcastle newspaper on 6 March 1972 and doubtless totally ignorant of this development far off in Hampshire, his report on the Heads is dated 10 March 1972. Here in full is this first punch thrown during the 'Rumble in the Academic Jungle'. [1]

'Both heads are made from the same material which is a very coarse sandstone with rounded quartz grains up to 2mm. diameter in a calcite cement. The heads with the incisions representing hair is weathered to show the surface character of the stone admirably.

This material could well have come from the vicinity of Hexham. Officers of the Leeds Office of the Institute of Geological Sciences inform me that such sandstone occur below the Durham "Millstone Grit" and especially in a bed just below the Little Limestone, north of Hexham. This sandstone is not shown on the Hexham Geological Survey Sheet (No. 19) since it was not then the practice to map the thin sandstones in this part of the geological succession. It seems to me to be rather unusual material to be selected for carving because of its coarse, gritty nature. However, since it was so used, it perhaps adds weight to the idea that it was local because it would appear to have no special properties which would warrant it being brought from afar.

The head with a groove extending from behind the ears over the high forehead, shows the hair region to be particularly smooth – an effect which I doubt could be achieved by polishing such coarse sandstone. Close examination reveals that a surface coating of fine material has been applied. Most of this surface is now blackened, perhaps by some altered pigment. The immediate underlying material is an ocherous yellow colour. Examination of a minute scraping of this by X-ray diffractometry shows it to be calcium carbonate. It thus seems that the head region was plastered over with lime to give it a smooth surface. Possibly this was to provide a surface suitable for colouring. Within this smooth region are small white patches which may more nearly represent the original plastered surface having been protected by "paint" only relatively recently lost.

The left eye socket also contains white material which has minute spots of green substance. This is also possibly the same plaster in an undiscoloured condition preserved under a pigment now almost completely lost. Permission to remove a fragment would be necessary to determine the exact nature of this "eye" but, whatever the substance, it has been inserted whilst plastic and is not a specially shaped "jewel" inserted in the socket'.

At this stage Anne Ross was highly sceptical of Des Craigie and happy to accept Frank Hodson's findings. In a personal letter to Dr David Smith, Lecturer in Archaeology at Newcastle University and Keeper of the Museum of Antiquities, she apologised for cancelling a trip north in which she had hoped also to see 'the Robsons'. No doubt the finders and not Douglas and his wife, as she continued:

'I want to interview the lorry driver who claims to have made the heads, because, unless he can produce very convincing proof of his skill, I simply don't believe the story. In the first place, the report, made by the Dean of the Faculty of Science here, tells a very different story. He himself said that of all the heads I have given him for analysis, these are the most interesting and sophisticated. It was a common Celtic custom to pigment and then plant their cult heads, and to set them up on pillars – and the elongated necks of these suggest that this is what they were inserted into. The stone is real, not a mixture such as the lorry-driver suggests: I have seen many heads made by non-experts as a kind of "doodle", and all have been immediately recognisable as such'.

Having just returned from a three-week tour of French museums, she then related that she 'saw similar small heads with hair depicted in the same manner from the Source of the Seine, and commented to Dick how they resembled the Hexham examples. These are the questions I would like to have answered. Why, if he was not a sculptor by trade, did he suddenly make such extraordinary stone heads for his daughter (out of sand, lime and cement?) .. How did they come to be buried in the garden? There are only three possibilities that I can think of: that he had seen Celtic heads of this kind and copied them – and Professor Hodson's report closely argues against this, and it would take a very skilled artist to do this. Or that he unearthed the heads himself, and covered them with pigment and painted them to amuse his daughter – and again Professor Hodson's report indicates that the pigmentation is

Historic Environment Record Report

HER number 8768

Site name

Description:

Two small heads found in 1971 at No 3 Rede Avenue, Hexham (NY 94006365). Heads have different hairstyles, and the necks appear to have acted as tenons. Examined petrologically by Professor Frank Hodson in University of Southampton. One head revealed it had a surface coating of fine material; it may have been covered in plaster. (1)

Location:

Parish/District: HEXHAM   Tynedale

Grid Reference: NY94006365   LO

Classification - Type and date:

CARVED STONE   FIND   UNKNOWN

Status and other references:

SHINE CANDIDATE STATUS NO

OLD NORTHUMBERLAND SMR NUMBER   NY 96 SW 52

Associated Events/Activities

The relevant Historic Environment Record Report, which gives the Ordnance Survey grid reference and states categorically the Heads were carved and not reconstituted concrete.

ancient. The only other possibility is that we have another example of someone coming forward and claiming to have made the head (sic) in the past, just as when a murder has been committed, people go to the police and say they have done it, when they haven't. I have had several experiences of this, and on each occasion, close questioning of the person concerned has revealed that they are talking non-sense. In one case, the person was proved to have been <u>four</u> years old when the head was unearthed next door! So unless very convincing evidence is produced, and I see the lorry-driver carving sophisticated heads with my own eyes, I simply cannot accept the claim. **There is something very queer about the whole business** [my emphasis], and as soon as another visit is possible (and I hope it will only be a tem-porary postponement) then I shall do my best to get at the truth – unless you can manage to do so yourself. The copy of Professor Hodson's report is for you – he gave me one for you; I myself regard it as conclusive'.

Hodson's findings were eventually printed in the magazine *Archaeologia Aeliana* as an appendix to illustrated Heads 4 and 5 from Hexham. Before the report's words 'Both heads … 'there is a short addi-tion – 'So far as can be determined by surface examination', making clear Hodson had (virtually) not subjected either to physical scrutiny.

The appendix was preceded by a brief paragraph on the Heads including a reference to their different hairstyles and the observation 'the necks would appear to have acted as tenons'. Despite something of a muted disclaimer, Dr Ross obviously favoured an ages distant provenance for the Heads:

'Before attempting to date them firmly, fieldwork in the area is essential. They have an archaic appearance, and their find-spot would be in accordance with an early dating. But, whether or not subsequent research proves them to be early or late in date, their very existence and discovery, and the fact that they are of local material, has an inherent value and interest that cannot simply be ignored'.

The article was illustrated with the evocative line drawings depicted in Chapter One. The only subse-quent public comment Dr Ross made on the report appeared after a reporter from Newcastle's *The Journal* rang her in 1974. The brief account she gave was:

"We had full tests carried out and it seems unlikely that they were made recently. Analysis showed that they were carved from a local rock. Of course, the analysis could be wrong". [3]

Anne Ross wrote a short personal letter to Dr David Smith shortly afterwards mentioning Hodson's report and frustration at Dr Robson's lack or urgency in analysing the Heads:

'I wish you would get Dr Robson to look at the heads. I am particularly interested in the patina detected by Professor Hodson, and the substance apparently set into one of the eyes. The Leeds Office told Professor Hodson that the sandstone in question comes from immediately north of Hexham, so it will be interesting to have this point settled one way or another. … Would you be very kind and send the offprints (enclosed) to Mr Coulson [Craigie, I assume] and the owners of the Hexham heads? I have sent everyone else mentioned in the note a copy'. [4]

As for Douglas Robson's report , from the title it certainly relates specifically to Anne Ross's article.

Whether it was published subsequently or had limited circulation is conjectural. These are the conclusions in full:

REPORT ON HEADS 4 AND 5, FROM HEXHAM

'**General observations**. The material from which the heads have been fashioned consist of uniformly large grains of quartz – 2mm diameter on average – set in a very fine-grained matrix. The latter is calcareous. The grains are extremely well-rounded and polished, with no indication of partial solution or of secondary growth. There are numerous sandstones, belonging to the upper Carboniferous succession, which outcrop in the Hexham district, but none of them bear any similarity to the material from which these heads have been formed. Indeed, this material is unlike any natural sandstone.

Specific observations.

1. In a natural sandstone, there is invariably a predominance of grains of a particular diameter, but also with a fair proportion of grains of greater and lesser diameters. On analysis, such a sandstone provides a cumulative with one prominent peak. The material of the heads would no doubt form a curve with two marked peaks – something which a normal sandstone seldom provides in nature.

2. In a natural sandstone, the grains are closely packed, and in contact with one another; any fine interstitial material introduced after the deposition of the sandstone, would occupy the small pores between the grains. The material from the heads consists of a large proportion of very fine grained matrix with the very much larger quartz grains imbedded in it but generally not in contact with each other.

3. In a natural sandstone, the quartz grains generally show a considerable degree of singularity; this is certainly true of all the local sandstones. Only sand grains which have been subjected to desert conditions or to intense wave action on a sea-beach show the degree of rounding exhibited by the grains which come from the Hexham heads. Moreover, grains from a desert sand show a pitted, rather than a polished surface.

4. In a natural sandstone, there is generally some indication of bedding or a layering of the grains; no such pattern can be detected in the material from which the heads are formed.

Conclusions. The material from which the heads have been formed is an artificial cement. The sand grains in it are probably derived from the sea-shore, where wave action sorts out material to a very uniform size and produces a high degree of rounding and polishing. There are often well-rounded calcareous fragments – from sea-shells – in such a deposit though, without disaggregation, it would not be possible to confirm this point in the case of the Hexham heads. If the heads are of modern origin, no doubt the quartz grains come from a builder's sand. If they are of ancient origin, presumably some enterprising Hexham Briton, struggling through the swamps of the Tyne valley, may have visited the seaside and have come back with a satchel of sand which he subsequently mixed with ground-up limestone and water. There is an adequate local supply of limestone.

No further comment regarding the polished surface of the heads, beyond those made by Professor Hodson, needs to be added.' [5]

JAN 75 ?

Professor's stone heads mistake . . .

A LEADING geologist yesterday admitted that he had probably made a mistake over two stone heads, thought to have been of Celtic origin.

Prof. Frank Hodson, Professor of Geology and Dean of the faculty of science at Southampton University conceded his mistake last night.

The two heads are now lying in Newcastle University Museum of Antiquities.

And last night Hexham lorry driver, Desmond Cragie, was having a quiet chuckle at the thought of having fooled geologists and archaeologists alike.

Mr. Cragie, of Prior Terrace, maintained he made the Celtic idols for his daughter back in 1956.

The heads, thought to be at least 1,800 years old, were first examined by Dr. Anne Ross, an archaeologist, who said they were probably Celtic religious symbols.

The heads were depicted in magazines and were analysed at Southampton University.

There seemed no doubt that the heads were genuine, Dr. Ross, herself, said: "There very existence and discovery, and the fact that they are of local material, has an inherent value and interest that cannot simply be ignored."

Prof. Hodson examined the heads and believed them to have been made of sandstone from the Hexham area.

Only one academic was sceptical—Dr. Douglas Robson, a senior lecturer in geology at Newcastle University.

He inspected the heads and declared they were not natural stone. Yesterday he said the heads were made out of a compound similar to that used by builders making mock stone for housing.

Yesterday Prof. Hodson said he was again looking into the head structure, but had not yet completed his examination.

But, he said, it was more than likely that Dr. Robson was right and that Mr. Cragie had indeed made the heads.

"Anyone can make a mistake. In many of these matters you cannot win. "If you get it wrong and leave it you will eventually be made a fool of, but if it happened to be genuine and you destroyed it while examining its structure you would obviously be reprimanded," said Prof. Hodson.

Mr. Cragie said last night: "It is just what I have been telling them all the time."

Pilloried in public

Frank Hodson was drawn into the public glare over the anomalies between his conclusion and that of Dr Robson. Journalists can be mischievous, particularly when they spot 'expert' authority figures such as academics and scientists at loggerheads and a hack on Tyneside (doubtless primed, for how else could he have got his story?) became aware of a Heads saga development. A sub-editor headed the expose 'Professor's stone heads mistake . . ' The news item was naturally anchored by the local angle of Des Craigie's modern-origin Heads claim, but introduced Anne Ross's endorsement of them being Celtic after the Hodson report made her believe as he did they were made from Hexham area sandstone.

But *The Journal* had Douglas Robson declaring they were not natural stone, but 'made out of a compound similar to that used by builders making mock stone for housing'. The uncredited reporter rang Frank Hodson, who said he was again examining the stone structure, but had yet to complete his examination. Obviously an honourable man, he conceded that it was more than likely his counterpart was correct and that Des had indeed made the Heads. Admitting:

> "Anyone can make a mistake. In many of these matters you cannot win. If you get it wrong and leave it you will eventually be made a fool of, but if it happened to be genuine and you destroyed it while examining its stone structure you will obviously be reprimanded". [6]

Willing to admit a fundamental mistake is praiseworthy, but this was hardly a display of magnanimity.

Contempt for his Newcastle opposite number is barely disguised. Hodson's disapproval of the 'destruction' is plain. Additionally, did he suspect Robson deliberately passed his report to the media? It certainly shows that the stakes were high and feelings also.

Even more pertinently, not everyone – even scientists – has been convinced by either petrological conclusion.

Naturally, Des Craigie was told the news and his response of, "It is just what I've been telling them all the time" was the least surprising aspect, having already stated earlier that "the heads were made from a mixture of different sands and cement". [7]

The academic ding-dong as reported by *The Journal*.

Curiously, Anne Ross's oddly brief comment in *Archaeologia Aeliana* spookily mirrors the opinion – and even wording – of archaeologist Roger Miket, in Newcastle:

> 'The necks appear to have acted as tenons, which combined with the pulled-back hair on one of them have led to speculation as to a possible Celtic origin. They were found in a garden at Hexham by some small boys who were throwing stones – the national pastime of this age group which in this case may have had a constructive result! We would be grateful for your opinion on these two heads, both to complete our records, and also to included as an article in Barbara's [Harbottle's] Newsbulletin [*CBA*] if this is agreeable to you'. (8)

During all this academic knockabout routine, the finders had not been entirely forgotten. Anne Ross, in her letter to David Smith, asked if he would forward 'offprints (enclosed)' to the Robsons. These I assume to be relevant pages from *Archaeologia Aeliana*. As the undated letter from Jenny Robson I have comes from the Museum of Antiquities file, I assume it was addressed to Dr Smith and the 'little book' she thanks him for would be the *AA* offprint. After saying she and the boys found it 'very interesting', she gives the go-ahead for the Heads to be tested:

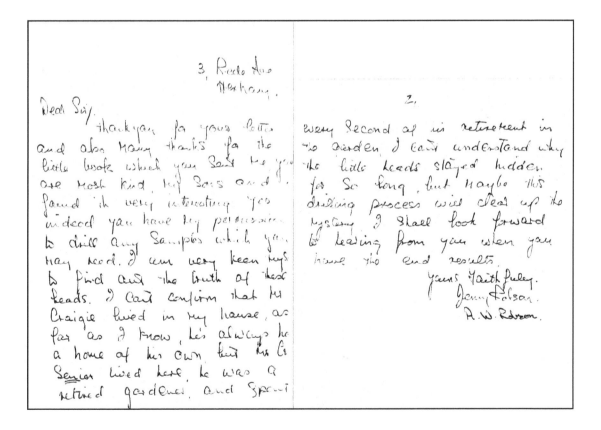

The Robsons permit drilling – not sawing!

'Yes indeed you have my permission to drill any samples which you may need. I am very keen myself to find out the truth of these heads. I can't confirm that Mr Craigie lived in my house. As far as I know, he's always had a home of his own, but Mr Craigie <u>Senior</u> [her emphasis] lived here. He was a retired gardener and spent every second of his retirement in the garden. I can't understand why the little heads stayed hidden for so long, but maybe this drilling process will clear up the mystery. I shall look forward to hearing from you when you have the end results'. [9]

The letter was signed from Jenny Robson and A. W. Robson. Critical correspondence now shifts to the time following Douglas Robson's 8 May 1974 and the finders are mentioned among others in Dr Smith's letter of thanks to his Newcastle colleague for his analysis, beginning rather formally:

'Dear Dr. Robson,

This is to thank you, a little belatedly but nonetheless warmly, for your report on the Hexham heads. This is a positive step towards bringing this affair to an end. A copy has been sent to Dr. Anne Ross and, unless you have any objection, I will next week send copies to the finders of the heads and to the lorry driver who claims to have made them. If the latter contacts the press, and if the press contact us, our comment will be that we have never been anything but intermediaries in the matter and have absolutely nothing to add to what may already have been said.

With thanks again, and kindest regards'. [10]

To Des Craigie, he simply enclosed a copy of the Robson report on 'those heads' and apologised for the delay. [11] Yet it seems he waited until 1975 to contact the Hexham Robsons (presumably no relation; it is a very common Tyneside surname), despite his avowed intention to do so contemporaneously with Des. His excuse when finally getting around to contact was to blame expectancy of a further analysis and the last paragraph seems chronologically ambiguous, so it's best I give the letter in full:

'Dear Mr. and Mrs. Robson,

I apologize for the long delay in writing about "the Hexham heads", but I was under the impression that the geological examination of them was still proceeding and that there would be another, more positive report on them. I find, however, that I was mistaken. In any case, the report by Dr. D. A. Robson of this University's Department of Geology, dated 8th May 1974, is sufficiently conclusive to justify my closing the file on these heads. I enclose a copy of his report and a copy of a Memo which I have just received from him. I am sorry if you and the boys are disappointed by the report, but so are we.

Thank you again for allowing us to keep the heads for so long, and in particular for permitting samples to be taken from them for microscopic examination. Without this the nature of the material could not have been conclusively determined.

I am sending copies of Dr. Robson's report and Memo to Mr. Craigie of Hexham, who claims to have made the heads, and also to Dr. Anne Ross. The heads themselves are being returned to you, as they were found on your property, under separate cover'. [12]

The memo being referred to by Dr Smith is dated 16 January 1975 and suggests Dr Robson was either being very co-operative or rubbing salt into Hodson's wounds. For someone who seemingly 'binned' his initial report Robson seems to anticipate another report from Southampton supporting his scepticism. Worth printing in full in the spirit of non-favouritism and as an inclusionist, here it is:

'THE HEXHAM HEADS

Yes, the only Report is that dated 8th May, 1974. Subsequently – on 26th September last – a note was sent to Professor Hodson enclosing three thin sections, two from the Heads [sic] and one from a cement block which was made at about the same time as the Heads, by Mr Craigie, with similar material. There was no accompanying Report to Professor Hodson, only an observation that the three thin sections are very similar and confirm the conclusions stated in the Report dated 8th May, 1974.

Professor Hodson has acknowledged receipt of the sections, in a letter dated 27th December 1974, and hopes to send his report soon'. [13]

Despite Dr Smith's assurance to the Robson family regarding the return 'under separate cover' of the Heads, he framed a brief letter to the parents in what might be determined to be a mildly menacing tone:

'Forgive me for troubling you again, but I really would be grateful to know if you want to have the two "Hexham heads" back. If not, I will send them to Mr. Craigie, who has expressed his wish to have them'. (14)

Jenny Robson duly replied apologetically a month later:

'I am sorry I am late in replying to your numerous letters, but I have been away in Hull staying with my daughter. Yes! The boys would love to have the little heads back. They have talked about nothing else since we got back from Hull. Thanking you for all your help'. (15)

Well, the boys might have welcomed the Heads return, but it is certainly contrary to their mother's feelings as expressed in the media at this time, as reported earlier. And despite being clearly signed 'Jenny Robson, Mrs', Smith addressed the reply to 'Mr Robson', obviously unaware of Hexham's matriarchal supremacy. Suffice to say it involved transfer of the Heads to Prospect House, a council office in Hexham, where the family would find them labelled 'to be called for'.

David Smith, probably feeling thankful that he could finally tie up any loose ends, wrote what amounts to his virtual fading from the tale. To Douglas Robson, he informed him the Heads had been returned to the Hexham Robsons, Des Craigie was informed a day later and he stated 'I have now closed my file on these heads' with a valedictory 'my grateful appreciation of the time and trouble you have taken over the objects'.

A frank interview with Professor Hodson

I actually spoke to Frank Hodson about the Heads. The circumstances themselves are somewhat shrouded in mystery. Some jotted notes of the conversation I found late in the investigation are headed 'Hodson interview 28/5/81'. The date is critical as it dates our chat post-publication of *Tales of the Hex-*

24·3·75.   3. Rock Ave
                              Horsham.

Dear Sir,
          I am sorry I am
late in replying to your
numerous letters but I
have been away in Hull
staying with my daughter.
Yes! the boys would
like to have the little
heads back. They have
talked about nothing else
Since we got back from
Hull. Thanking you for all
your help. Yours Sincerely,
                 Jenny Robson. Mrs.

A woman of few words – Jenny Robson replies to the museum.

ham Heads. More mysteriously, more frustratingly I cannot recall the circumstances. The fact they were scribbled on both sides of a single sheet of A4 paper, one side of which was printed with a sub-editorial page planner from my workplace suggests the conversation was unplanned, unprepared and took place at the *Hartlepool Mail*. Also I see no reason why I should have chosen to ring Hodson as I assumed the subject was then in my past. My impression today is that he tracked me down to set the record straight after reading my booklet, although I was meticulous about recording to whom and when copies were sold – and his name is absent.

The notes begin with an intriguing and wholly baffling "can't recall at the moment" and a line to indicate, presumably, a change of subject. With the remainder of my notes, I have elected to flesh out the scant phrases and key words to make the most probable dialogue possible in the circumstances:

> "The heads came to me as rather precious objects. I studied them under a microscope and scraped a milligram [from one of them?] to look at it under an x-ray machine. Thus I established the matrix. They were made of calcareous sandstone. Previously they had been sent to [the Museum of Antiquities] to Dr Robson in Newcastle and he made a destructive analysis. He took a great slice. He said it was artificial".

The notes then suggest that at this point I asked if he concurred with Douglas Robson. He replied in truly fortean fashion:

> "I have no opinion on the matter. All I could do was say the grains contained calcium carbonate. If artificial it was sand and cement ... calcium silicate ..."

For this book I had been wrestling with the troublesome timeline, the pieces in the jigsaw taking shape but a glaring gap existed between the Heads arriving back in Hexham in 1975 and their reappearance in Southampton for further onwards movement by early 1976. Did the Hodson chat clear up the mystery? Well, yes … and no.

> "Dr Ross sent me 50 to 60 ['Celtic' heads] in her time. Perhaps R [my unhelpful appreviation – Ross or Robson?] sent them back to me. Anne brought a young chap [to see me. Presumably Dr Don Robins].

At this point Hodson's narrative introduces the opaque comment, "I think what must have happened to justify his claim", is I guess a reference to Robson when I told him my friend Don Robins had been highly critical of Robson's butchery of the Heads. At this point, Hodson seemed ready to cease sitting on the metaphorical fortean fence.

> "I think they [the Heads] are artificial. The material was not accumulated by natural means. Perhaps he [Robson] sent them back with the slices".

This suggests the unclear 'R' reference mentioned earlier referred to Robson, but the correspondence referring to the samples for further analysis does not mention the Heads themselves being part of the package. But how else could they get from Hexham to Southampton? Charles Fort himself coined the term 'teleportation', but I think even with the multi-level mystery here, that notion's too off the wall!

At this point it seems I switched the conversation to Anne Ross and elicited his opinion that, "I suspect in her heart she realised the heads weren't Celtic," and "I think she lost interest [in them]".

Most trips down memory lane prove to be a dead end track, but I had got Hodson to be frank and admit he thought the Heads were artificial and modern and the suspicion, too, that Anne Ross was of the same opinion. It only needed him to vindicate Des Craigie and – apart from the still unresolved chronology – tie up some loose ends. But, of course, it was not to be. Despite Des's describing how he flattened the bottoms so that they stood up, Hodson was adamant that …

> "He tapered the necks [i.e. created tenons]. Most people would squash them so
> they would stand. [He must have had to] press the bottom".

At which it seems the dialogue ended. As I recall, it was a friendly chat with a cheerful, articulate, knowledgable and straightforward professional. It had been a pleasure to have made his acquaintance.

CHAPTER SEVEN
THE SCIENTIST

Anne Ross and Frank Hodson should by now be familiar figures to the reader, whereas Don Robins has warranted only fleeting mentions. Don's academic credentials are acknowledged in a number of fields; from the hard science of materials chemistry to the soft science of the paranormal and espousal of the controversial stone-tape theory. His books have covered such disparate subjects as a major study of stone retaining memories of past events through solidified energy and which might account for the presence of ghostly or psychic phenomena; earth mysteries analysis of infrasound at prehistoric sites; and a collaboration with Anne Ross on a popular but erudite investigation of Lindow Man, a bog burial sacrifice with added speculation.

As for my involvement with Dr Robins in the 1970s, this came about as a result of our mutual interest in the Hexham Heads and earth mysteries research in general. Hence (as with Des Craigie), having a rapport with Robins I refer to him with familiarity as 'Don', although there was a momentary blip in our friendship while having a drink after a moot organised by *The Ley Hunter* magazine when we were sat outside Hampstead Heath's splendid Jack Straw's Castle pub when I made some comments and as Don went to the bar to recharge our glasses, his companion observed, "Don doesn't like being spoken to like that!" I recall just laughing and obviously smoothed over any sleight. I recall we corresponded on the Hexham Heads (but as with the subject of our focus, the whereabouts of Don's letters is a mystery – particularly annoying as he was scathing about Dr Robson's methods).

Before I knew Don, he trained as a chemist but took a PhD in magnetism or solid state chemistry (his own book blurbs can't agree) and been variously described as an organic chemist and

A somewhat youthful Don Robins in the late 1970s.

materials chemist. He worked initially in industry before becoming a lecturer in applied science, during which time his interest in prehistory and archaeology grew. An early ecologist, he was appointed Reader in Conservation Science at Camberwell School of Art and lectured at the Institute of Archaeology in the University of London, where he developed the technique of electron spin resonance which became influential as a means of analysing food remains in archaeology and undoubtedly played a major role in the scientific aspect of his book collaboration on *The Life and Death of a Druid Prince*. [1] During this time his twin interests in archaeology and the properties of stone had led him to join the Dragon Project. This was an interdisciplinary group of volunteers, some of whom had scientific credentials, who banded together to study the elusive 'earth energy' theory so beloved of Sixties hippies and Seventies New Agers. Pre-empting his fellow researchers, Don chose to publish a book on the incomplete survey of infrasound data detected at various prehistoric sites, but particularly Oxfordshire's megalithic stone circle Rollright Stones. At the time, I was regularly visiting ancient monuments throughout the North with fellow megalithomaniac John Watson. But the eccentric here was Don himself, whose book *Circles of Silence* [2] appeared dull, a shambles and inconclusive. I reviewed it but admit I could not finish it. For thoroughness, I have finally managed this as a point of personal inclusionism and only now understand its enigmatic title – don't ask!

Meanwhile, Don went on to lecture worldwide upon his cutting edge work in archaeological science, holding a number of visiting professorships in the US, while forsaking academia for more lucrative consultancy work. Of his personal life little is known, although the blurb in his first book stated he was living in Middlesex, married to a psychologist called Zofia and they had a son 'and a large army of cats'. I believe she was of Russian nationality. Also, I understand that there was some ill feeling from others in the Dragon Project – details of which, known to me, are best not recorded in print – one of whom, when I inquired of Don's current whereabouts and status, told me he didn't know and that if he never heard his name again it would be too soon. According to the blurb in his 1988 book *The Secret Language of Stone*, he was moving to Malibu, California, to work for the Getty Institute. This was the book he produced in amongst all of this international jet-setting and immersing himself in bog burials. It attempted to give the stone-tape theory credibility and doubtless there was no-one better qualified to tackle this avowedly fortean aspect of science and parapsychology. Don seemed to be one of those rare maverick boffins who could move easily between the worlds of academia, global big business and weekend hippiedom at the megaliths (with one suspects a rat-like cunning plausibility, eccentricity, charm and I suspect psychological flaws).

If *The Secret Language of Stone* [3] was inspired by the Hexham Heads, his collaboration with Anne Ross took him back to the same historical period, but with a more personal emphasis on a real person rather than stone artefacts. Frankly, I have not had the time to obtain and read the 'bog book' (one for my dotage), but I am aware of its contents and in a strangely personal way I feel a faint affinity as I have many time travelled along Lancaster Road, Hartlepool, where an even more spectacular double human sacrifice bog burial was unearthed at the liminal point on the edge of The Slake, an estuarine former swamp excavated to create the docks upon which West Hartlepool's prosperity was created. If you're reading this while hangin' out in Malibu with Bob Dylan, Mel Gibson, Janet Jackson, Jeff Bridges and Angelina Jolie, drop me a line, Don, and we can compare mythologies.

Whatever anyone thinks of Don Robins as a person or his scientific dalliances, he has a keen mind, a sympathy for paranormal research, rare among scientists in general. In fact, an article he published in *Alpha* magazine in 1980 is the best and most concise comparison between the scientific and paranormalist approaches and I would urge anyone interested in any aspect of the 'supernatural' or science theory to seek it out. This is especially important as he acted as necessary whistleblower on colleagues who, when even the tightest of experimental designs often throw out inexplicable results, these were conveniently ignored in many disciplines: the equivalent of admitted paranormal non-repeatability in laboratory conditions. He also even mentions scientific oddities such as brain opiates, which to me must logically indicate all drug laws are inadmissible on the grounds that drugs are naturally created by the human body. Don told me he and his wife picked (magic?) mushrooms in the shadow of a Russian nuclear power plant. [4]

Although I have tried to contain discussion of the various theories pertaining to the Hexham Heads mystery until later in the book, to put Don's strategic involvement in context I need to explain the stone-tape theory briefly. It will also be dealt with subsequently, but suffice to say it relates to a concept of place memory and stone memory and has a long history, best exemplified by the scientific studies of archaeologist Tom Lethbridge, the speculative fiction of Nigel Kneale and influence upon shamanic author Alan Garner.

In summary, the notion is that traumatic events – murder, rape, torture – leave a record of their occurrence, explaining why spooks haunt concentration camps, asylums and dungeons. Somehow dramatic events supposedly become impressed upon the fabric of their environment: buildings or landscapes and even a personal object associated with the person at the epicentre of the trauma. As a sympathetic sceptic in all matters, I have tried to empathise with this 'playback' place memories notion, but without much enthusiasm. So what chance scientific objectivity; particularly as it proves elusive to scrutiny under laboratory conditions? Don has pushed a selling point for this support as to how we instinctively feel places have atmospheres, citing how estate agents play on an almost tangible happy feeling some houses exude and I have personally experienced a difference in ambience when a lazy miserable pub landlord has been replaced by a jovial workaholic.

But to get back to the Hexham Heads, Don explained how they seemed to have a role to play in his investigation:

> 'As I became more involved in the considerations of energy storage and transduction in stone, I increasingly wondered about this phenomenon and the likelihood of establishing an energetic basis for its reality. It seemed that to do this it would be necessary to investigate a well-established case of "playback", if possible viewing the phenomenon directly before any definite hypothesis could be put forward. It was at this point in my awakening interest that I chanced upon the strange story of the two Hexham Heads'. [5]

In this article, Don then gave a resume of the Heads history up to early 1978. He was particularly intrigued that they might be modern and as Des Craigie maintained all along not designed with any close reference to Celtic style, but as Don oddly phrased it, 'for some **undisclosed purpose**'. [my emphasis] Don went on to stress that removing the Heads from Dr Ross's home did not banish the werewolf. At this point Don recognised that here was a rich opportunity to pursue his stone-tape theory investigation and to this end began by seeking the Heads whereabouts. In true narrative style he recorded how his tracing of them progressed from having written an article on the possibility of image encoding in stone using the Hexham Heads to illustrate aspects of the problem, to how after the article appeared in *The Ley Hunter* [6] magazine, its editor, Paul Devereux, contacted Anne Ross over certain points and in passing inquired of the Heads whereabouts. She assumed they were either back at the Museum of Antiquities or had been returned to the finders. She confirmed the phenomena in her home but said it 'only ceased when her entire Celtic head collection was removed from her home'. Observant readers may have noted that even Dr Ross contradicts herself here, as she was quoted in the Reader's Digest compendium as saying 'the thing' had **not** gone with the collection.

Heads left neglected for two years

Don then introduced one of the still unexplained aspects of the mystery. Having doggedly pestered Anne Ross over the Heads whereabouts, his persistence paid off. In the late summer of 1977, she replied to say the Heads 'were, in fact, still in Southampton University', although in the keeping of Frank Hodson. It gets even weirder. Don continued, 'Apparently they had been returned to him from Newcastle some two years before, and they had lain neglected in a cardboard box ever since!' Which begged more questions: did Hodson specifically request them, if so for further analysis but if so why 'neglected'? Two years previously takes us back to the Heads being back in Hexham and being moved from Rede Avenue down the road to Allen Drive and back again, plus Jenny Robson saying the family wanted them returned, then saying she hated them and planned to rebury them … yet they ended up in Southampton! But let Don's narrative continue:

> 'On 21st September 1977 I travelled to Southampton for the meeting, feeling very disturbed about the prospect of encountering the heads. I was aware, of course, that such an attitude was not at all conducive to dispassionate objectivity, but I was nevertheless prepared to keep all my options, subjective and objective, open. One thought constantly on my mind during the journey was that while I started out from the standpoint that the phantom was some type of play-back phenomenon, I had increasingly come to wonder whether there was more to it than that. One possibility that hovered on the edge of my awareness of related phenomena was that of the "elemental" or "guardian" that is sometimes associated with particular places or things, and this added a whole extra dimension to the simple concept of 'playback', one of which far outstripped the tenuous links I had tried to retain with scientific objectivity in the whole pursuit of these heads. It also added a sinister undertone to the quest itself'.

At which point Don met Frank Hodson and as they discussed the Heads, his host 'was at pains to tell me that, as far as he was concerned, there seemed to be no basis for Dr Ross's accounts of the phantom'. To emphasise his scepticism he made the significant point that, 'In the two years that he had the heads in his possession nothing had happened'. But were the Hexham Heads then wholly isolated – probably in their box in a desk drawer? Had Dr Ross introduced him to subsequent examples for analysis as she had on many occasions and which had tarried awhile in his room between laboratory visits? Not as at Rose Road where they had enjoyed resonance with similar company in the form of fellow idols?

Yet more significantly, Frank Hodson returned to the ancient versus modern championship. Stepping into the metaphorical ring again, he dealt a blow which was worthy of Rambo to Robson's certainties:

> 'The main peculiarity of the heads, in his opinion, was the material of their construction: they were reputedly made of cement by Craigie, but spectrographic analysis indicated **no sign of calcium silicate, the major component of cement**.' [my emphasis]

So, does this imply the Heads were not modern? This was a private observation gone public – or at least put into the public domain – and maybe makes Hodson the eventual victor.

Back in the Southampton University study that day, Don seemed disappointed that Hodson had not unveiled the objects and purpose for his journey with a flourish, but as they were withdrawn from a small cardboard box was hardly awestruck, only experiencing surprise at their smallness. He then drew attention to how his host's rival had treated the Heads:

> 'Both heads, when placed on the desktop, sat squarely on smooth flat neck surfaces. This, however, was not their original form, since the necks had ended in cone-shaped tenons. Examination at Newcastle had proceeded by sawing off these tenons to give surfaces for petrographic analysis, leaving the heads with a smooth surface. It is interesting to note that this tenon feature is also distinctly Celtic (probably related to the placing of heads in wall niches). On handling, the heads were unexpectedly heavy and dense, and whether holding them or looking at them on the desk top, I did not feel at ease. My immediate impression was that the female head, the girl, was the one that disturbed me. Wherever the head was placed on the desk, one of the eyes seemed to be on me, and I only felt at ease when the head was turned around so that the eyes were facing directly away. Anne Ross then joined us and during the rest of the day I discussed the heads with her and Professor Hodson'.

Well, permission to drill as granted by Jenny Robson does not, surely, extend to 'sawing off the tenons'! In correspondence, Don continued to express anger at this dubious professional behaviour and I was sure he would take care of the Heads and conduct his own less destructive analysis, to which end I took a very small sample from my Craigie-made doll/idol and posted it off for Don's opinion. As for that fateful day in Southampton, Don then had a real surprise coming:

> 'As our meeting came to an end, I was offered the heads to examine on an indefinite basis, and whereas I had expected only to look at them and photograph them, I now found that my quest had succeeded rather too well, and it was with some trepidation (greater than I had at the outset of the quest) that I walked to my car with the heads in my briefcase … That night I kept the heads at the end of the garden after letting my animals (four cats and a German shepherd) inspect them. The cats showed no reaction, but the dog immediately fastened his teeth on the heads, an action difficult to see any significance in! I kept the heads at home for some two months, transferring them to college for another two months before I parted with them at the end of January 1978 [subsequently altered to early February]'.

Doctor puts spin on story

The next chapter is devoted to the even more elusive Frank Hyde, to whom Don loaned the Heads. For any information of Hyde's involvement I have had to rely on Don's account and the one in his book on properties of stone has the best account so I will here pass over this episode in the *Alpha* article. With his erudition in matters pertaining to petrology, I find it odd that with the Heads in his possession, my sliver from one made by Des Craigie and perhaps slivers from Hodson, why Don did not carry out his own examination as an arbiter between 'Black Douglas' and 'Fearless Frank'. In the *Alpha* piece he blamed the Heads being loaned for his own tardiness with the lame admission that 'I had intended to carry out other tests on the material from which the heads were made, but these were never to be done'. He then made the observation that 'the question of the heads' construction is still equivocal' and moved from solid science to the paranormal by continuing:

> ' … although I personally felt the veracity of Anne Ross' experience was beyond reasonable doubt. A number of factors in the "haunting" seem to be common to other more prosaic encounters with apparitions: the appearance in the bedroom, the association of the spectre with stairs, the feeling of intense cold on manifesta-

tion, and the sense of atmosphere associated with the heads themselves. Much could be written of the energetic of these phenomena in relation to manifestation and "playback", although it falls outside the scope of this article, but I am still left wondering whether there is another deep, and more sinister, dimension to the whole affair [and actually earlier] there is no tidy ending or explanation to this story'.

At this stage in my personal quest for the truth and the Heads whereabouts, I wholeheartedly agree with both sentiments – that it goes deeper, there is no easy answer and perhaps never will be.

In *The Secret Language of Stone*, Don reprises his pivotal trip to Southampton, so I'll only mention any additional information of consequence and a couple of discrepancies with the *Alpha* account. He first met Hodson in mid-morning as Anne Ross was in a meeting. The professor impressed Don with his pragmatism and 'was extremely sceptical of any attempt to explain the phenomenon since he maintained it did not exist, and noted with some good-humoured force that he had never experienced a thing during the two years they [the Heads] had been in his possession'.

Yet Don repeated that final petrological revision:

> 'The only peculiarity he would concede was in the chemical analysis since no trace of calcium silicate, the major cement component, had been found. He had assumed it was concrete based, of course, upon Craigie's comments about how the heads were made although "artificial stone" as he described it does not have to be cement, for example it could be crushed and moulded limestone or marble, although this would not accord with the generally observed denseness of the stone'.

Was this further evidence that 'Fearless Frank' was the moral victor? Another nail in the Heads are modern argument?

Don then described his initial encounter with the Heads, emphasising their 'extreme denseness' and Hodson describing 'the conical tenons being sawn off at their base'. He also recorded his growing anxiety in the presence of the Heads: not from the 'skull-head' with its 'gaunt, vestigial and even serene features' and a 'neutral' feel, but the 'wall-eyed hag' disturbed Don. Then when Don came to retelling how he came to be the Heads custodian, in this version he puts an extraordinary spin on the offer:

> 'Both Professor Hodson and Anne Ross concurred on the archaeological worthlessness of the heads because of the **certainty that they were indeed modern**'. {my emphasis}

So, any prospect of a rematch between geologist heavyweights looked over; 'Fearless Frank' had thrown in the towel, his reputation bruised and a resigned realisation that it was time to move on. And anyway it had just been fantasy boxing, hadn't it? But what of his No. 1 supporter? Give Don credit, he had not been phased by his lunchtime companions' scepticism, yet had Trainer Ross forgotten her attachment to matters paranormal? When offered the Heads he 'came near to panic', but 'it was definitely an offer I could not refuse'.

OPPOSITE: Hardly a new theory despite the title's boast, but nevertheless seemingly the last throw of the dice for the stone tape theory.

THE SECRET LANGUAGE OF STONE

A new theory linking stones and crystals with
psychic phenomena

DON ROBINS

Well, Don, it was the equivalent of being the one taking a Lonsdale belt home. Next stop London and don't spare the horsepower.

Back with Don's book, doubtless embarrassed that he had mentioned his Alsatian biting artefacts in his safekeeping (despite some now regarding them as academically worthless, though valuable in contemporary mythology), the extended version has him depositing the Heads in their box wrapped in a plastic bag under a tree in his garden while surrounded by his 'inquisitive cats and dog, who showed **no interest** in the heads'. [my emphasis] Or should I be charitable and accept Don could have had a momentary lapse of memory?

Following the role played in the Ross household of the werewolf's presences on the staircase, Don deliberately placed the Heads on a bookcase in the upstairs study facing the door which led to the stairs. Planning to go to the Chemical Society Library, in Piccadilly, for the afternoon, he set off for the Tube after silently challenging the Heads to reveal their supposed powers when he returned. After going a few hundred yards he realised he had forgotten a volume which required its immediate return to the library and with trepidation returned home. Opening the door of his Edwardian abode where the weatherworn windows and doors allowed for draughts on a blustery day such as this, Don felt an unexpected 'electric tingling breathless tension and silence' within. With apprehension rising, he ventured into the study where the claustrophobic atmosphere seemed even more dense:

> 'I looked out of the window and saw branches waving in the wind, but in that room was the stillness of the tomb, no curtains moved in the draughts at the window, no sound seemed to penetrate. I felt more and more mesmerized by the sightless gaze of those mad eyes, but I managed to pick up the book and leave without a backward glance'.

When bookworm Don returned, the draughts had returned, the tingling atmosphere had dissipated, but the foreboding around the Heads had increased. It was time to be rid of them.

CHAPTER EIGHT
THE ASTROLGER

Ａs for Don Robins, we left him in the last chapter wanting rid of the Heads. In his *The Secret Language of Stone* he related how several people of his acquaintance knew he had become custodian and requested to borrow them for various techniques of testing. Seeking their removal, Don was willing to consider some of these approaches as he had a foreboding that if he retained the Heads he was in peril and that some shadowy 'climax' was heading towards its conclusion. Inspired by reading fantasy writer J R R Tolkien, he pondered the possibility of the Heads working through the folkloric process of ostension like the mythical Ring to blindly seek a new guardian in the furtherance of some unspecified ghastly destiny. Don mused, 'After my electric experience in the study *anything* seemed possible'.

With so many seemingly interested people wanting to test the Heads, Frank Hyde would seem to me to have been an unlikely candidate, but maybe Don was desperate to be rid and in reality no-one else was interested. Having already pointed out there are many on the fringes of the scientific world who believe in parascience and the occult realm, but who are shadier and less transparent than your average earth mysteries follower like myself, Don's articles had attracted the attention of those in this twilight world whose participants normal researchers would shun or discourage. Not Don, who allowed himself to be introduced to Frank Hyde.

I found a few facts about Hyde during a 2007 internet trawl which suggested a career in engineering and a fascination for pseudoscience. After the name F W Hyde came the letters FSE, FEng and FRAS. Born on 10 September 1909, it seems he was a consultant in technology with special attention to space exploration and space medicine. He was also a consultant in parapsychology and operating a unit of interface between man and his environment, including mysticism and related practices. One internet site which mentions a Frank Hyde in astrological history appears to summarising *The Astrologer's Manual*, by Landis Knight Green, which mentions in a chronology of some society's history for 1977 a publication, *Recent Advances in Natal Astology*, compiled by Geoffrey Dean and assisted by Arthur Mather, and among 22 collaborators is the name Frank Hyde. (1) Parascientist David Taylor contacted the Astrological Association on my behalf, but it replied on 2 February 2011 that there was no record of Hyde on its 2002 database, despite his having given the AA a lecture entitled *Astronomy and Astrology* around 1977. David made several such fruitless approaches to find more of the elusive Hyde. He struck lucky, however, with his friend and fellow author, Peter Underwood (See also Chapter Four), who recalled:

> 'I'm afraid Frank Hyde didn't make much of an impression. [Author] Dennis
> [Bardens] introduced him to me at a Ghost Club meeting, saying he was some-

thing of an expert on astrology and might be a speaker for us one day, but it never materialised. I have no idea whether he is still alive'. [2]

For whatever motive, it was Hyde's expression of keen interest in experimenting with the Heads utilising his dowsing experience which won the day. The diviner lived in Kilburn, North-West London, and one evening in early February 1978, Don drove to deliver the Heads. As he unpacked them from their cardboard box, Hyde asked if before Don returned home he wanted to witness an experiment? Panicking that this might imply that the total extent of the amateur's investigation was about to be enacted and he would again be encumbered with what had in his eyes turned from treasure trove into fool's gold and a metaphorical albatross tightening around his neck and squeezing him into realms of anxiety and paranoia, Don agreed with reluctant.

Hyde and seek

Anyone with the slightest interest in practical earth mysteries, at some stage tries their hand at dowsing. Personally, I had some good and some bad days, positive ones and not a flicker of response ones. Don had also reached the same rudimentary stage and entered into the spirit that evening. Firstly Hyde tried to get a response with a pendulum, followed by my speciality angle rods and finally using a long thin metal rod supposedly most sensitive of all. Then Don tried his luck. Not surprisingly, whether in close proximity or distant from each other, the positive reactions came from the wall-eyed hag Head. 'She' activated the pendulum and had it performing a merry dance and had the divining rod twitching away; while the skull-head 'He' remained moribund, a mute testimony which made it crystal clear whomsoever of the couple carried the spark of alien intervention.

Doubtless still anxious to retreat to his cosy home, *sans* Heads, Don witnessed the next stage in the research programme, whereby the traditional techniques gave way to a more 'Mad scientist's laboratory' experiment with the Heads wrapped firstly individually and then together and put into a network of copper wire which Don compared to a Faraday cage. Don was impressed but the latter demonstration to show that the procedure diminished activity has left me baffled. In Don's account he admitted he had no 'clear idea of what further experiments he [Hyde] proposed to do', but after the demonstrations felt sufficiently confident to leave them in Hyde's hands. Or – and am I being cynical? – washed his own hands of his custodianship? Not really, as he did admit relief at fostering the Heads out and Hyde had given him an assurance to keep in touch regarding further experimentation and to return the Heads for others, too, to examine them.

When after a reasonable time Hyde had not communicated with him, Don tried to contact him by letter and telephone but to no avail. Later that spring, Don met the acquaintance who had introduced him to Hyde and was to receive bad news. Shortly after Don left the Heads in Kilburn, Hyde had been injured in a serious road crash. The messenger with bad news had no idea as to Hyde's current whereabouts. Throughout that summer of 1978 Don tried to contact the injured Hyde without success. Private and professional priorities took prominence and Don put the Heads out of his mind. But others had not forgotten and over the following five years persons who Don had contact with asked after the Heads welfare and situation. Many of these knew Frank Hyde personally. Or rather, had known Hyde – 'because to all intents and purposes he seemed to have vanished as completely as if he had walked into a fairy hill in a folk tale!' Don still mused upon whether Hyde had a private agenda as to his interest in the Heads, but despite unresolved questions he put them to the back of his mind. Out of sight, out of mind for him, but not for me. The quest for the Hexham Heads was on in earnest. However, I needed first to speak to some more people with a close involvement or who might offer valuable background information.

CHAPTER NINE
THE BRAINS TRUST

A t this stage in late 2011, with vacillating opinions from the experts; I had spoken to (Hodson), been rebuffed by another archaeologist (Robson) and with a rookie third (Robins) remaining stoically in favour of an ancient origin, I decided to seek a second tranche of three further opinions. I had no particular hopes of resolution, but I'm a dogged investigator and had nothing to lose as I remained as bemused as the next person, had no academic reputation at stake and was certainly neutral as to how matters had developed and might change in the future. All three persons I approached are graduates and experienced in their scientific fields and whose opinions should be relevant.

A verbal caning administered

A number of people involved in the quest were drawn in by serendipity, such as Lindsay Allason-Jones. She was a member of the audience at the *Fortean Times* UnConvention 2011 when Dr David Clarke and Andy Roberts gave a talk on cursed heads and as part of this showed the familiar picture of my hands holding the Colin Robson and second tranche Des Craigie head in my possession and wrongly – despite my previous protestations to the former – claiming it depicted the **original** Hexham Heads! Lindsay stood up and denounced the whole business as modern and not Celtic, leading to Stu Ferrol and Graham Williamson, also members of the audience, to approach her for more information on the subject and suggested a filmed interview.

Lindsay was not some dilettante armchair mysteries pundit challenging speakers' wisdom, but an experienced archaeologist and administrator, who moved to Newcastle in 1978 to take up the role of Assistant Keeper at Newcastle University Museum of Antiquities and deputy to Dr David Smith when Roger Miket moved on. Upon Dr Smith's retirement in 1988, she became Keeper, remaining its director until 2008, when the museum closed prior to the contents being moved to the Great North Museum: Hancock. Lindsay, who gained a Master of Letters degree, still carries out some teaching of archaeology and museum studies. She is also President of the Society of Antiquaries of Newcastle upon Tyne.

Subsequently, I interviewed Lindsay for film *Heads!* In late 2011 in a private office at the Great North Museum and will select from an hour-long interview the pertinent points for this book. An agreeable and enthusiastic subject, she had never seen the Hexham Heads, as by the date she took up her position they were no longer on museum premises, so I produced my Craigie creation for a visual comparison. She was intrigued but unimpressed by its crudity of fashioning, commenting firstly on it being "considerably smaller than any true Celtic head" she had seen and likening it to "the sort of thing a child would make out of plasticine … It's a very basic thing". Even more dismissive was her opinion that "if someone brought this in for identification today, I would immediately presume, without knowing the background, that this was a modern head". [1]

There was, however, one other head for her to see and Lindsay's comment upon seeing the ugly sculpture made by Colin Robson was to declare it "awful" and subsequently, "This looks more like a vampire hedgehog". Yet indicating Des's example, declared, "It's quite similar, in a lot of ways".

Several of my points were to establish how factual previous information I had collected could be substantiated. Such as how the Heads came to be in the museum. Had she any idea of whether there was a chain connecting Betty Gibson and Professor Bailey. I made the error of misremembering him as Charles and not David, but eventually we were satisfied that Bailey passed them to yet another intermediary, Barbara Harbottle, a local archaeologist and adult education teacher, who in turn passed them to the then Assistant Keeper, Roger Miket, who organised drawings of the Heads and sent these with photographs to Dr Anne Ross. Phew!

In Chapter Four I referred to the Heads having been allocated to the reserve collection as if they were in detention and hidden from inspection. It has been a fortean gripe that museums harbour all manner of embarrassing artefacts as if in some 'dungeon of the Damned'. Had that been the Heads fate? Lindsay patiently explained:

> "Oh, they weren't hidden, no. They would only have just been put in a secure cupboard out of the way, because the museum didn't own them and so we wouldn't have been able to put them on display without permission. And it was all very hazy about who owned them. So, you know, David Smith was dealing with these as yet another enquiry, and you have no idea how many enquiries that museum had to deal with every year. And some of them were very fringe indeed. And there was no way we could have put any of them on display until it was decided exactly what it was. So when you say reserve collection, it would have been put in the cupboard in which items brought in for identification would have been stored until they were collected by the owners".

I mentioned Des's visit to view the Heads and reference to a woman saying another person would need to be present. That, too, had a simple explanation:

> "I think the person he's talking [of] when he says 'custodian' means the lady at the reception desk. Which is why she said, 'Are you the man who made them?' She would have thought, 'This is something I would have to pass on to David Smith or Roger Miket'.

I showed Lindsay the undated and local unspecified picture of Des with the Heads (see Chapter Four) and introduced the vexed question of the extent of Douglas Robson's physical intrusion upon the Heads. Lindsay was impressed by the difference between photograph and line drawings, remarking: "I wouldn't be able to tell one brick wall from another! What I do find interesting about it is that these heads both have quite long necks. As for Robson's permission to drill, she elucidated:

> "I think in those days it would have been quite tricky to take a sample without making quite a large hole. Nowadays you don't need to make a hole at all. But in the early 70s you would have to take a substantial piece out of the stone – in inverted commas – to get an analysis. And it's quite clear from this letter from

Lindsay Allason-Jones fielded dozens of inquiries about the Hexham Heads.

Mr. Robson that he had given permission to drill "any samples which you may need".

But did Dr Robson overstep permitted protocols? Lindsay replied:

> "David Smith would have been very concerned about that, because geologists do tend to like to take large hacking lumps rather than just small samples. I have spotted that in my own time! The vital thing was, he got a good analysis and sent slices down to Professor Hodson as well. The problem is, since I've never seen the real heads, I can't comment on how big a piece he took or where he took it from. I mean, what I would have expected him to do would have been to drill into the bottom, so he wouldn't have been in any way affecting the face or the visible bit. I mean, certainly that was the normal way when we were taking archaeological samples; you would drill in to the bit that wouldn't be seen. But I don't know how much supervision Dr Robson had when he was doing it ... I think the problem with trying to analyse something which has been made up by grinding down stone and then reconstituting it, if you just scrape some bits off, what you're scraping off is basically stone. The stone fragments that sticks it together may not be in your sample. That's why you need to drill to get a good-sized sample of it. That way you can get a proper thin section and see what's going on!

When asked if had there been tenons, they might have been sawn off, Lindsay agreed. And if that had been contemplated?

> "I certainly wouldn't have encouraged it. I know that where people have been getting thin sections where I've been involved, I've either been watching them do it or giving them very strict instructions on where these should be. But certainly I know in the early days, the geologists would need quite large bits. They used to hack great lumps off a thing! If you think that these are fakes then you're not going to be bothered about hacking a lump off. But if you think these are genuine you're probably going to be a bit more nervous about it. So I think that's where he's [Don Robins] coming from".

As for the non-academic phrasing and sneering tone of Douglas Robson's analysis report, Lindsay commented:

> "I think he thought it was actually quite funny that they just turned out to be made of cement. I think that's where the sarcasm's coming from. That by doing a proper analysis and using thin sections he had been able to prove to his satisfaction that this was reconstituted stone".

So, Dr Robson was content to close the matter and so it seems was his archaeological opposite number." In fact," said Lindsay, "David Smith has a wonderful quote about 'I have now closed my file on the heads', which I think means he didn't want to see them again!" And as for the closed file, when she left the museum, Lindsay retained the file for posterity and subsequently made it available for thankful researchers.

Jolly Roger in, not out

Having been the person Lindsay Allason-Jones replaced at the museum, I rang Roger Miket, in Wooler,

Museum technician Roger Miket with the two stone heads.

Heads— and tales— of doom

By Journal Reporter

THOSE allegedly "evil" stone heads were back in Newcastle museum last night.

And Roger Miket, the man in charge of them at the university's Museum of Antiquities, said: "I don't regard them as being sinister at all.

"They are just archaeological material to me."

The two roughly carved heads, thought to be Celtic religious symbols, were sent to an expert in Southampton for analysis.

But after "strange happenings" at her home, Newcastle-born Dr. Anne Ross sent them back.

Last night, it was not clear what will become of the carvings.

At the moment, they are in the museum's reserve collection and are not on public display.

Mr. Miket said: "We are interested only in establishing whether they are genuine Celtic carvings or not.

"But I suppose the public would be far more interested in the supernatural side of it. Anyway, they don't worry me."

The heads were uncovered two years ago in a garden at Hexham but, while experts were examining them, the owner of the house said he had made them himself for his daughter.

But next-door neighbours left their home, claiming they had been haunted by strange supernatural beings, similar to those described by Dr. Ross.

Roger Miket regarded the Hexham Heads as "just archaeological material".

Northumberland, on 30 December 2011 and had a chatty hour-long chin-wag about matters of relevance (and a few tangential mutual concerns). His reason for relinquishing his post was his appointment as Keeper of Archaeology for Tyne & Wear County Council. Later, he quit the North-East and moved to the Hebrides for around 15 years, setting up a museum service for these remote Scottish islands. Now aged 63, he took early retirement 13 years ago. When he casually introduced early in the conversation that he was an occasional reader of *Fortean Times* and recommended I read it (I have every single copy!), I felt nothing I said was going to be misunderstood nor an embarrassment. Consequently, I asked him outright what he thought of Douglas Robson's invasive sampling of the Heads:

> "I don't believe he butchered them. Every care would have been taken to obtain the minimum amount needed for analysis. You wouldn't take pinking shears to the Turin Shroud".

Next, I introduced the nagging problem of tenons and just how 'pre' and 'post' Robson they had been modified? Never mind about cameras never lying, so many depictions are undated, unclear, or partly obscured by hands holding them, nor do they necessarily tally with verbal and written commentary. Probably the nearest we have to 'real' images are the set of drawings by Mary Hurrell, drawn for Anne Ross's *Archaeologia Aeliana* article as depicted earlier. Roger told me:

> "The illustrations were probably done before analysis. Mary believed the heads to be Celtic and drew them as such, which reflects the heads before intervention".

Certainly the drawings show one has virtually no neck and the other what might be regarded as half a tenon, although may have had a sufficiently level bottom for it to stand up.

As a young man in the 1970s, Roger had been photographed holding the Hexham Heads and quoted as saying he wasn't spooked by the Heads. I asked him if anything had developed after that burst of media interest had passed or whether he had any further feelings or hunches:

> "They caused no concern for me. I found there was nothing malevolent about them. My wife would say that's typically insensitive of a man. I felt nothing of any sort from them. As objects they were totally inert to me. I felt no force associated with them, but for years on they still exert this interest which is more than you'd expect from a couple of pieces of concrete".

Roger elaborated on the last point, as so many academics and lay researchers have shared with me their willingness to concur that the age when the Hexham Heads were created was basically irrelevant; that it was people's perceptions which mattered, whether it be prior knowledge, occupation or whatever, emphasising:

> "It doesn't need to be anything more than a trigger to what's in people. Whatever they are or were could stimulate a response in people who would respond. It could well be concrete or modern [for a response] and [they would react differently] if I were to tell them it was Celtic or modern".

Roger made another telling point by asking, hypothetically, why there had been no similar cases where anyone else had come forward to say, for instance, that a retrieved artefact such as an Anglo-Saxon brooch, was actually their handiwork.

> "It is remarkably strange there has only been, as in the case of the Hexham
> heads, that you have had someone coming forward to say they made them. It
> is very unusual. It is a strange thing to do and then claim to have made a
> third".

These are the relevant points from a long conversation with us joshing about our experiences in Scotland and my going off at a tangent talking about my editor sending me off to the remote island of Berneray to dig up potatoes planted a week before by Prince Charles and fearing a Wicker Man denoument as I helped two crofter women gather in the last of the harvest as a full moon set in the west and after stacking the last stook I set off back in the dark. It could have easily been 1,800 years in the past. Reverie aside, Roger brought me back down to earth as he refused to voice an opinion as to whether the Hexham Heads were 1,800 or 55 years old. Nor could he recall how the Heads arrived at the museum.

Calcium compounds the confusion

One of those who joined the quest late on was scientist and homoeopath Steven Cartwright, who along with partner psychometrist Kathy Stranks approached David Taylor after the paranormalist gave a talk on the Hexham Heads at an Association for the Scientific Study of Anomalous Phenomena conference in Bath. After some correspondence with Steven and phonecalls to Kathy, their interest was sufficiently piqued for Kathy to envision a ritual landscape around Hexham and Steven to delve into the constitution and fabrication of the Hexham Heads. I punningly referred to them as 'Kathy cum Homoeopath', although Sapphire & Steel would suffice. I've noticed Steven spells it 'homeopathy', which is the American way, whereas I prefer 'homoeopathy', which is British and technically requires a grapheme. Where Steven uses it then US prevails; where I do UK wins.

Steven's credentials and area of specialist interest made him an ideal person to approach for an independent assessment of the Heads. His background is as a research biochemist with a PhD from Edinburgh University. He is currently working at an Innovation centre just outside Oxford leading a research programme investigating the physical chemistry of homeopathic medicines. He has also trained as an archaeologist with an MSc in archaeology from Oxford University. In the field of archaeology, Steve's particular interests are the Neolithic, Bronze Age and Iron Age periods; ritual – especially the place of water in prehistory (e.g. deposition of ritual objects in watery places such as bogs and rivers, holy wells, siting of ritual monuments near rivers) and use of chemical analysis in establishing the provenance and age of artifacts. Again, I prefer the UK 'artefacts' and Steven the US 'artifacts'. No wonder there's so little agreement in this book!

As for an assessment of the Hexham Heads without recourse to visual or tactile contact and using only written sources and his specialist knowledge, here is the result of Dr Cartwright's deliberations:

> My current thinking is the heads *may* be either recent *or* ancient! Here's why
> - Putting aside issues such as the tenons, artistic style of the heads and Des
> Craigie's abilities or lack of as a sculptor, and concentrating solely on the
> material the heads were made of, there are a number of crucial points:
>
> 1. If the heads were made of cement (calcium silicate) they would have
>   to be modern as cement as we know it had its origins in the late 18th
>   century, but Prof Hodson's later analysis showed them to have no
>   trace of calcium silicate in them. Douglas Robson's report says they
>   were unlike any natural sandstone with well rounded quartz grains

(as perhaps one would find in quartz subjected to wave action) set in a compact calcareous (calcium carbonate) matrix. This means the material *is* sandstone but of a type not seen naturally and therefore may be modern or ancient.

2. Don Robins said the heads were very dense and heavy. Cement as we know it isn't that heavy (not as heavy as sandstone anyway).

3. Dr Robson himself says "if the heads were ancient they could have been made from quartz grains mixed with limestone" Lime was certainly known to the Romans and Prof Hodson had already commented on traces of lime plaster on the heads (something which the Romans frequently used).

4. There are three possibilities really – the heads *are modern* artificial sandstone (but I don't believe Des Craigie had the ability to make them); or they were made from quartz grains mixed with lime in antiquity (likely Romano-Celtic); or they are natural, formed in an unusual way not normally found in nature. Its perhaps worth noting that carvings were often made in antiquity from unusual natural substances as such materials were held to be more powerful. Coming back to the tenons, the artistic style of the heads and the fact that Dr Ross had seen similar heads in France together with the above arguments leads me to think the heads were/are most likely ancient'.

Permitting my usage of his views and stressing that these were only opinions without the advantage of personal examination, Steven added:

'Without any trace of calcium silicate in the Hexham heads it's difficult to know exactly what the binder was, as neither Frank Hodson or Douglas Robson say, but I am assuming it was some kind of calcium carbonate/lime/gypsum(?) mix. Someone other than Des Craigie could have had access to that kind of primitive technology but not Des himself, as he would have had easy access to modern cement and not been aware of older methods. That does raise the interesting possibility, I suppose, that someone unknown who was familiar with ancient methods made the heads in recent times – but why complicate things even further? The simplest explanation to my mind is that the heads are old. Hopefully one day the heads will be found and all this can be cleared up once and for all'.

INTERLUDE ONE
WEREWOLVES, WULVERS & WERESHEEP

Logic suggests I start chronologically with the were-beast in Hexham. However, a werewolf with hairy human body and vulpine face trumps a sheep with human head, which let's face it is almost farcically pantomime-like. All manner of experts have analysed why humans seem to actually enjoy being scared out of their wits – psychoanalysts, historians, cryptozoologists and folklorists have all pontificated. But we do so from cinema seats, television viewing or reading - not actually experiencing it. Indeed, thankfully, few of us ever have such encounters. This makes the experience of the Feachems in Southampton so extraordinary and a pivotal point in this book. As already chronicled, Richard 'Dick' Feachem, his wife Anne Ross and their children Berenice and Richard Charles experienced a werewolf (although Dick seemed strangely immune to seeing it - only hearing the intruder). Even well-documented evidence and honesty of witnesses can never be 100% foolproof testimony, as the reports given in so many fortean cases have been found, despite seeming bombproof as far as credibility goes. For umpteen reasons witnesses can have been fooled, events misinterpreted or a hoax perpetrated, as sceptics and debunkers never tire of pointing out. Consequently in this inquiry I have remained passionate about the material and the story, but as far as possible been an observer rather than participant. I trust none of the facts nor any of those involved – least of all myself!

Cryptozoology and hybrid fauna

Cryptozoology deals mainly with cryptids; that is animals whose existence is doubted in scientific circles. Its major founder was Bernard Heuvelmans, who half-a-century ago, stated memorably that 'terror is all the more powerful when it wears a human face' . But what if the face be animal and the body human? More? – or less? – scary? There may be a case for a <u>physical</u> hybrid human and animal combination – the werewolf. Cryptozoology prefers to deal with the physical and is also comfortable with what represent out-of-place animals; those known to exist, but <u>not</u> in that particular geographical location (and hence suspicious). A third category is more contentious and involves apparitional wildlife whose examples are quasi-physical and have been dubbed 'zooform phenomena' by this book's learned publisher, Jonathan Downes. [1] and denizens of 'daimonic reality', another term coined for a specific non-rational realm, invented by Patrick Harpur. [2] Yet broadly speaking, each was describing the same phenomenological landscape which liminal beasts inhabit. It is maybe significant that mainstream cryptozoologists can themselves be sceptical of the zooform theory explanation, but hostile to the extent of shunning any suggestion of supernatural intervention. When I see the Loch Ness Monster washed ashore dead or an abominable snowman captured I might have a change of heart. Hence forgive me for giving short shrift to the physicality of even more controversial fauna as werewolves and weresheep. I suggest this book will be more popular today than at any time since the Victorian era for there is a *zeitgeist* in which vampires and werewolves are being devoured by fans of the macabre as the twin tensions of adolescent sexuality and anxiety at being on the threshold of adulthood and the prospects of earning a living loom; those twin liminal realms of hormonal and educational readjustment are comfortingly fictionalised in that twilight territory of escapism between childhood and maturity reflected by the borderline between human and animal. And I'm not falling into the trap of us being animals, too. Yes, I admire Page 3 of *The Sun* and if I was flicking through *Penthouse* it wouldn't be for fascinating articles on vintage cars, so I do recognise mammalian features. But **we** are not animals as such; we have a divine spark within (Jeremy Kyle excepted). But putting God and biology to one side and before questioning my beliefs, there was nothing natural in a Hexham were-sheep nor Southampton werewolf.

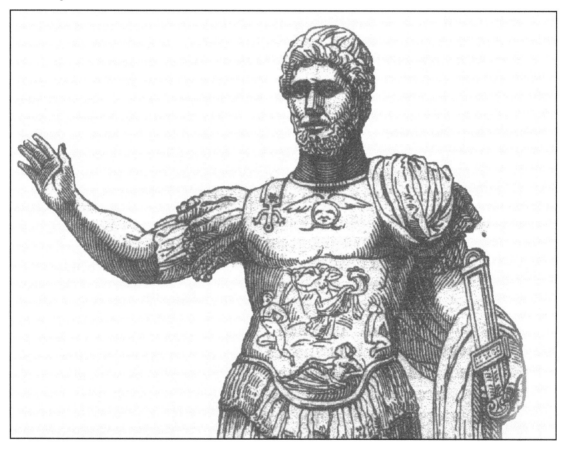

Emperor Hadrian: *PWOAR!* - Now that's what I call a <u>breast</u>plate! Arguably the Hexham Heads saga is historically the most significant event to occur in this sleepy market town since the wall-builder Hadrian billeted mercenaries and slaves from his empire in the vicinity, becoming the best-known warrior brickies until Winston Churchill took up the craft as a hobby. Even the Hexham Riots of 1761 – over a form of unpopular 'national service' – are eclipsed by the fortean focus on this Tynedale centre of the most sparsely populated area in England. Anyway, just because women have mammary glands doesn't make them animals, any more than the claim by Dr Susan Blackmore to *The Sunday Times Magazine* (26 June 2011) that "some little robots in Bristol that imitate each other and so build an artificial culture of robot memes" does not make them human.

Werewolf and the Feachems

A cultural nod in the direction of *Bigfoot and the Hendersons*, but there the archetype and happy family analogy ends. Hollywood, the small screen, publishers galore have embraced this Western World phenomenon of transmutation and turned legend into a purported reality of sorts. As at 6 Rose Road in floral suburban Southampton. No wonder the public has shown little enthusiasm for the reintroduction of wild wolves in Britain. It matters not that all species of dog are descended from wolves and that they proved to be successful carnivores, as witness their successful domination of a huge geographical area, but there has to be a reason for their universal persecution – and dread, and folklore, and legends of shape-shifting.

Should wolves be reintroduced?
Is this what we want – a pack of snarling carnivores on the hunt for food?

In its physical characteristics, the werewolf Anne Ross described is stereotypical. Its behaviour was not that of a pack animal such as wolves most definitely are in the wild, but a loner. Its appearance had common werewolf features: canine head (though it does not seem to have bared menacing fangs), pointed ears, large claws, dark shaggy body, padded feet, walked upright and had the semblance of human features in its basic body structure and above average height.

As a Celtic scholar, if the native tribes of Roman Britain had a term for it Anne Ross would know, but *werwulf* itself is Anglo-Saxon in origin: *wer* meaning man and *wulf* being wolf. European variants include *loup-garou* in French, *lob ambre* in Spanish, *lob omen* or *loborraz* in Portuguese and *lupomanero* in Italian. Lycanthropy, the process of becoming a werewolf, comes from *lykos*, meaning wolf, and *anthropos* equalling man. The change to becoming semi-bestial has to be physical; certainly not entirely hallucinatory in all cases. Of course, psychiatry argues it is all delusory; anthropology sees it as rooted in totemism. Politically, the Nazis of Germany were steeped in a deep-seated nationalism, whose heritage and mysticism embraced werewolves which, according to Nuremberg trial testimonies by Hans Fritzsche and Albert Speer were under the control of the missing Martin Bormann. As for British werewolves, several authors have tackled the subject, noting the paucity of accounts, their dubious reliability and acknowledging their debt to pioneering work by Montague Summers and Elliott O'Donnell. In this context, many modern commentators have also tackled the Hexham Heads association with varying degrees of accuracy and insight (none blindingly original and the giveaway that my Eighties writings have been plundered is the repetition of February 1972 as time of discovery). As far back as 2,000BC, when the *Epic of Gilgamesh* was written, werewolves have appeared in the literary record and in England a werewolf of 940AD was associated with Flixton, near Filey, East Yorkshire. Both sexes first appear in an encounter recorded in the 12th Century by Giraldus Cambrensis. In relatively modern times, naturalist and anomalous big cat sleuth Trevor Beer wrote about one on Exmoor in the 1970s.

While in the 20th Century, there is a modern account which eerily echoes the Feachems' ordeal. A contact of Jon Downes, the parapsychologist Robin Furman, recalled how his home in Grimsby, Lincs., became the location for a wolfman manifestation. His daughter complained of an unwelcome presence watching her from outside the bedroom, and when he offered to exchange rooms he, too, noticed a tall figure watching him through the doorway. He recalled that, "It was definitely the figure of a human, but the head was that of a wolf!" It did not terrify him. In fact, as the form faded from view, Mr Furman conceded it had probably only been curious. Maybe so sufficiently satisfied that the family never saw it again.

What is it about Cannock Chase?
They may not qualify for inclusion in the next edition of Dr Sir Christopher Lever's superb study *The Naturalised Animals of Britain and Ireland*, but the media is still reporting occasional sightings of werewolves in our countryside or what the public, fevered newshounds or paranormalist field researchers assume to be such. In this murky area of rumour and supernatural suggestion, one factor seems to have gathered substance; that Staffordshire's Cannock Chase district is a 'window area' for the weird. It is certainly the werewolf-spotting 'hot spot' of the moment. According to one estimation there have been 20 werewolf sightings reported over the past 30 years on Cannock Chase, which also has a notorious reputation as a UFO sightings focus. [3] As long ago as April 1975 a 'suicidal lycanthrope' was recorded from Eccleshall, Staffs., regarding a bizarre report concerning phonecall between teenagers, one of whom claimed his skin was changing and he was becoming a wolf. To add an element of satanic involvement, the lad was supposedly found dead at a village crossroads after seemingly stabbing himself with a knife. [4] I guess all this can be taken with a pinch of salt (thrown over the left shoulder not obligatory) and the monitor of this lore is an anonymous character with the pseudonym 'The Hob Goblin'.

But stay with me as there are seemingly some relatively substantial accounts with media interest. West Midlands Ghost Club was called in to investigate after there were several encounters in the vicinity of a German war cemetery between Stafford and Cannock. These included a postman who in 2007 saw what he assumed to be a large dog, but when he approached, it got on its hind legs and ran away. In 2010 a woman walking her dog on Cannock Chase confronted an enormous wolf-like animal that stared at her before turning and disappearing into woodland. [5]

Cabinets of vulpine curiosities

Of course, if there were no bodies or skeletons, werewolves as physical entities could be dismissed easily, along with Big Foot and the Loch Ness Monster. Yet a correspondent offered an 1888 find in Wales involving a 'werewolf skull', but according to an intriguing account in the magazine *Fortean Times,* whole skeletons exist today. Displayed at a secret location in London, among the Thomas Merrylin Cryptid Collection of animal specimens there are a juvenile dragon and preserved foetuses of werewolves, vampires and other legendary creatures. And just to add a human touch, Rasputin's right hand. The prize possession discovered by a mysterious Edward Harrell was a young male lycanthrope which he had exhibited at the centre of his drawing-room. Its provenance also never being explained satisfactorily. This, and a lycanthrope young of which he had collected several, was depicted in the article, and just to add more bizarre aspects, most had been taken from executed mothers Harrell had hunted while studying nomadic tribes of northern Europe and their migratory patterns. This gentleman psychopath assumed his genocidal spoils to belong to an elusive offshoot of primitive man, homo lupus, a symbiotic hominid sharing no actual genetic traits with the common wolf, other than what all mammals do. Harrell concluded they were intelligent, problem-solving animals with an eight-month gestation period and generally giving birth singly. [6]

The 'Brampton Werewolf' (Baffling the detectives)

That lycanthropy was alive and well (sort of) in Tynedale was suggested in a faded cutting I came across from The Journal. A man, drenched in human blood, was arrested by police as he walked through the market town of Brampton on suspicion of burglary. All he would say was, "I am a werewolf", leaving a bizarre mystery. He eventually gave his name as Robert Forster, of nearby Walton, and the 27-year-old was remanded to prison. Forensic experts deduced the amount of blood was consistent with a 'severe injury' but were unsure if it came from the man or a victim and appealed for information. [7]

As a fortean I clipped the news item and it entered that Sargasso Sea of lost souls which purports to be a filing system, but like the elvers which are carried by the Gulf Stream that is serendipity, it surfaced on cue, as did the ministering of the library angel that is the *Fortean Times* message board forum. Here were some addi-

"I am a werewolf" – delusional man had only a nosebleed which fooled police.

'Werewolf' case still baffles detectives

POLICE investigating the "Brampton werewolf" mystery yesterday appealed for help in tracking the man's movements in the half hour before he was arrested.

The man, drenched in human blood, was arrested as he walked through the Cumbrian market town, after allegedly burgling a house near the village of Walton 30 minutes earlier.

He told police "I am a werewolf" but has refused to tell police anything that might solve the bizarre mystery.

On Tuesday, a 27-year-old man appeared at Carlisle magistrates court charged with burglary and assaulting a policeman.

Robert Forster, of Knorren Lodge, Walton, near Brampton, was remanded to prison for three weeks for

psychiatric reports. Reporting restrictions were lifted.

"Anyone with any information concerning this man and his movements on the morning of February 5, between 9am and 9.30am, should contact Brampton police station or the major incident room at Penrith," a police spokesman said.

Forensic experts say the amount of blood on the man's clothing is consistent with a "severe injury" but are having to make further tests to find out whether it came from the man.

Police fear an injured person could be lying undiscovered and have checked with lists of missing persons.

They also want to trace a black leather jacket containing documents discarded just before the man was arrested.

tional facts of relevance. After combing missing persons records and dragging a river, the police learned that Forster had escaped from a local asylum, Garlands, and it took several days to establish the simple truth. The 'werewolf' had suffered a massive nosebleed. But, of course, the link between lycanthropy and mental health issues is hardly original …

The wulver – remove its relics at your peril!

I was comfortable in my monograph 30 years ago to endorse the comparison already made that what the Feachems encountered in their home was likely a wulver. Wolfmen had long been associated with Celtic folklore and certainly Anne Ross and her husband would have been aware of this aspect. Bearing in mind that what is being discussed has probably no actual reality at any time, but functions as an archetype, albeit a shape-shifting one and finding itself unfamiliarly dwelling in a suburban house, must test even the most tenacious mind monster and require exorcism, just as squatters require the attentions of burly bailiffs.

> 'The wulver was a creature like a man with a wolf's head. He had short, brown hair all over him. His home was a cave dug out of the side of a steep knowe halfway up a hill. He didn't molest folk if folk didn't molest him. He was fond of fishing and had a small rock in the deep water which is known to this day as the "Wulver's Stane". There he would sit fishing sillacks and piltaks for hour after hour. He was reported to have frequently left a few fish on the window-sill of some poor body'. (8)

Of the many authors who have reproduced this rare account none to my knowledge has tried to explain the meaning of sillacks and piltaks. They would seem to be Shetland/ Orkney dialect words. The nearest I can come to answering the meanings is sillacks to probably describe cod and the best I could do with piltaks is the dubious near-term for porpoises.

Another curious account I came across is from a book of 1963 which an American friend passed to me when his company recalled him to the States. Despite the blurb announcing –

> 'You are holding in your hand one of the most profoundly EVIL books ever assembled ... A catalogue of inhuman horrors, unfit for any person to know - too much about'.

The first time I saw this uncredited artwork it was captioned 'wulver' and seems to fit the description.

- but it is no worse than paperbacks by better known writers such as Brad Steiger and John Keel. Following that caveat, here's Bernhardt J Hurwood with a fascinating tale:

> 'In England and Scotland particularly, there are tales of werewolves that would more accurately be described as ghosts. They are depicted as human in shape, covered with shaggy gray fur, and having hairy, clawed hands and the heads of wolves. In one story, such an apparition was seen by a young Englishman visiting his grandfather in Scotland.
>
> Both were interested in geology, and during the day they had been exploring the pits and caves of the surrounding countryside. In their search for fossils they found a strange skeleton at the bottom of a small, dried-up tarn. The body structure was unmistakably human, but the skull belonged to a wolf. The grandfather identified the bones as the remains of a werwolf [sic], explaining that in olden times the island was infested with them. With that they dug out the bones and carried them back to the house for their collection.
>
> Later that night the whole family was out with the exception of the grandson. He was reading when he heard a loud knocking on the windowpane of the kitchen, where incidentally, they had placed the skeleton found during the day. He went back to the kitchen to find out what was causing the noise. When he looked out the window he froze in his tracks. There with its muzzle barely touching the glass was a werewolf! The mouth was half open in a hideous grimace, revealing both rows of sharp teeth. The eyes glowed balefully and seemed to penetrate to the very depths of the young man's soul. Anchored to the spot, he stood staring and trembling. Then as it raised on paw, as if to smash the glass, he regained his sense, spun around and fled from the room. Later when the family returned he told them what had happened. They searched around the house to no avail, not even a footprint could be found. The experience was chalked up to an overactive imagination. Nevertheless the next day they took the strange bones back to the spot where they had been found and reburied them. The wolfish phantasm was never seen again'. [9]

This story would seem to suggest that it involved more than an apparition as it involved bones – from a flesh and blood creature, even suggesting a hybrid existed. Perhaps an atavistic individual or even species? If the latter, a holy grail (poisoned chalice!) for cryptozoologists? But also note the 'cursed' relics aspect as with carved heads which should not be moved from their familiar or even sacred dwelling place.

As with all such yarns this one has had its accretions over the years. By 1986 Graham McEwan introduced the grandfather as 'an elder in the Kirk of Scotland' to give the story added authority figure status and explain the absence of other family members that evening. [10]

Nick Redfern recycles the incident, including an extract from the grandson Warren's own account:

> 'I immediately turned in the direction of the noise and saw a dark face looking in at me. At first dim and indistinct, it became more and more complete, until it developed into a perfectly defined head of a wolf terminating in the neck of a human being. Though greatly shocked, my first act was to look in every direction for a possible reflection – but in vain. There was no light, either without or within, other than

that from the setting sun – nothing that could in any way have produced an illusion.

I looked at the face and marked each feature intently. It was unmistakably a wolf's face, the jaws slightly distended, the lips wreathed in a savage snarl, the teeth sharp and white, the eyes light green, the ears pointed'. [11]

As I re-read the Scottish account alongside a Welsh one from 1888, the similarities became apparent despite the widely separate locations. The Merionethshire tale is also set in wild countryside during a summer holiday. The geologist is replaced by an Oxford professor with his wife and friend and both feature a cottage, in this case rented in a mountainous area. The dried up tarn is substituted for a full lake, in which the angler professor mysteriously found the catch of the day to be a huge, dog-like skull. Again a relic is taken from its natural resting place and moved inside a human dwelling space. No explanation is given for the men's absence when the supernatural comes a' callin' when there is a lone person in the relative safety of the remote location homestead. Then comes the face at the window, part-wolf/part-man, glaring with intelligent red eyes. She bolted the door and heard it prowling around the cottage. Finally its snarling and growling subsided and she heard the comforting voices of her husband and his companion. Having told the men of her terrifying experience, they extinguished the lamps, armed themselves with a gun and makeshift weaponry and began a long vigil. Whatever the creature was, it eventually returned and they saw it looking through the kitchen window, its eyes red with rage. Grabbing the firearm they rushed to the door, but the beast anticipated their purpose and was off in a trice, last seen passing through the garden gate as an undefined shadowy shape which headed for the lake, which it entered without disturbing the surface water with its bulky frame reflected in the clear mountain air starlight.

Next morning the professor was up early to fulfil a mission. Carefully carrying the skull, he returned to the boat he had used for fishing the previous day and rowed a little way out from the shore and without ceremony threw the accursed bone head into the depths of the lake. Apparently appeased, the spirit of the wulver/werewolf did not trouble the trio for the remainder of their holiday, nor has it been reported since. [12]

I suggest these two tales will suffice to make my point. There are great similarities between the two accounts, but each retelling adds and subtracts from the original as is the way with storytelling. But that said, there is usually some basis and substance in an actual event at some time however misinterpreted and mangled in the retellings. Perhaps werewolf remains have been found, including those of a relict population of wulvers. But it is essentially fictional and as with all folktales has a purpose. The moral of this story is that if you find ancient remains it's best that you leave them well alone.

Of course, the era which produced such tall tales was also one before television and the programme *Would I Lie To You?* and suchlike, where friends would meet in public houses and hold contests to see who could spin the most fantastical yet plausible yarn. This is how so many of the stories told today to credulous sightseers by tourist guides found their genesis and how ghost hunt entrepreneurs honed their skills. Many's a tall story which has led the naive folklorist astray, not to mention the most cynical journalist, sent a wannabelieve cryptozoologist off on a wild-goose chase or hoodwinked the beguiled disciple into some pseudo-spiritual group with alleged ancient antecedents or mesmerised a neophyte seeker into a more sinister mind-bending cult. This is the territory where the Scottish and Welsh tales as retold would be regarded by forteans as giving added veracity through geographical difference, whereas the contemporary legend collector and analyst would point to story migration. One sees the same data as strengthening an argument, the other as weakening it. I can happily wear both hats – but I also know it's sensible only to do so metaphorically.

The Great God Pan in a Norfolk garden?

We have three members of the Feachem family witnessing a werewolf, but the sole witness in Hexham was Nellie Dodd. Two of her children I've spoken to are adamant she saw a sheep with a human head: not that of a ram, nor that of a goat. And anyway, I know of no descriptions of a female satyr (outside of erotic fantasy art). Always male and overshadowed by the Great God Pan. I have no reason to disbelieve the original account by Mrs Dodd and her veracity, nor the honesty of her children Brian and Sylvia, and the rehousing issue has already been discussed and rejected. There is, however, a similar earlier account, but significantly it was not published until six years after the Hexham encounter and, without wanting to cast aspersions on the writer involved, it needs to be stressed it appeared later.

In this East Anglian story, an old sea-dog away from the briny discovered a vaguely similar artefact to those in Northumberland in his Norfolk garden. Taking with it a proverbial dose of salt, the account was written by Nerys Dee (who we met back in Chapter One). Here's an extract from her 1977 account regarding her uncle, a Captain Pearson, just retired from a 40-year naval career to a quiet county cottage existence, including unfamiliar gardening.

> 'On a spring morning in 1966 his fork met with considerable opposition, a few inches below the surface. Believing this to be a large stone, he set about its extraction. The Captain was right, it was a stone, but one with a difference. It was a crudely-carved, stone head.
>
> The day following this discovery, my uncle had a very strange experience. While looking into the garden from his kitchen window, he saw what he believed was "the devil". A more detailed description of this apparition revealed that whatever it was, it had the torso of a man and the legs of a cloven-hoofed animal.
>
> Over the next four years , until his death in 1970, this creature appeared in my uncle's garden at least ten times. The only association he ever noticed between this weird visitor and the stone head was that they both arrived at much the same time, which fact he viewed as purely coincidental'.

She concluded this article of dubious scholarship, sandwiched with anecdotage, by recalling:

> 'In May I visited Norfolk and called at the cottage. It was empty, up for sale for the third time since 1970. Although there was no sign of the stone head, the feeling persisted that it was there, somewhere in the undergrowth. If the previous occupants left because of the stranger in the garden, it can only be hoped that the next one, if he finds it, will rebury it as quickly as possible' [13]

I have very rarely bought *Prediction* magazine but the head cult article caught my eye. It obviously also caught a young David Clarke's attention as he contacted the writer seeking to learn the fate of the contentious artefact. She replied:

> 'I remember my uncle and stone head well because finding it was such a dramatic event, and of course, the aftermath. What I did not say in that article was that he told my mother, who used to visit him a lot, that when the devil came into the kitchen he would die. He was actually founded dead in his kitchen , but we shall never know if the devil came in.

Did this idyllic *Satyr & Family* scene as depicted in the 16th Century by Albrecht Durer reflect what was going on at the bottom of Nerys's uncle's garden?

'I do not think it was the devil he saw, but more a satyr – you know, the goat-hoofed nature spirit. Apparitions of these have been seem from time to time and you may have heard about the "devil's footsteps" that were found in the snow in Devon about a hundred years ago. They went for miles and miles, hopping over houses and haystacks in a straight line, and even jumping over river estuaries.

Unfortunately I do not know what happened to the head but I presume it was left in the garden. The actual place was on the outskirts of Norwich, but I cannot remember its name'. [14]

Randy couple experience '*coitus interruptus*' courtesy of Goatman

If I had doubts about the authenticity of Ms Dee's ancient mariner and his garden satyr, then I had even less trust about the true physicality of tales of an American Goatman. However, here the actual lack of constancy bolsters validity, as the developments in the burgeoning and ongoing narrative are consistent with accumulation from other aspects of urban mythology. Here the prime location is the US state of Maryland and to be specific Prince George's County. Claims of sightings began in the late 1950s and have continued to the present. The entity is generally described as having the legs and hooves of a goat, upper body of a man and the horns of a goat, being partially covered by fur. Height averages around seven feet and weight estimated at 300lb. For something so macho its utterances consist of high-pitched squeals (think Michael Jackson).

According to the *Unknown Creatures* website the first recorded encounter was made by a couple parked along a deserted country track in dense woodland. As might be expected they were not playing I-Spy, but deeply involved in paradise-by-the-dashboard-light carnal calisthenics when the love-making session was not rudely interrupted by banging on the car bonnet. The unlikely source of the intrusion was an excited 'dogging' spectator, but not a goat-like creature, staring at them while wielding what appeared to be a double-edged axe. The terrified couple were then relieved to see the humanoid monster turn and bolt off back into surrounding woodland. As with all such traditional teen tall tales there is an underlying moral: pre-marital chastity is best, sex before leads to unwanted pregnancy, STDs, promiscuity, prostitution, drugs and total moral degradation. [15] The webmaster linked the sighting to the Pan and satyr archetype, drawing a parallel between the earthy lustful nature of the woodland denizens mythical realm and the all-to-real and familiar behaviour of adolescent humans and the components of contemporary legend such as automobile worship and teenage copulation. An axe or hatchet also often figures in these slumber party apocrypha, being a metaphor for the male penis or intended physical harm, so there's no great surprise there except for how come the chimera acquired such an implement.

A fuller inquiry and with greater depth of analysis has been provided on the Goatman legend from the Essortment website. Here the compiler is more circumspect, noting consistencies such as an angry, upright manimal but noting variations such as some accounts reporting Goatman to have a human body with a goat's head similar to the general perception of Satan, whereas others encountered a creature with a goat's lower body and the torso of a human, much like the satyr of Greek mythology. Geographically several localities in Prince Geoge's County seem favoured, particularly focussing upon the Bowie area, but his perambulations also seem to favour Lottsford Road and Fletchertown Road, between which just happens to be located Glendale State Asylum. The webmaster in this instance notes the ubiquity of the same legend in other states, including Texas, Alabama, California, Kentucky, Oklahoma and Oregon.

When outbreaks of monster creature sightings occur the rumour mill often goes into overdrive and all manner of ordinary felonies are blamed on the mythical marauder as the social panic gathers momentum. In Goatman's case there were reports of disturbing him during break-ins and a struggle yet no physical evidence, pet mutilations and damage to cars inflicted by that anachronistic axe, which blurs into such high-school favourites as 'The Hook'. Not unnaturally there has been much speculation as to the Goatman's origin and more than one theory has emerged. It is worth reproducing this dissection for reasons I will explain at its conclusion:

Beware the bogeyman

At the centre of this moral crisis lies the United States Agricultural Research Center of Beltsville, Maryland. Two common variations involve a scientist working with goats at the facility. In one story the scientist simply went mad, for reasons often improvised by the storyteller, and ran off into the woods screaming. Ever since that accursed day the madman has stalked the woods of the area with an axe. The second and more fantastic version claims that the scientist's experiments with goats went horribly wrong and he ended up becoming mutated and goat-like in appearance. After this occurred he went the way of his mad scientist counterpart, fleeing to the relative peace of the woods with an axe and a chip on his shoulder.

'Beltsville is situated at the outskirts of Washington D.C.'s suburbs and has an abundance of wooded land that could provide shelter or an escape route for the Goatman. There is a third assertion about man's scientific wrongdoing involving a botched attempt at creating a cure for cancer. As the story goes this occurred back in the 1960s in a Pittsburgh lab using techniques that are known to modern medical researchers to be redundant with no hope of facilitating any breakthroughs in the battle against cancer. However, this was unknown to the unfortunates involved in the experimentation and, through methods as yet unrevealed, the cancer cells were caused to grow into none other than the Goatman. The abominable beast then broke loose and has ravaged the countryside ever since. Furthermore, this legend claims that the Chubacabra phenomenon is in actuality the mistaken progeny of the Goatman creature that was created in the lab. No explanation as to how he multiplied has been ventured at the time of this writing.

A fourth theory involves the mental health facility housed within the confines of the Goatman's known territory. Some locals have grumbled about rumored experimentation on inmates while others have speculated about "regular" insane persons escaping in the night to commit the crimes that the Goatman has been blamed for. And finally there is the assertion that the Goatman is the embodiment of none other than the arch fiend himself, summoned to this earth from time to time by the rituals of satanists. The connection between this origin and the attacks on cars and dogs would seem tenuous at best. Other sources site parental license in the use of a deranged old hermit loose in the woods wielding his axe against children, generally residing in whichever area the parents wanted their children to stay away from. Examples are: near busy highways, under bridges, around certain electrical towers, and any other dangerous places.

As recently as the August of 2000 a group of construction workers sighted a sasquatch-like creature that, in their estimate, was twelve feet in stature traversing an area of Washington's suburbs. Whatever is happening in the region, whether imagined or bizarrely real, the story of the Goatman will not only persist but thrive. Publicity has come from many different sources in the past originate? An area of Western Japan called Kinky! Yes, really!

Fairway to grow old?

Ever wonder what happened to those kung fu warriors of the 1970s. What are they doing now they're too old to fly through the air to kick the foo-yung out of their week will 'force the golfer to swing correctly every time,' he says. And if you don't you can kill the caddy with it. The Toski Trainer costs a mere £79.95. Sounds a bit implausible to us, but we haven't got the nerve to tell him . . .

Naked, hairy and confident and pictured in men's mag *Mayfair*. The illustration, however, is not from the 'bush era' but surprisingly a depiction of a werewolf and not a modern shaven nubile pneumatic nymphette.

few years including feature articles in the press in tandem with the inclusion on cable specials where the Goatman was featured with the monster elite, Nessie and the Yeti. Cryptozoologists, those who study the so-called extinct or nonexistent animals, have been drawn to the story in droves. Until the myths can be sufficiently proven or disproven the Goatman will continue to be the object of both ridicule and fear for residents outside of Washington, D.C.'. [16]

When I asked Maryland folklorist/cryptozoologist David Puglia if there had been any recent Goatman sightings he said not and no activity on 'a bunch of upcoming films that never materialise', but he has an article on the history of the legend scheduled for the next issue of Contemporary Legend magazine.

One of the factors regarding the Hexham Heads saga which has irked me greatly over the years is the misinformation peddled in articles and books. But as the webmaster here points out, storytellers which change factors in an account and this is done for umpteen reasons – age and type of audience, giving it a familiar location or whatever – and it almost seem willful not to alter a tale in some way so as to prove their skill at honing a narrative to give it a personalised spin. The journalist in me greatly disapproves, the failed novelist empathises and the raconteur is tempted. I suspect many of my own speculations in this book will eventually become holy writ as fact as the canon of the Hexham Heads undergoes many metamorphoses over time.

The human face of sheep farming

At the grave risk of alienating any book buyers or readers in Hexham, here's a joke, 'What do you call a sheep tied to a lamp-post in Hexham?' – 'A leisure centre'. Apologies, but I have a point to make (and you are welcome to make the connection that as I'm Hartlepool-born, yes I've endured a lifetime of monkey-hanging ribbing from non-Hartlepudlians). Hexham is rural and Nellie Dodd was adamant that what she saw that fateful night was half-human and half-sheep.

Whereas werewolves would seem to have some demonstrable existence and obviously exist beyond pure folklore, be it reality or some brand of ostension, and wulvers also seem to take their place in the pantheon of chimeras, er, weresheep!? However, it must be admitted this must be the most enigmatic of the Hexham Heads saga quasi-fauna. As I shall reveal, the weresheep image not only figures in the seemingly flesh and blood creature encountered in a bedroom of the Dodd family home in Hexham, but in an anecdote told to this author and also in the folklore of a slaughterhouse opposite in Rede Avenue. So I have found some substantial evidence for a reality of sorts for weresheep. That said, in the fictional literature of male and female werewolves you won't find a weresheep – not even a walk-on part.

So, ignore fiction, go for facts and ask an expert. Who better than author on paranormal subjects and a professional psychologist - Dr Robert Curran. Bob kindly sent some information, but as I expected it is scant yet unexpectedly focuses upon human bestial deviation:

'There are a couple of instances of were-sheep in England that I know of, but these ideas probably grew up around the births of deformed children. These were generally regarded as the result of sin - i.e. bestiality on the part of one of the parents - and were to be killed. Around 1580, there is mention of an 8 year old boy living near Shrewsbury which was said to be the result of bestiality between his father and a sheep. It is said that "both his feet were cloven as was his right hand" and this was taken as the result of an act of unutterable deviance in defiance of God's laws. It is probable that the child was simply grossly deformed. Another incidence of a were-sheep was mentioned at Birdham, near Chichester, in 1647. If memory serves, when the child - I can't remember what gender it was - was nailed to the church door after being killed by locals. This was to remind the congregation regarding the terrible results of bestiality. Johannes Mayer in his *Tuefelbuchen* (published in 1690) tells of the birth of a deformed child which was the result - according to Mayer - of sexual congress with a horse. The woman was publically stoned to death. By the same token he also mentions a woman who in 1692 gave birth to a cask of iron nails - what sort of congress did she have I wonder. These interpretations were probably used to explain deformities in children - the *monstrum* or evil omen brought about by serious sin such as the Man-Ox in Wicklow, Ireland alluded to in 1185 by Giraldus Cambrensis. Their deformities were probably severe but they had become that way because either they or their parents had transgressed God's laws'. [17]

The strange business of a man carrying a sheep carcass during the night, a slaughterhouse haunted by a human/sheep hybrid and the role of the mysterious Barry Scott will be revealed anon.

But as demonstrated, when dealing with weresheep, sex is never far away from the agenda. Just to show dirty minds are the same worldwide, in the Patagonia region of Argentina the Mapuche folklore tells of a hybrid known as the calchona, which resembles a black sheep and is active at night. The popular story goes that it is a female witch who mutates when magical creams are applied. In the classic version, a suspicious husband, believing his wife to be a sorceress spies on her, sees the transformation and destroys the salves. When she returns the spell cannot be broken and she roams the night bleating pitifully for food. Oh, the sex angle? No ram involved, but the name calchona derives from the Mapuche term 'kalch', which means pubic hair, referring rather graphically to the manimal's long, curly fleece. [18] And if you thought it couldn't get any worse, I canvassed Robert Schneck, in the US, who came up with human-sheep hybrids called grunches, which he believed were located around New Orleans, adding that he 'knew a guy who passionately believed that Mexican sheep ranchers fathered grunches on a regular basis. What a moron!'

Having surely made you nervous of visiting the real and splendid leisure centre in Hexham and also made the reader a little queasy with bestiality, finding a way of capping what has come before has not been easy. My solution, and my favourite subject, contemporary legend, has come to the rescue and once again thanks to my publisher, who is involved.

Having related several West Country werewolf tales, Jon repeated one where a member of a probably prominent local family committed various misdemeanours while out and about in lycanthrope mode, but these were covered up and he was dissuaded from his activities by chaining and barring him every night. Jon tells how a similar legend was attached to a house in Abbotsham when he was at school in nearby Bideford, North Devon, in the 1970s:

'It was very much a foaf tale – everyone knew about the "beast" and its predations, which were supposed to be on sheep, although the creature – whilst in human form – was said to make homosexual advances towards various local schoolboys. Needless to say no-one ever admitted to having had first-hand experience either of the werewolf or the pederast, but one suspects that the story is still deep in the labyrinthine memories of a whole generation of pupils of Bideford Grammar School'. [19]

American readers will probably be best acquainted with the 'Bray Road Beast' and eyewitness Lorianne Endrizzi said, "My eyes popped out of my head", when she saw this likeness in a 1976 book of the mysterious.

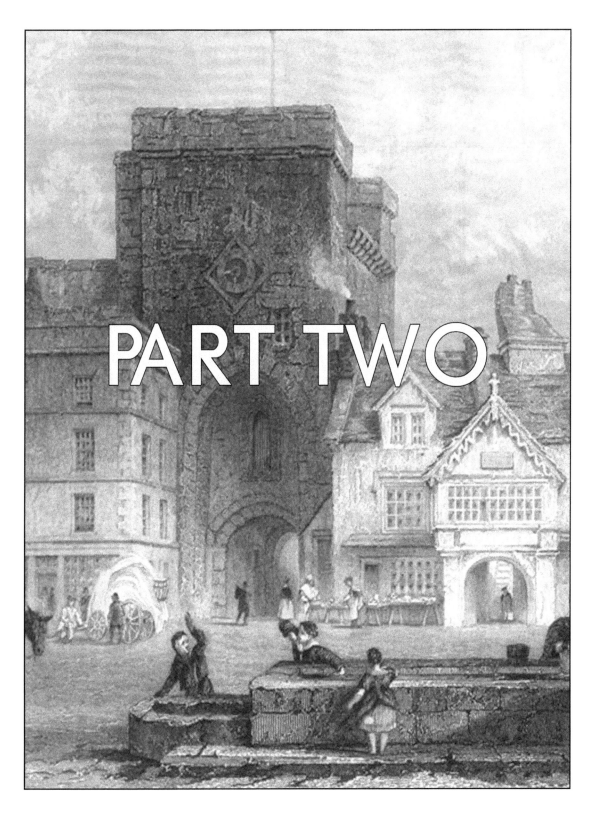

PART TWO

PUB GHOUL'S NASTY HABIT

Dirty old monk who can't stop groping

PRETTY barmaid Kate Archbold is used to being touched up – by one customer who refuses to be barred.

Kate's problem punter is a groping ghost who's been giving staff and customers the willies.

For five months the sexy spirit has been touching up 18-year-old Kate, but now he's turned his attentions to other women in the pub.

The passionate poltergeist – believed to be a mediaeval monk – has a habit of turning up in his hooded cassock at the Grapes pub, in Hexham, Northumberland.

But young Kate's taking it all in her stride.

She said: "I saw him for the first time when I was standing facing the mirror behind the bar.

"I saw a black-hooded figure walk across the pub. I turned but there was no-one there. The pub was empty.

"When I turned back to the mirror, the spook re-appeared.

Friends

"Now he visits me nearly every night. He always touches me on my shoulder or back but it is not hard. It is quite affectionate.

"I call him Jack. We've become quite good friends. It's a good job my boyfriend's not jealous."

Landlady Julie Shell said: "He seemed to take quite a fancy to Kate. But now he just can't keep his hands off any woman.

"At first I was quite

SPOOKY: Julie Shell has seen him

By STUART QUALTROUGH

scared. But now I feel quite relaxed with him about.

"When I first started in the pub, regulars told me about funny goings-on, but I didn't believe them."

Daily Sport stunna Tara Bardot last night offered some reassuring advice to Kate.

The sexy model said: "Don't let him put the willies up you.

"If he does, just chuck a pint of bitter over him!"

Ghost experts believe the spook appeared from the crypt of nearby Hexham Abbey.

But Julie's husband Brennan, 28, is unconvinced.

He said he wouldn't believe the tale until he saw him himself.

Mind you, he can't explain why he has to change at least one light bulb a day while one particular bulb never goes off.

An electrician checked the wiring and said it was fine.

But even during a power cut, that one light still keeps shining . . .

How *Daily Sport* readers were titillated by the tale of an amorous spirit at *The Grapes*.

CHAPTER TEN
PAGAN CELTIC (OR ROMANO-BRITISH) TRADITIONS

This may not be a particularly conventional way of tackling a book of this timbre, but my work generally focuses on the personal rather that the abstract. Here I focus upon a modern-day Celt, rather than shadowy nameless figures existing in a misty past. This being Anne Ross, who is now familiar to readers and would surely approve, being co-author of a book which had as its central character a very real – but very, indeed sacrificially, dead subject – a Celt like herself. And who else better encapsulates modern Celticism than Anne Ross? Not a dewy-eyed New Age buffoon turning a blind eye to a savage head cult, but an educated and pragmatic academic willing to get her boots dirty, a wife and mother, a Gaelic-speaker of Highlands stock who forsook the college high table port to drink a few drams with the natives while collecting oral traditions before they became extinct, who embraced the supernatural as almost normal and also was born with the gift of second sight.

A curious Peak practice

Dr Ross and her producer, Ray Davies, gained the trust of the Peak District community of Longdendale when making the BBC2 Chronicle programme *Twilight of the English Celts*, broadcast on 27 October 1977, and doubtless this valley is not unique in its locals' heritage. Perhaps an authentic secret pagan pan-Pennine tradition could embrace Hexham? It seems this insular 'secret community' still practised a 2,000-year-old Celtic tradition aimed at retaining the fecundity of the land and livestock rather than worshipping pagan idols. In fact, it would seem today to be simply a worship of God and sadly on the brink of extinction. The Seventies documentary claimed there were between 200 and 500 people in the scattered homesteads of the High Peak retaining an Earth Mother belief protected by a small coterie of 'guardians' whose role was never explained satisfactorily. Truly, A Land That Time Forgot!

Also a similarly-themed TV documentary to that on Longdendale on 'Celtic-style' stones found at Mouselow, also in the High Peak area, was broadcast on Hallowe'en in 1986. Archaeologist Glynis Reeve excavated on a hilltop for several seasons and received menacing late-night phonecalls and verbal abuse or stony silence at the dig's headquarters in Glossop. Anne Ross aired her view on the film that Reeve had unwittingly stirred up "a strong local feeling about certain stones which had been sacred, which were believed to have certain powers". [1]

Farther north in Scotland, up the bleak Glen Lyon in Perthshire lies an even more significant archaic heritage site. Had I been aware of it in the Nineties when my wife and I spent a week at a hotel in

Killin, I might have made the pilgrimage to the most remarkable of British Celtic survivals. But there again I might not; it was a time when I had become totally dispirited with earth mysteries squabbling and my 'chauffeur' to megalithic monuments had chosen instead to pursue historical re-enactment. I am referring to what is known in Gaelic as *Tigh nam Cailliche*, a stone-built shrine in the valley which goes by the ancient language name of *Cromgh learn nan Clach*, which translates as 'the crooked glen of the stones'. The gateway to this long and mysterious glen is the village of Fortingall, with its historic yew, the oldest tree in Europe and at around 2,000 years old predates Christianity [2] and is where Jesus Christ's crucifier, Pontius Pilate, was traditionally born under its shade and played there as a child, supposedly the illegitimate son of a Pictish girl and a Roman ambassador sent to pacify the natives ; whereas to spoil a good story, the Roman invasion came later and anyway hardly touched a place so far north, plus there are similar myths in Spain and Germany that he was born there. [3]

Fascinating though this local lore is, it's the remote primitive shieling which is of concern here, an isolated, crude rocky shrine, a house of the goddess or 'the Hag's House'. Believed to be the last surviving example of its kind in the British Isles, it too has a guardian – not genius loci, but a living person. Things may have moved on, but a couple of decades ago a lone shepherd followed generations of his family in continuing the tradition of taking stone figures formed by the River Lyon out of the shrine at Beltane (April 30 / May Eve) and returning them inside at Samhain (31 October). The thatch would have been replaced in olden days although now it is covered in boulders and all orifices would be filled to keep the interior warm and safe from the elements for the representations of the fabled family. This was told to Anne Ross, a fluent Gaelic speaker, when she met the shepherd guardian.

Anne Ross twice visited the sacred glen. Having heard of the shrine while studying at Edinburgh University and accompanied by a colleague, they trekked 16 miles from Crianlarich across snow-covered mountains to find the shepherd had carried out the tradition and all the stones were outside the shieling looking down the glen under their protection. She again made the pilgrimage, 30 years later, no less hazardously, making a long hike over treacherous bog before ascending to the glen led by a special marker atop a rock outcrop. Again the idols were all gazing down upon their protectorate; not just the mother, father and child, but three companions. Shaped similarly to dumb-bells, not carved but created by water action at one particular stretch of the burn flowing below the shrine, here the Hag stone appears to have both a face on its top and torc-like neck ornament, while in special light and shade conditions appears to take on human features.

Naturally, there is an oral tradition to explain this numinous presence and Dr Ross recorded that it is said that centuries ago in unseasonal Beltane weather a monstrous man and his even larger pregnant wife sheltered in Glen Cailliche. When they ventured to the burn, local villagers built them a thatched stone house. After the daughter was born, the couple blessed the valley, an enchantment which will remain so long as the ritual is continued. The traditional procedures seem to be kept even in the 21st Century, but it is unclear by whom.

One public talk given by Anne Ross of which there is a record took place at *The Ley Hunter* moot in 1991, held in Dinas Mawddwy, northern mid-Wales. At this time Dr Ross was winding down her career, lecturing at the Extra-Mural Department of the University of Wales at Aberystwth (an email reply from which on 21 November 2011 claimed she had never been on the staff!). Much of editor Paul Devereux's report echoes material already covered and which I extracted from David Clarke's fine book *Twilight of the Celtic Gods*. Apparently she spoke with 'eloquence, grace and great charm', making the telling point that in Celtic cosmology, goddesses were bound and rooted in the landscape, while seasons and other constituents ruled the gods. The Celtic affinity with terrain included sensitivity to specific locales where they willingly placated the genius loci. Slanting her talk towards a core earth mysteries audience, she selected three ritual landscapes for discussion, one of which was the familiar Glen Cailliche. [4]

I first read of the remote Breadalbane glen in the context of a reader connecting garden gnomes as successors to guardian spirits with the same shieling and the book *Magic Mountains* in which author Rennie McOwan described finding the site with great difficulty as 'it would be possible to pass it by and not notice it'. [5] Another account claims Anne Ross took one of the stones for closer inspection some 30 years ago, but 'returned it to the gamekeeper [shepherd?] who looked after the stones "looking really distraught and dishevelled – as if she had been haunted".' [6] When plans were submitted in 2011 to flood the glen for a hydro-electric power station, Glenlyon History Society held a protest walk to the shieling and there were dire warnings of trouble if the plan went ahead. David Clarke also wrote of his concerns stressing the site's uniqueness. [7]

What's in a name? Celtic or Roman-British

Of course, I have been using the term Celtic willy-nilly as it is a term which conjures a historical period in the mind and for this I have been pulled up by purists. Perhaps, rightly so. In order to place the era when the Hexham Heads were supposedly created, here are some expert opinions on that era – and the favoured term Romano-British.

In the Head's study for six of the best

Stan Beckensall is a former headmaster and prehistorian, specialising in cup and ring markings. With a prominent local author and archaeologist in Hexham, it seemed natural to me to approach him with Anne Ross's notion that a Celtic shrine could be in the vicinity of Rede Avenue; also Stu Ferrol's catalogue of possible anomalies in the immediate area chimed with my growing feeling there was a definite genius loci associated with the spot. Who better than to seek for confirmation or otherwise for continuity of peoples dwelling here for centuries than Beckensall himself, best known for his prolific and pioneering work into prehistoric rock carvings? Unfortunately my 20-minute phone chat became one of the most unpleasant, sad, and rudely dismissive and humiliating put downs of my long career. Admittedly, he said he had written a history of Hexham which might have answered all my points and of which I was unaware, but I plodded on hoping we could concentrate on the one specific small area which interested Stu and I, even trying to butter him up with the promise of a pint in The Forum ("Humph, I don't drink in Wetherspoon pubs; more a Tap & Spile man"). I laboured on, trying to humour him with saying I had taken photos of cup and ring markings in Northumberland at Weetwood Moor and that two were not credited to a particular site and maybe he could identify whether it was Roughtinglinn for me? That made him more annoyed and he told me that "if you had done your homework" I would know of his Newcastle University archive and I could Google his umpteen illustrations to check for myself. "It's had seventeen million hits!" Had I been physically facing him he would have risked making that seventeen million and one with the bonus of a bloody nose.

It got worse. I had missed his pieces in The [*Hexham*] *Courant*. "Don't you read it? Don't you read *The* [Newcastle upon Tyne] *Journal*." Ah, fell into a trap of his own making there, assuming I was local. "No, neither of those papers are stocked here in Seaton Carew." That inflamed him even more. "Anyway, I'm too busy with my fortieth book," which sat uneasily with his wife telling me that morning that I'd just missed him and he'd be sunning himself in the park. After some more castigation for not being thorough - what did he think I was doing asking his advice? - he berated me for sounding as if was taking a "mystical" stance instead of the disciplinary approach he took as an archaeologist. Then he launched into a diatribe about "shamanism and archaeology" being a recent trend which he abhorred and thought that might be where I was coming from. Exasperated, I retorted: "Well, actually, some of my friends regard me as a modern shaman myself - a suburban shaman." That shut him up - briefly. I asked if meeting him was definitely off? "Yes, we'll not see eye to eye." Oh, well, we were in agreement on that point at least.

Oddly enough, the conversation had begun more amicably with him mentioning he was studying misericords of the Green Man motif in Hexham Abbey. Well, if that's not 'mystical' and bordering on the 'shamanistic', even post-hippie New Agey ... oh, forget it! Well, not quite. In his lecture to me as if I was an inattentive, unacademic, lazy schoolboy, he also chastised me for being unfamiliar with the 'Acomb Man,' a sculpture of a smiling head from Watersmeet re-erected in the nearby village of Acomb, which top regional experts had deemed to be of Romano-British origin. Obviously not Celtic - and Beckensall hated all that romanticising of the Celts and Druids.... except there was no such thing as Celtic.... Actually, I think I had a lucky escape there and better off by the exorbitant price of a pint of real ale for Hexham's most celebrated citizen. Glad I had copies of a couple of his humourless pot-boilers down my trousers for that caning. Bet he's a bundle of laughs in the Tap & Spile. [8]

An antiquarian friend of mine suspects Beckensall is of the old school of archaeologist who thinks rigidly and without imagination. He told me: "I've never met him, but one of the criticisms I've heard of his work is that it fits in with the current thought in rock art research devoted solely to the narrow cataloguing and description of sites and images with no attempt to expand into any interpretation of such pictures and places whatsoever. What he's doing is a form of collecting, which has more in common with people who collect stamps, old bottles, etc. which can take OCD-like forms".

A modern industry based on two lines in an ancient book
David Clarke, whose degree is in archaeology, gave his opinion, both for this book and the film *Heads!* during the section of interview I conducted at Sheffield Hallam: [9]

Dave: Well, the whole idea of a Celtic people even existing, never mind all the stuff about mistletoe and human sacrifices, is regarded as nonsense by archaeologists. Propaganda by the Romans! So the idea that there is a Celtic connection with this is just total speculation, because who are the Celts? I just think that the word Celtic is used to add mysticism to the subject, in the way that people in the 19th century used refer to things out in the East, in India, like the Indian rope trick, as if it was something exotic and mysterious, and Celts are our equivalent of that. Whereas, really, it's meaningless. All we're talking about are the indigenous peoples who lived here in the Iron Age; who some people have called the Celts.

Paul: Yes, well, of course, there's people who've plugged into the whole industry of books with 'Celtic' in the title ...

The Acomb Man now takes pride of place in the village of that name near Hexham after being renovated after lying buried in a riverbank for close on 2,000 years. After flooding dislodged it, the sandstone carving led a chequered career, including storage in a barn for many years, and basically when its owners emigrated it was bequeathed to the parish council, which had it restored to its former glory. Such carved deities have been rediscovered throughout northern Britain. At another spot named Watersmeet, in Piercebridge, County Durham, was found one inscribed 'Mars Condatis'. Such sites have offered up other votive offerings such as carved heads, skulls and weaponry. (Paul Screeton)

Dave: Including me! [*laughs*]

Paul: I was just about to say, yes! I do remember some sort of book with Celtic in the title [*Twilight of the Celtic Gods*] ... [*both laugh*]

Twilight of the Celtic Gods – great title? Dave Clarke told the author he can't remember what his original one was, "but it wasn't as good as that!"

Dave: I blame that on the publisher! I think the bottom line was "If you don't have 'Celtic' in the title it won't sell". It didn't sell anyway, but by the by. I think basically the thing about the Celts is, the Celts are associated with the Western areas of the British Isles .

Paul: Oh yes, even though they were a pan-European race?

Dave: Yeah. But the whole point I was hoping to try and put across in the book – I can't remember exactly what I wrote – was you could go to East Anglia, you could go to Kent, you could go to Sussex, places that aren't normally associated with – [*makes air quotes*] – Celticness, and you could find all the same beliefs and traditions there. So using the word Celtic is meaningless. It doesn't devalue the beliefs and the traditions and the supernatural aspect of it. All that I'm saying is that people have those experiences regardless of whether they're in the Scottish Highlands or Amsterdam. It makes no difference, them being Celtic or not Celtic, people still have extraordinary experiences.

At this point in the filming, Graham took over to ask questions specific to the film, but returned to the subject of Celticism:

Dave: The word Celtic has got, rightly or wrongly, all these mystical and spiritual associations that have accrued to the word Celtic in the same way that, in the 19th century, when going to, say, the Orient was seen as something very very way out, very few people did it […] and came back with all these stories about priests and whatever they're called in India and the Himalayas who could levitate and do all these fantastic things. Most of it, we now know, is complete nonsense. But those stories came back, and so there was a lot of mysticism about the East. In the same way there's a lot of mysticism about the Celts, and people know bugger-all about the Celts. All the stuff about the Druids – there's been thousands and thousands of pages written about the Druids, but what do we actually know about the Druids? Two lines in a book by [Julius] Caesar. That's our entire evidence of the Druids, written by Romans who hated the Celts and wanted to destroy the culture of the peoples they encountered in France and Britain! So they made it out that these were bloodthirsty savages who enjoyed human sacrifice. That is the only evidence that the Druids even existed. And yet whole theses have been written on them, books have been written about them – and I think it's basically because people know so little about them that, basically, it's an empty pot into which you can pour anything! You can say anything about the Celts because who's going to disprove it? That's why it's got this mystical aura about it.

A federation, but only loosely

John Billingsley has also written about Celtic heads, but his book *Stony Gaze* takes a wider perspective and John prefers the term 'archaic' to describe the phenomenon of carved heads to cover any and every era when they have been created. Also for his film *Heads!*, Graham Williamson travelled to West Yorkshire to interview the editor of *Northern Earth*. Here's the relevant passage from the interview: [10]

Graham: Perhaps we should define what we mean by Celtic here.

John: Yes. We have to see Celtic as a cultural term, not as an ethnic one. That's clear. The implication of the current research is that the Celts didn't invade, but that Britain took on a Celtic culture. That's putting it as simply as possible. The jury's still out on certain aspects of that, but the point about the severed head, the archaic head motif, is that these are aspects of Celtic culture no matter what the people involved are in Western Europe at that time. That's not to say that it was only the Celts doing it because the Germanic people were using the severed head as well, and you see it coming up in cultures all around the world. So it's not an exclusively Celtic thing. But the Celtic culture, as Anne Ross has shown, both in Europe and in Britain, seems to have had a particular fascination with the carved head. So we're talking culturally.

Graham: And Celtic was a term that encompassed many subgroups of tribes as well, wasn't it? There wasn't a monolithic Celtic culture.

John: Certainly not. That seems to be part of the idea of Celticism now, if you like, is kind of a federation of related cultures. But a loose federation, not one which is self-conscious at all. The Greeks knew who they were and paraded themselves as such; the Celts weren't, really. They just knew who their friends were, and would go against or work with anybody who it was in their interests to work with – it would seem. So that idea of self-identity is quite crucial, I think, in the history of Europe.

No head cult before Roman invasion

Lindsay Allason-Jones, too, shared similar views. Here she was discussing ancient archaic heads: [11]

Lindsay: Not a single one from the North of England has ever come from an Iron Age context. All of the ones where we have a good context for them come from a Roman context. And I don't think that the Celtic heads in the North of England represent pre-Roman religious belief. I think what they represent is the troops coming from Gaul in the Roman period, because we have lots of evidence of Gallic peoples coming to the North of England. And they're bringing their cult of the head with them. They're not bringing their heads with them – they're carving them out of the local sandstone when they get here . There's not any single piece of evidence for the cult of the head in the North of England before the Romans got here.

Paul: So we can more or less throw all those books out of our library!

Lindsay: Well, no, not exactly – I mean, certainly the Celts – the problem is the word 'Celts', because the Celts were basically a wide range of tribes across the whole of Northern Europe who spoke an allied language. And there has been a tendency for people to presume that if they spoke the same language they worship the same gods and have the same beliefs, and I think that is pushing your luck a bit. We know they didn't have the same laws, necessarily. And just because Tacitus says the people in Germany did this, that or the other doesn't mean that's the case. I think that every tribe will have had their own beliefs, and it is quite possible that the tribe who lived in the North of England were inclined to chop people's heads off. There's no evidence either for or against that. It may be that they worshipped those heads, but I have no evidence at all archaeologically that they carved those heads in stone and worshipped them until you start to get the Gallic troops coming in. And, in fact, at the Mile Castle on Hadrian's Wall at Sewingshields there is one of these heads carved on the stone wall which is part of the Mile Castle. And that is on display in the museum.

Paul: So they're Romano-British?

Lindsay: They are Romano-British. Oh – no, no, that's pushing your luck a bit as well, because the term Romano-British implies they were carved by people who were British and lived in Britain when the Romans were here. What I'm saying is that they are likely to have been carved and worshipped by people who have come in with the Roman army from France.

Paul: But wouldn't they be Celts?

Lindsay: They would be Celts, but the problem is they're Celts because they speak the Celtic language. I think you can't say, therefore, that these heads imply there was a pre-Roman worship of the head in the North of England.

Paul: Aren't we playing semantics?

Lindsay: We are playing semantics, but we are inheriting – inheriting a long tradition of playing semantics when it comes to the word Celtic!   [*Both laugh*]   A lot of people use the Celtic heads to imply that this is an indication of pre-Roman religion in the North of England. What I'm saying is that no, it doesn't prove that, it just proves that during the Roman period there was a cult that used the head as a favoured symbol.

Paul: Assuming therefore, then, that the so-called... ah... that the Hexham Heads are ancient and not made by Des Craigie, what age would they have been?

Lindsay: If the Hexham Heads were genuine, they would probably have been second century AD. But what I'm saying is they are of Roman date, let's put it that way. If they are genuine. But as I say, I have never seen a genuine Celtic head from Britain that small. Um... and certainly it's quite clear from this one that the features have been stabbed in while the material was still plastic. Enough to take – And I have never seen any need to doubt what Dr Robson – it may be a rather sarcastic report, but it's a very thorough report, and I see no need to argue with it. What I do find interesting about the Hexham Heads scenario is how over the years many people have not wanted to give up the mystery, even faced with a solid piece of analysis. I think that's very interesting psychologically!

Paul: The curious thing is that everybody associated with them sort of doesn't really like them. Yet they all end up claiming ownership

Lindsay: I think that it's very interesting that so many people got sucked into a sort of Celtic twilight of their own imagining when it comes to these heads. People were seeing and imagining things which I think shows a very interesting power of suggestion from an artefact. And I am not saying that they didn't see those things, but I'm not entirely sure that they can entirely blame the heads for that!

Celtic bubble - boom and bust

Of course, Dr Anne Ross was unavailable for comment on this issue. It was she, to a large extent, who was responsible for the post-hippie, new-agey Celtic industry. After *Pagan Celtic Britain*, a rare serious academic work which struck a common chord, she only partially cashed in on the Celtic publishing phenomenon with her collaborative effort with Don Robins. This was hardly a coffee-table votive offering high on pictorial spectacle and low on intellectual scholarship. It was a serious but popular offering by two accredited experts in separate but conjoined fields. It appeared at the right time, before inevitably, as with all frivolous fashions the bubble burst and remainderers struggled to shift acres of trivial, pseudo-historical, pseudishly-written, cynically-marketed tosh.

As mentioned, Anne Ross did appear on TV, but in her capacity as 'the' expert and not some New Age airhead transformed from stone circles as observatories commentator or ley-line apostle. She acted as a talking head for *The Celts*, a six-part documentary series which was accompanied by a book written by Irishman Frank Delaney, whose questionable grasp of history was queried in *Private Eye*. [12] However, the *Eye*'s literary page contributor may have ended his review in the spirit of sarcasm, but Delaney hit the nail on the head when he was 'finally forced to admit that "the search for a Celtic heritage is spurious".' [13]

Apologists for the Roman occupation have a lot to answer for, as the authors of this book explain, for it was always – *UnRoman Britain*.

But as every fortean is aware, if there is one aspect of the universe we can predict with some precision it is that it is cyclical. From being taught as I was in the 1950s that Roman culture triumphed over barbarians, to the Sixties or Seventies of rediscovered astronomer-priests, on through the Eighties and Nineties of Celtic sophistication realisation, then there had to be a Romano-British backlash in the Noughties and in the last couple of years a total reappraisal of what the Romans did – or did not – do for us. Contemporary thinking is finally coming around to what I first wrote about in the 1960s, that Rome represented totalitarian imperialism and subjugation. (14) One recent book even utilised folkloric ostension in comparing Albion as the empire's Afghanistan' a Helmand on Brit earth, or as that book's title states simply – *UnRoman Britain*. (15) The view of Romans as a civilised society was a Victorian fantasy still taught by my grammar school Latin master, but it is pure tourismus moonshine, to put in folkloric lingo. The Brits – native Celts if you prefer – were akin to the Afghan Taliban. That's not to say all was bad and a local fashion's sales as exports helped the country's balance of payments. This being the woollen hoodie, which we shall meet again later in this section.

While taxes soared and resentment became ever more hostile, the population increased and agriculture and husbandry prospered. Hypocritically, the Romans claimed to deplore ritual sacrifice and any head cult influence, while they themselves organised gladiatorial 'games' and decimated the druids, yet allowed their mercenary or conscripted foreign legions to worship their own distinctive gods. It is obviously time to look a little deeper into rumours of a head cult, whether sacrifices were voluntary and … where did you get that hoodie?

Heads or tales? Cult or no cult?

With the scenario seeming less opaque, heads might have been chopped off in the Iron Age by Celts, but there's no certainty they worshipped them. The Romans imported Celtic soldiers from Gaul who carved and possibly worshipped heads. So there <u>was</u> a head cult – and it was created by Celts. Well, sort of …

I had sought and received contemporary opinion from experts in the field and praiseworthy though Anne Ross's pioneering work was, it had been eclipsed. It was she who in *Pagan Celtic Britain* had claimed the Celts 'venerated the head as a symbol of divinity and the powers of the otherworld'. Also, in the wake of the discovery of the Hexham Heads and other similar artefacts in northern England, she contributed to the regional academic publication *Archaeologia Aeliana*. (16) Here she was unequivocal about this aspect of Celticism:

> 'The cult of the head was the most potent of all Celtic religious expressions; in conjunction with springs and wells, the head reached the apotheosis of its power, according to popular belief. The Celts were head-hunters as well as head-worshippers. It was this barbaric aspect of their culture, together with the practice of human sacrifice which **allegedly** [my emphasis] caused so much embarrassment to the conquering Romans. As a result, the taking of heads in battle and their veneration in the temples would come under official censure and prohibition. When fresh heads became scarce, it would be inevitable that, just as human sacrifice was modified to mock execution, so the cult of the fresh heads would be transferred, to a great extent, to substitute-heads, fashioned from stone, as well as wood, metals, and other materials. In this way, a deeply-rooted native cult could continue, without offence on the one side, or fear of punitive measures on the other. It has been thought that the sudden crop of stones heads in Celtic areas in Roman times was due entirely to the sculptural tradition and the civilising influence of Rome. Where classical influences can be demonstrated in the artefact this is no doubt the case. But here again, we are faced with a fact, and a problem'.

THE HEAD CULT

The splendid illustration which accompanied the article by Nerys Dee in Prediction in 1977.

Dr Ross was viewing the past through rose-tinted glasses with the Celts as savage 'baddies' and Romans as sophisticated 'goodies', as if the Roman invasion rescued the Iron Agers from barbarism. I suspect she also foresaw the coming paradigm shift which 21st Century commentators have extolled in interview for this book. Call her stubborn, but she was not going to have her life's work challenged without a fight. That contentious aspect of dating returns to haunt this book and Anne Ross remained doggedly defensive and in favour of an earlier that Romano-British period for the creation of archaic heads, pugnaciously continuing her essay with:

> 'There is ample evidence for the fashioning of human heads from stone *well into the pre-Roman period* [my italics], by the Celts; and excavations at important cult sites in France, for example, are bringing more of these to light. The problem is the whole question of the dating of these heads when found within, or without, a Roman context'.

Dr Ross continued her essay by saying where heads were excavated from a level consistent with Roman occupation and display features distinctly of the era, there can be little doubt in the dating, though it does nothing to clarify their *significance*. Moving to more primitive and controversial finds, she warned:

> 'When heads of crude, or non-naturalistic nature are found in excavations of a recognisable Roman period, it is clear that they do not *post*-date this phase, but it is by no means certain that they do not *pre*-date it; they may well belong to an already established native shrine, rather than to the period of the occupation of the fort itself. This *pre*-dating may not amount to a long period of time; but the presence of an indication of Roman influence on native religious sculpture. Consequently, a more open mind is required even in dating heads found in a well-attested context. Moreover, there seems good reason to envisage native cult activity even in instances where a purely Roman situation would seem to be applicable.

At this stage in the critique, Anne Ross warned that it was never altogether certain that even in good archaeological contexts could it be guaranteed dating would be precise, particularly where the find was made in unstratified ground, such as where they were disturbed by ploughing or 'discovered in gardening activities', as with as here being discussed, the Hexham Heads. Continuing by tackling the vexed problem of just what constitutes 'Celticism', as opposed to Romanesque carving, a continuation through mediaeval times to the modern day and Des Craigie with his sculptural kitchen sink drama. For those like myself who had only a rudimentary knowledge of archaic heads, what Anne Ross wrote next would have come as something of a rude awakening:

> 'It will be found that the so-called *typical* Celtic head is, in fact, a myth; even a study of the human countenances on the rich metalwork of La Tene Europe will reveal the variety of ways in which the limited repertoire of facial features can be expressed; and in the case of the heads fashioned from stone, the varieties upon the basic anatomical theme are infinite. Eyes may be lentoid, or round or staring; they may be uneven in size, without pupils, or having deep-drilled holes for this feature. The pupil, or the eye itself, may consist of some inlay such as glass or coloured stone. Nostrils may or may not be depicted. The mouth may droop sombrely, or turn upwards in a humourless smile, or be lacking altogether. It may be straight and severe, or toothed and vaguely menacing. The hair may consist of scraped-back, streaked strands, ending, perhaps, in a single pigtail or two pigtails [remember, both the Hexham Heads had hair scraped back, one ending in a bun], or continuing the

short striation at the nape of the neck. It may also consist of elaborately curled locks, twisting and twining to create an elegant pattern. But, on must say, there must be *some* factor which links and unites all these heads and enables us to speak of certain heads a 'Celtic'. Perhaps the factor which welds them all together is the common, elusive, but indisputable quality of non-humanness. They cannot, for example, be said to be horrific, but they *are* non-naturalistic. They *are* not portrait heads; they convey an idea, an impression, not a likeness. It is this elusive quality that sets them so strikingly apart from the calm, naturalistic heads of the Roman iconographic tradition and the grimacing grotesques of the Romanesque'.

In conclusion, I get the impression the head cult notion is something of an embarrassment for archaeologists, bordering almost on a 'no-go' area. Take Aubrey Burl, for instance, who boasts to have written the first book 'solely about the rituals of prehistoric people in these islands'. So if you anticipate a measured explanation of a Celtic head cult, you find fewer than ten references throughout a lavishly illustrated coffee-table book on religious rites. [17]

Of course, I write here not as an expert but from impressions and opinions I've received by reading the relevant literature and talking to experts in the field and come to the conclusion that the head cult – if it ever existed – was symbolic rather than worship or the lesser impulse of veneration. General opinion suggests that to the Celts, the head was the seat of the soul, but if the soul moved on after death, the head had to be an empty shell with no special function – its essence being no longer there. This is the doctrine of transmigration of the soul. In this context I would endorse John Billingsley's speculation in *Stony Gaze* that in the triple ritual slaying of Lindow Man, the first act of a savage blow to the head was deliberate and a means whereby the soul could be released from the body via the head before the body itself was snuffed out. Another neo-antiquarian, the hirsute Anthony Roberts, as if anticipating his own death (of a heart attack on his beloved Glastonbury Tor at the full moon), wrote in response to an ugly and deeply personal insulting diatribe by Valerie Remy:

> 'My body may return to earth, but my immortal soul is *free* and will go where it fucking well wishes in accordance with my own true will under God'.

If the head <u>was</u> worshipped, it represented a cult. If symbolic, it was a ritual object. Subtle but crucial, and 21st Century opinion leans towards the latter. So, sadly, farewell Celtic head cult, R.I.P.

Flasher hoodies - a dimension beyond hugging

There is a deep-rooted belief that the most common historical ghostly apparitions can be doubly divided: by their colour and gender; White Lady and Black Monk. Beguiling though this conundrum may be, let's just concentrate on the latter as there is a Hexham connection. As I noted, the Celtic hoodie became a major export item from Albion. This pragmatic garb afforded protection from inclement weather and also offered a form of camouflage for those travelling through woodland or forests. It has only been in modern times that they have been usurped from the domain of the clergy; being adapted by track athletes and footballers in the 1930s; hip-hop, punk and skating fans adopting the style in the 1970s, along with fictional Rocky Balboa; while from the 1990s onwards it has become the product of fashionable labels and again camouflage uniform for shoplifters and looters, culminating in that non-fictional pugilist John Prescott calling for a total ban on hoodies on 2011.

Back in Roman-occupied Britain, a 'cult of the hoodie' certainly existed and there are carvings to prove it, including one near Hexham at Housesteads. This is how we know of the genii cucullati (hooded spirits of place), where the name comes directly from the cucullus, a full-length woollen robe with hood. These were not living beings but spirit beings, generally depicted singly in continental Europe but in triple in Britain, becoming cult figures associated variously with warrior cults, healing, fertility and regeneration, but without any inscriptions it's guesswork. Occasional continental iconographic versions have the cloak or coat open to expose the penis, while wherever they appear their hoods give them an undeniable phallic image. They are unusually for their age widely distributed geographically and may well have represented another aspect of guardianship.

The genii cucullati cult was big along Hadrian's Wall and this carving of a trio was found at Housesteads.

Among those who have done research into 'hooded entities' is Steve 'Pagan' Jones (**his** distinction, doubtless as he has so many namesakes, being in descending order of importance a *Sex Pistols* founder, ambitious Welsh TV presenter, an athlete and a snail geneticist with a predilection for skeptical controversy; his email being 'paganjones' and a correspondent who saw him give an UnCon talk described him as looking and speaking like 'Alan Bennett on acid'). In an article written at my request for *Folklore Frontiers*, (18) Steve recounted a number of persons' encounters with the phenomenon, in Ilkley and Leeds, West Yorkshire, and Bolam lake, Northumberland, where Centre for Fortean Zoology director Jon Downes witnessed a seven to eight-foot tall black shape with glowing eyes during a vigil for an

English Bigfoot variant in 2003. (19) As originator of the 'deck of cards' theory for entity sightings, Steve began collecting 'hoodie' accounts and found they could basically be grouped into two: either small hooded shapes, alone or as a trio, or seven to eight feet tall. Although they would be described as hooded, further prompting would invariably elicit that only a black shape with a pointed top of the head was witnessed and the garment assumed to be a cloak with a hood. The pattern of distribution also revealed a preponderance of sightings at or around ancient sites, particularly if these had been disturbed (such as an earthwork at Bolam lake) or rituals were being carried out there (as at Ilkley Moor's Backstone stone circle).

Steve regards such entities as guardians of genii loci; manifestations of the earth spirit. One pagan performing a ritual in a wood near Wakefield, West Yorkshire, looked up to find a green-hooded eight-foot entity watching him with what he felt to be an amused expression even though the face was hidden. As for accounts of red eyes, Steve believes these manifest only when the entity senses witnesses' fear, from which they gain power, as if a battery is switched on. A case report which involves both red eyes and large and small entities is also rather amusing:

> 'I was told of a sighting of both large and small hooded entities in Holywell Wood, near Castleford, West Yorkshire, in the 1980s. An army cadet group were practising digging trenches and camping in part of the wood. They were kept awake all night by seeing small hooded shapes and one large seven-foot tall one popping up from behind bushes. They had glowing red eyes. The cadets tried to practise their skills by surrounding and leaping on the bushes where they appeared, only for them to vanish and reappear elsewhere. My informant told me that it was like Snow White and the Seven Dwarves, of which she was seven foot tall and there were about nine dwarves!'

As a civvy-street patriot I find this heartening that would-be soldiers were not scared by these 'insurgents' and as a folklorist amused at the grafting of and Eighties event blending genii cucullati, ghostlore and a old fairytale.

Among various examples I have come across is an experience involving someone well known to me whose identity might best be cloaked in the anonymity of 'a veteran EM researcher' seeing as he was undertaking trance work helped by local fungi at the burial mound Miller's Grave, Midgley Moor, West Yorkshire, around 2003. Here he had an experience where he was visited by three very tall black-robed, hooded figures. The percipient asked rhetorically:

> 'Generally, if one is, for instance, drunk, one's report of UFOs or ghosts or whatever is usually discounted. Well, I wasn't drunk, and was in control of the work I was doing, but in circumstances like this, does the fact that I was not in normal consciousness detract or enhance from the credibility of seeing liminal entities? Or does it all depend on the hearer's predisposition?'

This British triplism has led scholar Bob Trubshaw to suggest they represent male counterparts to the threefold Matronae (mother goddesses), which they often accompany.

Groper of The Grapes

No self-respecting inquiry into paranormal territory would be complete without a spectre (nor a pub), and a traditional one appeared on cue as I was clearing out redundant files dating back to when one my journalistic duties was to write a self-explanatory column entitled 'Pub Spy' (200 in total, with drink and food on expenses). This tale I found had history, sex and mischief as constituents. According to the newspaper cutting, the over-friendly wraith in monkish garb of hooded cassock had become a regular visitor to *The Grapes* pub in St Mary's Chare, Hexham, and achieved national notoriety through his unholy habit of groping girls. (See p.114)

It was neighbour and landlady of The Grapes, Carla Rowley (pictured holding daughter Esme with partner Lee Briggs) who raised the alarm when a fire broke out in adjacent flats in May 2012. According to the local paper the Old Church district is known as the 'ring of fire' for its frequent blazes. (Picture courtesy of *Hexham Courant*)

The passionate phantom first turned his amorous attentions towards barmaid Kate Archbold, but after spending five lustful months courting 18-year-old Kate, the sexually-frustrated spirit became more gregarious and began touching up various female customers. The haunting made headline news in the *Daily Sport* in 1993 [18] and spooked serving wench Kate related:

> "I saw him for the first time when I was standing facing the mirror behind the bar. I saw a black-hooded figure walk across the pub. I turned but there was no-one there. The pub was empty. When I turned back to the mirror, the spook reappeared. Now he visits me nearly every night. He always touches me on my shoulder or back but it is not hard. It is quite affectionate. I call him Jack. We've become quite good friends. It's a good job my boyfriend isn't jealous".

Pub landlady Julie Shell corroborated the story:

"He seemed to take quite a fancy to Kate, but now he just can't keep his hands off any woman. At first I was quite scared, but now I feel quite relaxed with him about. When I first started in the pub, regulars told me about funny goings-on, but I didn't believe them".

The current landlady for the past ten years has been Carla Rowley, who when I showed her the cutting found the groping aspect amusing, so I asked if she had ever been groped. I meant by lecherous Jack, not some Jack the Lad patron, responding, "They wouldn't try it in here, I'd break their necks", so no wonder Jack keeps a low profile! However, Carla has experienced intermittent odd happenings in the pub, commenting dismissively, "A lot of daft things happen which you don't really notice. Ten years ago things would strangely fall down the cellar but nothing ever got broken". Absent was the traditional pub polt behaviour of mischievous breakages, disappearing objects and turning on and off of pumps, but when pressed, Carla, did recall that a few days previous to my visit (13 May 2011), her Patterdale terrier Pip had been behaving abnormally a few nights previously, "running out into the beer garden, standing up on the step and looking in the ladies' loo, back out again, back in again. It's the only time I've been freaked out here". It subsequently transpired the dog had sussed a rat and the vermin was dispatched.

Landlady Carla Rowley invited me to see this blocked-up ancient passageway in the cellar at *The Grapes*.

The Grapes was built in 1899 on the site of a demolished pub and has recently been used as a backdrop for period drama productions. It retains the original cellars, dating back to the 16th Century, which Carla showed me and pointed out where tunnels spread out, one supposedly leading to the abbey. The *Daily Sport* piece airily claimed, 'Ghost experts believe the spook appeared from the crypt of the nearby Hexham Abbey'. But I'm as sceptical of those 'experts' as was landlady Julie's husband Brennan of the supernatural goings-on, but he conceded he couldn't explain why he had to change at least one light bulb a day, even after an electrician checked the wiring and deemed in wholly satisfactory. Equally bizarre, one particular light bulb never went off, and even during a power cut that single light kept shining…

But should there be a presumption that the randy wraith emanated from the abbey – or had it more ancient antecedents? My long-time friend and fellow author Paul Devereux had similar thoughts when he identified the Black Dog, Black Monk and White Lady as a trio of most popularly reported forms of landscape spirit. After gazing at a small stone relief carving of hooded figure he reported:

'I wondered if it was possible – if I dare even think it – that the supposed monkish spectres seen by people today were actually much older wraiths, these *Genii Cucullati*? Perhaps we were seeing the phantoms as figures we could explain, mediaeval monks, when they were in fact something far more archaic?' [19]

Sheelas: the crack between two worlds

The *Genii Cucullati* certainly had their phallic cult aspect, but I am not presuming the corresponding *Matronae* of maiden/mother/crone lineage to have represented an overt vulva cult. But while we're there, it would be hard to ignore the presence of the sheela-na-gig within the book's terms of reference.

As one might expect, Dr Anne Ross had her own opinion on the matter. Guarded and tentative as she was in the face of

Known locally as the Whore of Kilpeck, this Herefordshire sheela-na-gig is often described as Celtic and survived the reformation and Cromwellian prudery. With her gaping vulva and lopsided grin, she could equally be a fertility figure manifestly displaying the blatant sexuality of mediaeval religion. Drawing kindly supplied by David Taylor.

proponents arguing it to be a Norman motif and those seeking to establish the figures as mediaeval creations, reading between the lines it is hard not to believe her sympathies lay with a pagan Celtic tradition; witness the title of an article she wrote, 'The Divine Hag of the Pagan Celts'. [20] Without having seen one in situ and probably with any red-blooded male's gynaecological fascination with womanly anatomy, I cannot but conclude that such elastical exaggerations of the fecund female form imply more than ritual observance and are suggestive of an apotropaic nature. Of course it could simply represent a yonic cult, but I understand there was a superstitious belief that women would display their private parts to ward off evil.

Pete Marsh, aka Lindow Man

According to archaeologist Professor Barry Cunliffe, 'ritual behaviour pervaded every aspect of life' in Celtic times, where variations in burial ritual was prominent, including cremation and ritual sacrifice, while grave goods usually accompanied the elite, and the fact that certain stretches of river appeared to favour others in the amount of artefacts found suggests such specific locations to be in the nature of genius locus. As for the ritual sacrifice, the Celts were far from being alone in practising such, as it was common to many ancient cultures. To 21st Century thinking the notion of propitiating gods with a 'blood sacrifice' to ensure fertility of land and fecundity of livestock, including humans, may seem anathema, but Christians such as myself symbolically drink the blood of Christ at Communion and donate blood at transfusion sessions to aid the wellbeing of others. When the evidence is examined of the 'bog burials' of the Celtic era, the likelihood is that the victims died willingly as their personal sacrifice was not the taking of blood, but the giving for the welfare of their fellow tribespeople.

About the only fact we have of the priesthood of those times, the Druids, was that they believed in the transmigration of the soul; that the essence of a person would be reborn in another body upon death and consequently life was not an end but a new beginning. Applying logic, this also adds to the notion of willing sacrifice, but runs counter to the parallel but contradictory idea that the head was sacred as it contained the enemy's essence. No one ever said Celts weren't obtuse – nor current anthropo(logical) opinion! As Dr Ross, herself, put it, the Celts 'venerated the head as a symbol of divinity, and the powers of the other world, and regarded it as the most important bodily member, the very seat of the soul'. [21]

In those far off times, it is tantalising to speculate from the Hexham site named Bogacres that the land around Rede Avenue – presumably in Celtic times a brackish tract fed by springs and with poor drainage – that into this non-agricultural land bodies had been deposited to propitiate a resident genius loci. And ritual sacrifice leads to an aspect in our narrative whereby it reunited Drs Ross and Robins, who we left bidding adieu at Southampton University in 1977 as he departed with a box carrying the Hexham Heads. In 1985, Don quit his university fellowship teaching post with the ambition of pursuing archaeological science full-time, to which end he set up a consultancy and analysis of 'the body in the bog', aka Lindow Man and the more tabloid friendly Pete Marsh, saw his practice bloom. This stroke of luck brought him and Anne Ross back into professional contact at a point where he had also begun to write *The Secret Language of Stone*. This he followed with their collaboration *The Life and Death of a Druid Prince*, a book savagely reviewed by I M Stead, who concluded that 'it cannot be treated seriously by scholars and it will undoubtedly confuse and mislead the general public'. [22]

Coincidentally, another body found at Lindow Moss a few months earlier by the same two peat-cutters told an even more macabre tale and offers a moral for archaeologists. Here the skull was tested and forensic evidence identified it as from a middle-aged woman. Further analysis had it change gender and experts became convinced it was that of a man and around 2,000 years old. Meanwhile, a local man came forward claiming it was female, modern and only twenty years in the ground. Sound familiar? Here the similarity with Des Craigie's challenge ends, for this claimant was convicted of murder. He confessed to having raped his wife, murdered her, dismembered the body and buried the parts in the Cheshire bog. [23]

A richer, true archaeological find and one in a more notorious context was made in my native Hartlepool. Workmen laying drains in Lancaster Road in 1985 found the entwined skeletons of a young couple, but police scaled down investigations when archaeologists assured them the bodies were ancient. [24] Speaking to the local newspaper, archaeological site supervisor Robin Daniels had concluded that:

> "It could have been a lovers' tryst. They could have broken the rules of society for that reason. A sacrifice would be unusual and it is more likely they took their own lives". [25]

Then Daniels had a change of heart and conceded that:

> "After every theory I've considered I keep returning to ritual murder. The care taken as they were laid together. The [jet] necklace on the [girl's] body. All of this indicates tenderness and respect for the couple after their death once they had been sacrificed as an appeasement". [26]

At the time of the couple's death the grave would have been on the edge of a large expanse of salt water marshes known later as The Slake before drainage to create a seaport for the new town of West Hartlepool. Fancifully, around this time a maverick Victorian antiquarian, Daniel Henry Haigh, made this the setting for a scene where the Anglo-Saxon saga *Beowulf* was enacted, and his wild speculations have continued to be substantiated beyond local legend by aerial photography and excavation, including the presence of a huge mead hall inland at Hart. [27]

CHAPTER ELEVEN
PSEUDO-PAGAN CONTINUITY & THE ARCHAIC HEAD

Anne Ross was not the only person to be obsessed with carved heads. In Yorkshire, the then Keeper of the Cartwright Hall Museum, Bradford, Sidney Jackson, was collecting, investigating and documenting stone heads. Entranced by the motif and recognising their significance in the sphere of folk heritage, he mounted a successful exhibition, which attracted national recognition. This was in the early Seventies and typical of that era was his definition of the carvings under the catch-all and erroneous nomenclature 'Celtic'. Enchanted by the mystique of the mythical, Jackson went on to publish a booklet, *Celtic and other Stone Heads*, [1] listing more than 60 examples of the crudely-carved heads he had noted in the West Riding. By the time of his sudden death in 1974 he had recorded in excess of 700 individual heads.

Whereas at this time Des Craigie had entered the picture claiming the Hexham Heads were not ancient and **he** had created pseudo-Celtic artefacts, Jackson's detractors claimed **he** also had created pseudo-Celtic carvings but passed them off as ancient. The way Guy Ragland Phillips tells the story, it has more than a whiff of urban legend about it, 'An official of a Yorkshire museum is said to have alleged that Mr Jackson carved the heads himself – which would make Mr Jackson a genius of gigantic stature'. [2] A strange reversal, but both themes are familiar to folklorists as sub-genres of ostension.

In fact, Jackson, who became Director of Bradford Museums Service, was a folklorist himself, treating his study in the manner of an ethnographer, collecting folktales about archaic and apotropaic heads, not only locally but from contacts who had heard similar tales while abroad. He made a survey in 1969 of extant heads and was one of the first researchers to recognise the connection between the carved heads he was cataloguing and the supernatural.

As for confusing ancient and modern carvings, John Billingsley, who could be regarded as Jackson's archival and spiritual heir, John told Graham Williamson:

> "Sidney Jackson, the Bradford Museum curator who started all this new interest in so-called Celtic heads in the 1970s, he – by the end of his life – had realised that, and that's why he called his book *Celtic and Other Stone Heads*, because he realised that something else was going on and they had misnamed it at a very early stage, but it was a bit too late to go beyond it because there had been so much publicity about the Celtic heads". [3]

Today, alarm bells would ring. As John put it, 'Few stone heads occur in a context by which they can be reliably dated'. He also made some interesting points in an article 30 years ago:

> 'Some doubt was cast as to the authenticity of certain of these carvings. It was revealed that a few of the heads were carved in modern times. For some people this instantly devalued the collection but Dr Anne Ross, the leading authority on Celtic culture, was impressed by the exhibition'. [4]

That should have given Jackson's exhibition the stamp of academic approval. As events have turned out, her blessing would seem to have had little benefit in retrospect. However, one aspect of his successful display and TV publicity was that a market for such artefacts suddenly mushroomed and a note in his card index recorded adverts from antique dealers, followed by a large jump in prices. Meanwhile, in the West Country, the late writer Rodney Legg (subscriber to *The Ley Hunter* during my tenureship) and archaeologist Chris Copson reportedly began a project to date and catalogue all the Iron Age stone carvings depicting decapitated heads they could find., stressing they were well aware of the dating difficulty. Copson also mourned the trend to sanitise our past, remarking, "The fact that we were once a nation of head-hunters appears, in modern times, to have been all but swept under the carpet". [5]

Mill-towns an eye-opener for ethnographer

Naturally Anne Ross was not only aware of Jackson's collection of heads, but as mentioned travelled to see them. Speaking about what she saw and acknowledging the pagan continuity aspect, she said:

> "What strikes me as above all significant is not so much whether this head or that is genuinely Celtic or not, but the extraordinary continuity of culture shown by this collection, Presumably without knowing it, there are local craftsmen of this very century in these Yorkshire industrial valleys, carving heads with specific characteristics such as the 'Celtic eye'. I had always imagined the West Riding to be an industrial hotchpotch in which all traces of past cultures would have been obliterated. I had failed to realise that each mill-town and village was, almost to this day, largely cut off from the others and isolated. It is a treasure house of continuity".

Again in this book I look without shame for guidance on this matter in general from Dr Ross and what she wrote back in 1973 is as relevant today as then:

> 'It would seem that the greatest degree of error is likely to occur between the modern "primitive" heads and those that are genuinely archaic: and here it is essential to employ every corroborative discipline possible. For example, the evidence of petrology is of major importance; geological analysis can indicate what is natural and what is artificial in the material employed. It can differentiate between natural fracture and marking on the stone, and that made by man; the constituents of paint, in lay and so on can be determined. Again, field questioning when there is a doubt about the origins of a head may be rewarding. One has always to bear in mind the fact that heads may turn up inadvertently in a context of archaeological interest, but not necessarily of interest to the finder; as a result, being fairy portable and decorative, heads would tend to be carried away from the find-spot and placed in some prominent place, while any related structure would be ignored and even forgotten. Again, the continuing folklore of the head, the belief in its powers of averting evil and keeping the

supernatural at bay is in itself striking and noteworthy and may offer some explanation for the persistence of this iconographic tradition. In conclusion, the very phenomenon of these heads is a most remarkable one, a predilection which seems to lie deep in the descendants of the former Celtic inhabitants of Britain and Europe. Little progress can be made in this sphere until a comprehensive corpus, devoid of prejudice and subjective thinking, is compiled, if this enigmatic aspect of our past – and perhaps our present also – is ever to receive the scholarly analysis it deserves'. [6]

'They could be anybody. They could even be nobody'

Sidney Jackson may have been the first to display and promote carved heads and Anne Ross the first to

John Billingsley ... gone native in the wilds of Calderdale.

capture popular imagination over Celtic heads, through promoting the notion of a head cult, but it was left to a modern antiquarian, John Billingsley, to delve deepest into the continuity aspect. It was he who claimed to have coined the term 'archaic' to encompass heads carved or created anywhere between prehistory and the 21st Century. But in the passage above Anne Ross deliberately uses the preferable term 'primitive' for modern reproductions and 'genuinely archaic' for Celtic/Romano-British examples. (I fear John has inadvertently caused confusion by this virtual reversal of usage of 'archaic' but it seems to have stuck and I'm not averse to using as an alternative to primitive. More semantics...) His superb book *Stony Gaze* (based on his 1992 MA thesis) brings together his scholarship, fieldwork and insights. [7]

An adopted 'tyke', John moved to West Yorkshire from Twickenham via various places, including a spell in Japan, but has spent more years of his life in Yorkshire than anywhere else. It appears he quickly 'went native' and has absorbed the customs, folklore and culture of Calderdale, writing a number of regional books based on his studies. Actually, I first met john at a *The Ley Hunter* moot in Glastonbury in the late Seventies and have written for the magazine he edits, *Northern Earth*, and am a spirited contributor to debates on its lively internet readers' forum.

It was while perambulating his new haunts that John noticed a proliferation of archaic heads. With a keen geomant's eye, he spotted effigies protecting conventional sacred spots, but they obviously also struck a chord with the secular sector, many being popular with urban householders for the mundane reason that they are decorative. While gathering material for his thesis, John quickly realised that many of the examples of what had established the notion of the 'Celtic head' were far from being ancient but creations by 17th century stonemasons. Also notable was that portraiture had never been a key aspect of the archaic head, or as John put it, 'they could be anybody. *They could even be nobody*, and this is crucial in the tradition of the carved head'.

Interviewed by Graham for his film *Heads!*, John was first asked for clarification that it was 'style rather than era' that he meant by the term 'archaic'? Agreeing, John expanded on the theme, explaining:

> "Yeah, that's the reason for the choice of the term, that 'archaic'. It gets us off the time hook, the dating hook. Now the dating hook is one reason why a lot of archaeologists like to keep away from carved heads. It's because it's so hard to date them, and you don't want to say, 'Oh yes, this is a Celtic head', for somebody to come back and say 'Oh, I carved it in 1957' – for instance! Yeah, that is a famous case, but it's not by any means an isolated case. If you just go on the idea of them as archaeological artefacts and let your mind be focused on that you can miss some important points about them. And the important point is that the style itself is pretty much ageless, it's timeless, whether it's 20th Century or 15th Century or Iron Age. There's nothing really between them. So that is archaic. We could make a head here now, and, you know... give it a bit of lichen, a bit of moss, spread a bit of yoghurt over it, take it outside, we could probably take it into an antique shop and blag it".

Discussing the apparent simplicity of the carved heads, which forms one of the cornerstones of the head cult's attraction, John explained that *raison d'etre* and pondered its guardianship role and Otherworld connection:

> "You're on kind of a philosophical level here, where – I think it was Plato –
> said that if you want to draw a picture of a table, one board with four rough
> legs is a better picture of a table than this nicely-turned surface with fluted

legs and maybe a bunch of other fripperies. Because the more detail you put into it, the more you come to "This table" or "That table". But as soon as you put a board with four legs in it... you know it's a table. That's all. If we extend that to the idea of a... we have to take a step back here and say, "These archaic heads, they appear to be threshold guardians, they appear to be speaking to a dimension which is beyond this world" These seem to be a vehicle; they sit at the threshold of worlds. And they're protecting against incursion of both the present realm and from the magical, the otherworld realm. Nobody quite knows what folk are going to look like on the other side! It's where the dead are, it's where the faeries are lurking, it's where there are all kinds of strange beasts beyond there. But if you want to set yourself to deter all of that lot, you need to have an image which speaks to both sides of that fence. That's the idea of the stripped-down template. It's recognisably human but it's not recognisably of either world. So it sits on the fence".

When later in the interview Graham asked about traditions associated with the Celts, John again focused on the head and its connection with the afterlife:

"*The Mabinogion* tale featuring Bran's severed head seems to tell us an awful lot about the power of the head to live on after death, and to entertain people with poetry and song and prophecy and to actually place people that it's with in a state outside time. So you've got issues of hospitality, you have the issue of prophecy, of inspiration – these are social values which are transposed into an Otherworld context. That seems to be the general idea behind the Celtic ritual of the head. There seems to be the idea that if you decapitate somebody and take the head, that's more than just a trophy, you're actually taking something of their power with it. And that it has some sacred value in that sometimes you can take the skull, gild it and give it to a local shrine. So from all these little clues we can assume that, yes, it's a guardian artefact for them, and it's a sacred guardian at a sacred threshold. These seem to be important".

Folk art enters the picture

An aspect pertinent to this inquiry which John draws attention to in *Stony Gaze* is the role played by humble quarry workers in the creation of modern archaic heads. Des Craigie was not a quarryman, but his workplace when he claimed to have made the Hexham Heads manufactured industrial concrete posts. John writes that such spare-time activity should be regarded as 'folk art rather than with any deeper significance', reflecting how Des claimed to have created those originals. Rightly, John does not belittle such amateur craftsmanship:

'Even if "only" folk art, such heads are significant in suggesting that the vehicle of transmission of the archaic or severed head motif may well have been the quarryman/builder, rather than the guild sculptor, which would further underline the rural peasant context of the motif, and its transmission via an anonymous thread of cultural tradition'. [7]

So Des could have been totally unaware of a force driving him to make archaic heads – and maybe there was an even more sinister element also at work, as introduced into the narrative shortly.

Craftsman creates rural whodunit

Echoes of Des Craigie's intervention in the Hexham Heads debacle resounded in the broadcast media after residents in various North Yorkshire villages awoke to find archaic heads turning up uninvited and mysteriously. The riddle began in August 2007 after a carved head was left at Arthington, near Leeds, and two more a fortnight later. Greatest beneficiary was Kilburn, in the shadow of the white horse effigy, where six appeared, and one took pride of place on the bar at the Foresters Arms, but almost all of a similar number in Goathland promptly vanished. More appeared in Selby, Collingham and Braithwell. To add to the strangeness, several were accompanied by a card inscribed, 'twinkle, twinkle like a star – does love blaze less (or "flourish", in Kilburn) from afar?' Most also included a sign resembling a chi-ro plus the word 'Paradox'. Just as Anne Ross favoured an ancient Hexham Heads maker, Des Craigie steadfastly maintained they were his modern creation of them and hence argued contemporaneity.

Pertinently, similar disagreement surfaced by 3 October 2007 when rival channels nominated separate champions: ITV supported Brian Cox, while the BBC backed Billy Johnson. Being linked to The Art House project in Wakefield, Johnson, of South Elmsall, is a craftsman of note and spokeswoman Judi Alston claimed 57 heads had been scattered at random as keepsakes, which finders or claimants were at liberty to do with as they pleased. As the story faded from the public eye it was to be noted that they did not all conform to the same style and the jury was still out on whether there had been one or several artists involved.

Meanwhile, a would-be film-maker was sufficiently intrigued by this seeming stunt to apply his nascent skills to making it a springboard for a documentary of the subject of carved heads, ancient and modern. Before approaching me with regard to the Hexham Heads saga, Graham Williamson, together with Teessider chum Olly Lewis, made several visits to locations where the riddle-me-re creations had been scattered, but was unable to film the elusive Billy Johnson (nor any Brian Cox), who happens to run a company called – Paradox. (8) According to an Art House internet page, since deleted, Billy Johnson described his heads as 'hypnagogic', as did Judi when Graham contacted her. That and the chi-ro deepen the mystery.

Graham and Olly did, however, follow the spoor of clues in the media and in response to a request offered the following geographical location information gathered:

> 'The heads we found were as follows: five at the Mouseman Workshops in Kilburn, four of which are still on display. Not sure where the other went - they were outdoors, so it may have been broken. One at the Foresters Arms in Kilburn, though it isn't there now - the landlady, Fiona Gould, took it with her when she moved out of town. Three outside the post office owned by Mike and Valerie Hoyes in Braithwell, two of which now reside with a friend and one of which is built into the wall of Mike and Valerie's new patio! One in Goathland, in the garden of post office owners Brian and Susan Taylor. There were, as you say, more, but Brian and Susan were uncertain of how many, or where they went. Three in the houses of three friends in Bishop Wilton - there was one more in this village, but it seems to have gone missing. One of these was outside the local post office too - perhaps the artist couldn't think of anywhere more appropriate to put a delivery? Three in Arthington, one of which is owned by a local bar owner and two of which were gifted by local artist George Griffiths to his daughter in Oxford. We were unable to locate heads in Selby, Collingham, Stamford Bridge and Husthwaite, though we did often meet people who could confirm the heads were left there. There was an amusing rumour of one being left

A selection of heads crafted by Billy Johnson with a blurred CCTV
image of one being delivered.

> at RAF Fylingdales - this seems to have arisen because some men from the base saw Susan and Brian in Goathland and helped them do a bit of research on what the chi-rho meant, etc'.

Then out of the blue this April came an email from Judi inquiring about progress with the film and my book, triggered by an unexpected visit by Billy after a year's absence. She had shown him various emails from myself and Graham regarding his handiwork and I responded by email to her a draft of my passage on Billy's endeavours. Judi immediately corrected the wrong assumptions that had been made and defended Billy's integrity and impressed upon me his private nature and skill as a traditional craftsman driven by a head-carving impulse. Most importantly, I had led myself astray by assuming that Judi's tenancy at the Art House meant that was how she became in contact with him. As it so happens, her film-making company needed a central base and The Art House was convenient for One to One Development Trust, of which she is creative director and chief executive officer. As for The Art House itself, its CEO and team had never met Billy, although he had been a member for a year in the past; also Billy's heads project was and is separate from any organization; a head <u>was</u> left at Fylingdales; and Billy's family is related to the late wood-carver Robert 'Mouseman' Thompson of Kilburn. As for Brian Cox, that 'was a TV blunder, I think, a cock-up or piss-take'. Judi added:

> 'Billy has never sought publicity and I certainly never intended to be his publicist. The situation of the heads escalated very quickly and became a good media story, without intent or knowledge from my part. It was a whirlwind and Billy disappeared leaving me to answer lots of questions. Partly me not getting back to you or Graham was purely not knowing what to say. I couldn't really give either of you what you wanted without compromising my loyalty to Billy. My partner and I made our creative response to what Billy did through an online project called Clearance (self funded) http://www.dreamingmethods.com/ clearance/ . There is no way Billy would ever talk to the papers or press, or appear on a film (bear in mind I'm a film maker and one of his best friends. If he wanted to be in a film I'd make it). He could have capitalised on the incredible attention he had and set himself up for life (or certainly made some good money out of it), but he chooses to continue to live a simple and very basic life style. Money, fame, ego, mainstream just don't interest him - this can be frustrating as his friend!! Billy is a prolific maker/carver, driven by his own complex thinking and compulsion. He continues making heads and carving stone, there have been several copy-cat imitations'. [9]

In a further email, Judi was at pains to emphasise that the opinions expressed were her's alone and not an interpretation of Billy's. Her observations broadened the notion that Billy was tapping some deep psychic resonance from mysterious realms while deepening the mysterious aspects. The relevant section of the email reads:

> 'The explanation or interpretation of this is only mine; the intrigue here was and will always remain around Billy and the heads - even to me it is a mystery. There are no answers to lots of the questions, very little obvious rationale and in a way it shouldn't need to fit into needing to be explained. There is a profundity about these carvings and their symbolism, that period of time and those places where the heads were found, an amazing unprecedented energy that happened that I think is true modern-day folklore'. [10]

Since then there has been a bizarre twist in that the recipients of two heads from the second wave belong to a group which call themselves Timebridgers and believe they will be reincarnated. Believing they can get in touch with their future selves, they have buried the carvings in Spain for their reincarnated selves to find them. They sound like a dotty cult in that they are channelling message from the cosmos, or the Pleiades to be precise. After noting Billy's 'Twinkle, twinkle little star...' theme and speculating that the distribution might be a reflection of the Pleiades and the constellation of Taurus's configuration, it seems Billy has never had any association with the Timebridgers. Odd, nevertheless.

More old mead in new bottles

While John Billingsley was rooting around Calderdale for signs of 'head cult' continuity, I was noticing a few such carvings myself in the seaside village where I have lived for six decades. I would often pass a house in Byland Grove whose meticulous garden had a few heads in its rockeries and two stone examples adorning either side of the garage and another two at the gateway. Not of these looked Celtic but a single crafted stone of a naked couple embracing did have an aura of antiquity. But dare I imagine it was very many centuries old? One summer's Sunday as I headed for the pub, the house-owner was tidying a rockery, so I introduced myself to him, though he was certainly familiar to me at least as a face in the local paper. Hartlepool borough councilor Jim Mason owned a demolition business and he told me his workforce was under personal instruction to put aside any interesting carvings they came across. Hence heads of humans, lions and so on dotted around his property. As for the sexy archaic lovers embracing, it had been made by a student at the local art college and presented to him during his mayoral year of 1977/78. [12]

Something wicked this way comes

Another thread of continuity links another local demolition contractor to apotropaic heads. When John Whitfield bought my nearest 'watering hole', the Station Hotel in Seaton Carew, he negotiated to have a Sainsbury's mini-mart built on the land and then flattened the pub. The inn's ancestry has been the subject of much debate. The latest attempt and one aiming to be as definitive as possible was by Marie-Louise McKay, who spent years researching a history of Hartlepool pubs to the present day. Entitled *The Lion Roars and the Monkey Bites* [13], here the monkey refers to the notorious legend of the primate washed ashore from a shipwreck at the fraught time of the Napoleonic wars and it was hanged as a French spy [14], while the lion alludes to the local Camerons brewery with its lion symbol. According to McKay, *The Station Hotel* (*The Station* and *Station Hotel* names seem to have been interchangeable) was built in 1871 at the behest of Michael Bell, a former stationmaster at Seaton Carew railway station, on the other side of Station Lane, then little more than a trackway from Hartlepool. It finally closed in 2010.But I always suspected its age to be greater and was not surprised when landlord Dave Boreland told me in 1990 that he had been in the loft and found a document relating to the pub dating back to 1850. My suspicion was that it was built either at the time the railway arrived, for the sustenance of travellers and accommodation for the stationmaster, or earlier as a coaching inn.

In 1991, I first published an article on interesting aspects of Seaton Carew, focussing on 'fortean' and 'earth mysteries' aspects, 'Strange Seaton Carew', which was published in two magazines. [15] A paragraph was devoted to the pub and I recorded that 'the lounge has a distinctly spooky feel to it, and I'm not the only one to have experienced this, though the adjacent bar has no peculiar feel'. Yet I certainly never heard of any ghost sightings or poltergeist behaviour. But why should I? From its construction onwards, the pub had been protected by apotropaic surveying the world from the protective porch. Painted cream on dark green woodwork they watched generations of families enter and leave refreshed, umpteen landlords come and go. Those archaic-looking heads saw everything but themselves were only noted by a few.

**Guarding Seaton Carew's Station Hotel, but no match for the demolition crew.
(Jon Whitfield, by kind permission)**

The *raison d'etre* for the sentinel heads became clear after a terrifying experience one sunny early morning three or four years ago when I had been down Blackberry Lane, the pathway between the railway and allotments opposite the Station Hotel. I had been to photograph a freight train and on my return paused where the road to the station forks on the left. All of a sudden I was gripped by a dread greater than I could have imagined possible. It was stifling, gut-wrenching fear, made all the more horrendous because the evil, oppressive threat was invisible. I actually felt as if my life was in imminent peril. It was so overwhelming I figured it was going to overpower me. Fight or flee? No option where the enemy is overwhelming in strength and indiscernible. In fact, I neither debated nor hesitated, I pedalled away furiously as fast as I could, cycling straight across the main road oblivious of the likely presence of oncoming traffic. I fled and I'm not ashamed to admit it.

Only later did I realise that my awesomely daunting experience occurred directly opposite the protected doorway of the Station Hotel. Surely a site cannot be inherently evil; there must be an entity to cause panic. Were those apotropaic heads present for that very purpose to deter some lurking demon from taking shape and terrorising drinkers in the pub or was it a warning to any visiting god that a swift half or bacchanalian session was off limits? These heads were symbols denoting a point of contact between the human world and the supernatural Otherworld – a territory where spirits and gods dwell, going about their business and a realm to which we mortals are only occasionally privy, but a shared and invisible domain which is just as <u>real</u> as our everyday landscape and far more dangerous and wondrous. As leading Romano-British era scholar Dr Anne Ross observed, the Celtic goddesses were bound and rooted to the land, whereas the gods moved with the seasons and conditions' and this applied to specific locales. [16]

But with trade in decline, the pub owners threw in the towel and the Station Hotel was bought by European Property Management. I was very tempted to approach property developer Jon Whitfield and ask if I might have the porch and heads when the pub came down, but fearing that might alert him to some value in them and not wishing to pay exorbitantly, I risked waiting for the demolition and then seeing if the workmen would let me remove them from among the rubble. When the building's demise came it was efficiently swift and a digger worked one March 2011 weekend leaving it virtually levelled. I couldn't spot the guardian heads and suspected they had ended on a bonfire. But in a desperate hope that the protectors had survived, I rang Jon Whitfield. He understood what I was talking about and had been aware of the embellishments to the sentimental extent that he had told his men to put them to one side. In an email he explained: 'Tried to save them but damaged too much when front wall came down. The front canopy and practically every other piece of wood in the building was rotten and full of worm'. [17] So after serving their community silently, faultlessly and faithfully for 150 years, they were cast aside and destroyed. What intrigues me about the functional glass architecture is the absence of a front door facing the evil spot. There is an ancient belief that evil spirits cannot turn corners, though I doubt it that was consciously on Sainsbury's mind when the automatic hi-tech door was placed to face south.

That two demolition-men of my acquaintance had what I would have thought an untypically sentimental relationship with the history and relics they were obliterating may have a resonance in an oblique passage by John Billingsley in *Stony Gaze*, which links to onomastic folklore, where stories are told to explain carved heads on buildings as memorials to workers killed during their construction. In fact, I raised with John Whitfield whether anyone had been injured during the Station Hotel's demise and he assured me no one had come to harm, but earlier this year a grandmother had a leg shattered by a car in what the local paper headlined as a 'freak accident' in the Sainsbury's car park. (18) Then there's the ancient tradition of interring bodies in walls as foundation sacrifices, which still exists as the urban myth of 'hardened criminals' embedded in concrete structures such as London's Westway by rival gangsters.

'Slag Alice and the 'Gateshead Flasher'

Also in North-East England, Antony Gormley designed his *Angel of the North* creation for Gateshead Council to outdo Newcastle across the Tyne, having already exhibited his installation of 40,000 tiny clay figures in a former railway maintenance workshop. Strangely, these resembled a multitude of Hexham Heads. Gormley commented, "*Field* could be said to be evoking the spirit of our ancestors and the unborn. We are the mediators between them". [19]

Farther north, whatever the impulse was to create landscape artist Charles Jencks's *Northumberlandia, Green Goddess of the North*, when she's open to the public in 2013, I for one will want to visit. The Yanks have got their Serpent Mound in Ohio, but at a quarter of a mile long our's will be the largest representation of the human body on Earth. Not surprisingly, the reclining female figure will be a prominent feature to be seen from the A1 for motorists, her ample hindquarters provide a generous eyeful for rail travellers and her breasts rising 100 feet into the air will welcome incoming passengers to

Newcastle Airport. All from the spoil created by open-cast mining activity. And as with any self-respecting lady courting public attention, this year she was getting a 'spray tan' in the form of hydro-seeded topsoil which will coat her in grass. Her connection to my argument comes not from the prudish complainants affronted by raw geophysical naturism, but the mistaken public belief that she represents a pagan symbol: the focal point in a new public park in Northumberland's Blagdon estate, wags have already demeaned this sham/shamanic landscape, dubbing it 'Slag Alice' and unhelpfully, philistine county councillor Wayne Daley sneered, 'If we wanted something like this, we'd ask Jordan to open a theme park". [20]

Head-bangers, head-impalers and head-kickers

Rock 'n' roll's fascination with legend, satanism, Pan pipes and the head in its various guises reached its apex the day members of a Los Angeles band named *Shiloe* decided to rebrand themselves with a new direction, image, logo and name – Hexham Heads. The personnel constitutes Ken Ramos, Melissa Pleckham, Lukas Judge and Jeff Cohlman, who came together to create 'an alternative/goth/ psychedelic soundtrack for your addled mind'. Despite that they're rather good! What doesn't help is their lack of PR nous, Ken explaining to me in an email, "We don't really like to give a lot of info out, so we don't have details up for each of us or any close-up pictures". They did, however, deign to grant a brief interview in 2010 explaining the name change (which is what really matters here). Interviewed by Ben, of band *Summer Darling*, Melissa recalled:

> "Basically, we were just never *that* crazy about the name *Shiloe*. It never had any special meaning or a cool story behind it; it was just the best of the names we came up with back when the band first started playing shows. Everything else associated with the word is kind of tame (i.e., Brangelina's baby, the Neil Diamond song, the puppy books/movies, the Civil War battlefield) and we never felt like it was very indicative of our sound. When we both happened upon the story of the Hexham Heads, it seemed like it was a much better fit for the band. Also, the name Shiloe never inspired any particularly cool band logos, whereas the logo we have now for Hexham Heads is completely awesome. (Thanks to our friend Iona Lie for masterminding the logo!) ".

Pressing on, Ben asked if the rumour that the name came for a ghost-hunting book was true? Melissa again:

> "This rad chick I know who plays the flute - her name is Kara - gave me a book called An Illustrated History of the Haunted World for my birthday. This book contained the story of the Hexham Heads, which are two ancient stone carvings of dubious origin which appear to have a werewolf that watches over them. While reading this story, I thought to myself, 'Holy shit, now there's a band name!' Later, Ken was flipping through the book, and said, 'Should we change the band name to Hexham Heads?' It was a true mind meld, and HxH was born". [21]

Another interview, only memorable in retrospect, was one I did with a new heavy metal band from Hartlepool called *White Spirit*. They debuted with an eponymous album and I afforded them probably their fist publicity in my Discdate column in the *Hartlepool Mail*. *White Spirit* is famous now only for spawning guitarist Janick Gers and I last saw him as I waved out of the office window and was almost run over as the a National Express bus arrived to whisk him away to fame, fortune and eventually *Iron Maiden* via *Gillan* and Bruce Dickinson. For Maiden's 1993 Raising Hell tour they had a grisly set of fake severed heads – including one impaled on a stake – created as theatrical props, which were last heard of being auctioned in Aylsham, Norfolk. [22]

Another North-East band was *Angelic Upstarts*, whose connection with severed heads is more tenuous but equally macabre. Members of the band would place on stage a pig's head wearing a policeman's helmet and give it a savage kicking: popular with audiences, the symbolism of this act was not lost on the Northumbria Constabulary.

From kicking a decapitated head on stage to sports arena spectacle is a short step and there has been speculation as to the severed head being used competitively. I parade the fabulist Nerys Dee once again with the contentious claim that 'football, believe it or not, began from the macabre scramble to kick around the head of one's enemy'. [23]

I doubt former cricket star Imran Khan is actually a more trustworthy commentator when he told television viewers that Alexander the Great played wild polo – nothing resembling polo as played today – with the severed heads of his enemies. Still existing in the mountains of Pakistan, rural villagers still compete, but without human heads. [24]

For his film *Heads!*, Graham rejected any involvement by band *Hexham Heads*, but approached a semi-local musician, who agreed to score the film. Bob Pegg, who found prominence with folk band Mr Fox, wrote a truly evocative and most relevant song, *The Stone Head*, describing the imaginary thoughts of a guardian head watching and commentating on the goings-on over time which he witnesses, concluding with time-worn weariness," you seem to have need for me, my friends, but I have no need of you". Not surprisingly, Pegg was inspired to write the song from being influenced by the archaic heads he noted whilst living in Hebden Bridge, Calderdale. [25]

Stamped on landscape and Mars probed

The image of the head – whether it be expressed however crudely as resembling the 'typical' Celtic depiction – also exists through the medium of simulacra. In nature, standing at the centre of Castlerigg Neolithic stone circle, I spotted it as a distinctly Celtic face on the hillside looking south. Very different geographical simulacra significance was spotted by Charles Shepherd, who assumed a connection between the cult of the head and the sacred islands around our shores which are shaped as such and with a neck such as Iona, Caldy, Bardsey, Holyhead Island, Northumbria's Lindisfarne, Cornwall's St Michael's Mount when the tide is out and Brittany's Mont St Michael. [26]

That notion is attractive to New Age thinking, whereas ufologists and lost civilisation proponents became excited when in 1980 a space probe photograph showed a face from the Cydonia region of Mars which looked eerily Celtic (extrapolated, it equals three options: Celts colonised Mars, Martian invaders are the Celts or its total twaddle).

Final thoughts on the continuing fascination for heads

Although I have maybe implied the continuity here has been smooth, the reality is not so simple. In fact, the development has never been constant and there have been punctuated periods of dormancy. The efforts of Des Craigie, Colin Robson and particularly the fevered creativity of Billy Johnson are instead part of a process of recurrence, as if the image lies dormant until provoked into existence once again by some subtle stimulus or more probably is responding to its own cyclical nature. In the Hexham reawakenings, I suggest a genius loci exerting an influence to manifest itself in quasi-human form. It's as if whatever the numen constitutes it seeks to express itself in a form we humans can comprehend. Similarly much ufolore speculation is based upon the suspicion that entities encountered manifest themselves in forms we can identify rather than 12ft lizards or whatever concoction even a sci-fi film props department could never possibly imagine. Billy Johnson's carvings have a traditional, ancient ambience about them; Des's the rugged simplicity of a novice sculptor and Colin's is frankly unhuman, primitive and smacks of the popular depictions of Neanderthals, but with less attention to dental care and hygiene. All three crafted quite different representations of the human head

CHAPTER TWELVE
CHRISTIAN CONVERSION &
PAGAN SUBVERSION

Beguiling though they are, the West Country tradition of Jesus being brought to these shores by his uncle, Joseph of Arimathea, and notions that He sought out the druids to learn their esoteric wisdom, need not sidetrack this inquiry. As I pointed out as long ago as the early Seventies, Christian missionaries were instructed by Pope Gregory to subsume and adapt paganism in Britain. [1] A Christian formulary was superimposed so places sacred to the 'Old Religion' were selected, such as prehistoric mounds for churches, magical springs became holy wells and primitive gods and goddesses took on the names of saints. Visit any mediaeval church and this persistence of pagan imagery can be discerned. Putting aside the dating controversies, the Green Man spewing foliage to represent fecundity of crops and the sheela-na-gig holding open her vagina may well be Christian in origin, but they are surely pagan at heart? Even harvest festivals were only invented by an innovative and eccentric Cornish Victorian clergyman, the Rev Robert Stephen Hawker. I have discussed this as an example of fakelore, or the public's belief that certain traditions are ancient and this becomes folklorismus when they are promoted locally to increase trade. [2]

What does seem more substantial is the evident smoothness in the transition between Celtic paganism and Celtic Christianity, with the inevitable differences in custom and practice.. In fact, there would be more friction between Celtic and Roman Christianities, even quibbling over correct tonsure. They also argued over methods of dating Easter. On this subject, Saints Hilda and Colman supported the Celtic Church, whereas it was opposed by St Wilfrid, who went on to establish Hexham Abbey. Of course, seasonal celebrations and various folk customs are survivals of elements of Celtic spirituality. The ascetic side is also discernible today in practices at some Welsh chapels, Scottish Presbyterian churches and the more 'primitive' independent Christian sects.

On a more primeval level, I have paraded the practices of Longdendale and Breadalbane and one only needs to look to the resurgence of neo-paganism, the revival and proliferation of modern-day druid groups and the thread of mock-satanism in heavy metal rock music to see echoes of the 'Old Religion'. But the number of abandoned churches and ones transformed to become art galleries or bathroom centres points to a grim testament to waning Christianity despite charismatic movements and the inspirational Alpha course. Culturally and psychologically, paganism has lain just below the surface in society and the psyche for millennia. This breaks through in country traditions, some quite recent, and lurid tales of urban immigrants practising voodoo and other tribal witchcraft superstitions in our inner cities. It would seem Christianity is but a thin veneer, I fear, and aspects which hardly conform to Christian orthodoxy can be found in Hexham's House of the Holy.

Undoubtedly the best book on pagan continuity in ecclesiastical establishments is *The Unpolluted God*. Strangely-titled and quaintly-designed by an East Yorkshire regional publisher, this labour-of-love by Guy Ragland Phillips had previously been serialised as *Behind the Church Door* in Mike Howard's pagan magazine *The Cauldron*. It may therefore come as a surprise that the author describes himself not as a neo-pagan, but a Quaker Universalist. One a personal level, Guy and I enjoyed some correspondence and after his death his widow Ivy kindly sent me one of his trademark scraperboards and a pen and ink sketch. He was a fellow journalist who was at one time leader writer for the *Yorkshire Post*; obviously recognition for holding measured views. His last published work was an article on the Croft-on-Tees sheela-na-gig (or 'sheila' as he preferred) for my magazine *Folklore Frontiers*. [3]

By 'unpolluted god', Guy was looking for simplicity in religion, before sectarianism, cultism, priests and rituals, to a pure relationship without intermediaries, a one on one interface with the natural universal force pervading. Somewhat similar in spirit to Gnosticism, I guess, circumventing manmade trappings to encumber the pure essence in creation which has become so tainted. Yes, Guy was a philosopher: pragmatic, with a journalist's hunger for knowledge, inquisitiveness and resolve. His survey of pagan survivals in English parish churches is a masterful study of continuity and absorption. It tells how the clergy have not in general hidden the past, but are in most cases proud to exhibit the long legacy of worship of whatever colour or persuasion has been entrusted to their safekeeping.

Earth mysterians get a kick out of crypts

Seeking a Hexham connection, I naturally found some in the abbey there, but as for the dancing lady whose breasts were worthy of Page 3 in *The Sun* and whose hair flowed with Botticellian grace to hide her intimate parts, verger Austin Winstanley assured me its depiction on a chaise longue for visitors' comfort as one enters was of Victorian origin. But I was not there to gawp, I was seeking my third visit to the crypt to finally persuade myself that Guy must be wrong about a passage in *Brigantia* which I feared was leading me on something I was now suspecting to be a wild goose chase. He had written:

> 'Natural holes through rocks seem to have been regarded as potently magical [in Celtic lore and] the magical properties of the holes through the walls in the crypts of Ripon and Hexham Cathedrals (sic), through which people were expected to crawl, may indicate substitutes'. [4]

There's definitely no hole in the walls down there, just massive, solid stone walls which have withstood centuries. No wonder Hexham historian Stan Beckensall described the crypt as being 'regarded as the best of its kind north of the Alps'. [5] Sadly, few remnants of the original abbey remain today, but the 7th Century crypt has been left to posterity. Descend the steep steps and enter its dimly-lit vaults and passageways. Here are to be seen Roman altar stones, inscriptions and decorated blocks (also in the nave), plus other items of later Saxon stonework on display.

In modern times, visitors to ecclesiastical crypts are often not the traditional pilgrims of yore, but either the casual tourist or 'crypt-kickers' (well that's what I term them, from the *Monster Mash* hitmakers *Bobby 'Boris' Pickett and the Crypt-Kickers*), who seek to experience that alternative spirituality that is perceived as earth energy and which can also have the kick of an intoxicant or even hallucinogen. From personal experience I almost passed out in the rarely-visited crypt at York Minster and felt the same

**Consort to the Green Man? More a Brown Woman on a Victorian settle for contemplation.
(Paul Screeton)**

power very strongly at Lastingham Church crypt, North Yorkshire. [6] Regretfully, all my visits to Hexham crypt have been notable for zilch reaction. However, an appeal seeking others' experiences in crypts and in particular Hexham's, via the *Northern Earth* Readers forum, elicited seven posts. Comments of special relevance included editor John Billingsley's insights:

> 'Hexham has given me some vibey experiences, as has, inevitably, Lastingham; but for me the most reliable location for what Jimmy Goddard calls 'head hum' is Ripon cathedral crypt. last time I visited, in October, it was a very strong intensity. It's noticeable that although the environmental factors don't seem to change very much, the 'head effect' does vary, in crypts at least. But then, it was also so above, in the body of Ripon. At the risk of being dismissed as a closet New Ager, I have noted that if one walks carefully and consciously (eyes as closed as possible) up a nave – with, I guess, a dowser's perception tuned – one can feel in some churches at some times a progression of sensation through the body, up the spine. I'll leave you to work out where the tower and crossing and (original) altar make their presence felt. Over and above the strongest case of that I've had was in Norwich cathedral last August. If I had to venture an explanation I'd suggest a mixed progression of ritual focus and gradation of sacred space, but that leaves other questions unanswered. Similar effects were noted at some Shinto shrines in Japan'. [7]

Adam Funk (can this be Adam Stout in disguise?) asked if Hexham's crypt was built partly with recycled stones from a Roman temple [8], to which Barry Teague commented [9], quoting from *British Archaeology*: : '...The walls, ceiling, floors and stairway of the crypt are built from enormous blocks of Roman *opus quadratum*-style stonework, each one weighing over a ton, and an astonishing volume of carved and inscribed Roman stonework, including seven altars, two imperial dedication stones, seven relief carvings bearing anthropomorphic or bestial designs, a cavalryman's tombstone over 8ft (2.5m) high, and massive sections of Roman architectural mouldings elaborately carved with bead and reel decoration, acanthus leaves, and dentil and cable designs. Stonework of this nature must have originated in Roman public buildings of the highest order'. [10]

Alby Stone spread the net wider, recommending the crypt of Boulogne Cathedral where 'the vibes are really strong' and the town has a legend of a sea-borne Virgin centred upon a statuette of a Black Madonna which is carried in a parade, Following my mention of almost passing out in York, Alby admitted he has 'never felt like passing out there – though knowing myself as I do, if I had it would have probably have been down to Stella Artois rather than Stella Maris … ;- ' [11]

Similarly, I later canvassed *NE*Readers specifically for earth energy effects at Hexham Abbey, as on one occasion, while contemplating the Night Stair/s and beside a memorial, I felt the familiar kundalini spiralling of a telluric current rising from the ground beneath and finding its destination in my brain. The Night Stair is a 13th Century staircase which gave the mediaeval canons direct access from their dormitory to the choir. The memorial is the one mentioned in *British Archaeology* and from the 1st Century, recognising the exploits and life of Roman officer Flavinus, a horse soldier of the Petrian Regiment and standard bearer of the troop Candidus. He died aged 25 after only seven years' service. I felt the same energy - but weaker – the last time I was there and on both occasions was accompanied by Stu Ferrol, who felt nothing whatsoever, as was my wife's inability to feel anything at York Minster. Does this indicate personal sensitivity or a different tuning? As Tony Hancock mused in the celebrated *Hancock's Half-Hour* 'The Blood Donor' episode," I always knew I was different from the rest of the herd!" Among those who took up the baton was again John Billingsley:

The memorial to Roman officer Flavinus in Hexham Abbey. (Paul Screeton)

'At the foot of the Night Stairs? Yes, I think it was there I picked up an atmosphere a year or two back. Ley power... Jimmy Goddard called it, probably still does call it, 'head hum'. Lots of people call it 'earth energy' or just 'energy'. As you can see, I often use the word atmosphere. All completely meaningless terms on their own (and not helpful when they invite all sorts of equally meaningless extrapolations), but I think a familiar experience to most of us in E.M. There are various ways in which a place can affect the sensory apparatus – lighting, draughts, colours, sounds, ionisation, prior information – but that doesn't mean such environmental factors can explain away such place experiences. And what makes it such that some people feel/see something when their neighbour doesn't, as in my visit to Walsingham's Holy House?' [12]

Carrying on the energy theme, someone called Carol (no surname) reported that on several visits she had experienced 'a slight sick vertigo feeling from the bottom of the Night Stair upwards' and having climbed many worn staircases in historic buildings had 'never had this sensation anywhere else'. [13]

Ghost-hunting Parasearch director David Taylor shared his trepidation at returning to Lastingham crypt to retrieve the camera he had left there and for 'a grown man I didn't hang around on my own'. He also mentioned that he had been unable to track evidence of the elusive 'ley power' using electromagnetic, geomagnetic, infrasound and ultrasound detectors. [14]

By now, dear reader, you may be wondering if the author is merely padding out the book. On the contrary, my purpose has been to establish Hexham's key role as a 'place of power' in the past and the present, somewhere worthy of pilgrimage, whether one be a committed Christian or an E.M. aficionado or spiritual 'crypt-kicker'. Remember the role the abbey staff played in giving brief sanctuary to the Hexham Heads on their convoluted and controversial journey from Rede Avenue to a Newcastle museum. And if one looks carefully enough further heads can be found within the north choir aisle. The guidebook also stated that here could be found in a glass case, the skull of John Fenwick, an officer killed at the 1644 Battle of Marston Moor between the Royalists and Parliamentarians. The verger had never heard of it and was equally baffled by a reference to Fenwick's helmet in the nave. When dealing with heads in Hexham nothing is ever simple.

CHAPER THIRTEEN
MEETING AN EXORCIST & DELIVERANCE APLENTY

O f course, the reason for my being in Hexham in 1977 was not to seek out information on the media-celebrated artefacts, but I had gone to that part of Northumberland at the invitation of Dom Robert Petitpierre. The Heads research was incidental. At his behest, I was to meet him at noon in the Hadrian Hotel at Wall, four miles from Hexham. Any purpose in our meeting made no sense then, and without discounting the fortean notion of destiny, makes no sense to me now. The veteran ghost-busting monk wrote to say he was spending part of his annual fortnight's holiday in the North-East and would like to meet me – **again**!

He added that he had read my book *Quicksiver Heritage* 'with great enjoyment and interest', and upon wondering how to get in touch, wrote in his letter to me that 'the other day I was hunting through my address book desperately looking for a chap's address, and, behold, there you were!' How? Why? Whatever! Even odder was the reference whereby he wanted to me again! At the meeting in Wall he was insistent we had chatted on a bridge over the River Wear in Durham City. Had we done so, it would have been sufficiently memorable for it to have stuck in my mind. We certainly hadn't met nor had any prior communication. So how was it I in his little black/red book? Anyway, we had arranged a date and a time.

On the day we finally met, having made contact with Heads claimant Des Craigie and made the pilgrimage to 3 Rede Avenue, I revisited the town centre, located the bus station, ascertained the times to Wall and still with time on my hands popped into the pub opposite. Fortified, I made the 15-minute bus journey to Wall and the *Hadrian Hotel*.

Remember, this was a hot summer's day 35 years ago and memories fade. Also, as this was a social invitation I made no notes, but incorporated a few recollections into my 1980 monograph. I can vaguely picture Dom Robert as a small, stocky figure with a good sense of humour and more worldly than one might expect from a man of his background and vocation. He had with him a rather shadowy character who was introduced as a schoolteacher with whom he was spending time in Wall and Wooler. I got the immediate impression that this benefactor had been the subject of one of the priest's many exorcisms (and it crossed my mind somewhat strikingly that he still looked spookily haunted). This other person did not, I think, take part in any of our conversation.

Dom Robert had travelled from Buckinghamshire's Nashdom Abbey, a Benedictine Anglican monastery of Our Lady and Saint Benedict, in Burnham, built between 1905 and 1909 as a private house by Edwin Lutyens for a Prince Dolgorouki. According to one internet site a writer had described the establishment as having become an 'Anglo-Papalist *Titanic*', having fallen into liberalised ways in the Swinging Sixties with its tightly-disciplined monasticism becoming diluted by a racy country club ambience 'with occasional music around the piano from the London shows in the evenings ... cassocks on the lawn, priests who called people "my dear" with dry sherry in urbane huddles ... Somehow serious intellectual and pastoral work coexisted with the Wodehouse stuff ... and all that is left now are ghosts on the lawn'. [1] Dom Robert would have fitted in perfectly.

Yet he was also, remember, an acclaimed 'ghostbuster' and when the Bishop of Exeter, the Rt Rev Robert Mortimer, convened a commission of Anglican and Roman Catholic priests on the subject of exorcism and its role in the Church and society, a large report was compiled and Dom Robert edited it down to a pamphlet entitled *Exorcism*. [2] When interviewed by author Richard Deutch, Mortimer gave some indication of Petitpierre's character:

> "It was a lot of fun. Dom Robert, for example, who tends to differ with people quite a bit – he once had a rather boisterous quarrel with his own abbot – is a remarkably stimulating man to be around. About six of us at a time would get together and discuss exorcism and we determined our views on the theology underlying the rite and in the end we drew up a programme for the training of clergy in the field ... In the end we had quite a large report and Dom Robert honed it down. There was some opposition". [3]

A moment of relaxation for Dom Robert Petitpierre (left), playing dominoes with a colleague.

In a colour supplement article, Russell Miller wrote of Dom Robert that, 'He drinks gin and French, smokes Capstan Full Strength and spends much of his life chasing ghosts'. In my company he was drinking halves of bitter and was full of wit on the subject of ghosts and demons. As I wasn't in Wall to interview Dom Robert quite a few gems are lost to posterity and I must mildly plagiarise Miller's article once more. Apparently, when the waiter in the London restaurant where they were knocking back wine and smoking like blastfurnaces asked how he would like his coffee, Dom Robert replied "khaki". Then he inquired if the waiter knew the limerick:

> 'There was a young fellow called Starkie,
> Who had an affair with a darkie,
> The result of his sins,
> Were quadruplets not twins,
> One black, one white and two khaki.' [4]

Such an innocent verse would be largely frowned upon today by the PC brigade, but that is quoted from the 1970s. When Dom Robert and I met he revealed a puckish sense of humour and the joke we laughed at most was his own. He told me that his book *Exorcising Devils*, attributed to him, was not wholly his own work – another writer 'ghosted' it. The 'ghost-buster' chuckled spiritedly about the book having been 'ghosted' (presumably by the Max Caulfield, who holds the copyright). He also considered himself to have a personal sensitivity 'to what might be loosely called psychic phenomena', having concluded that people derived from Celtic stock develop such a response to a greater extent than others. These people can be of the British Isles or from continental Europe, and though English-born, his parents both came from Swiss hill regions and were of Celtic hereditary.

Back then, Dom Robert had read my recently-published formative book on the nascent subject of earth mysteries, *Quicksilver Heritage*, and had developed an interest in the controversial matter of leys (latterly known as ley-lines). When I wrote my 1980 monograph *Tales of the Hexham Heads* I thought 'it worth recording his comments [on the book] in the light of his interest in leys and the possible special nature of the location in Hexham where the phenomena occurred'. He wrote to me: 'I enjoyed the book, as it is informative and clear. I do not really agree with all the outlook on the Universe which you proclaim, but I am recommending it to my friends as a first-class example of how and why Christians have failed your generation, and forced you to seek important slants on life'.

To that end, I felt I should read *Exorcising Devils*, which I did for my monograph. In fact, his book devoted a whole chapter to 'Ley Lines', which he felt exerted a baleful influence, declaring, 'I know from experience that where a "Ley Line" exists, its influence will not be helpful in clearing up later difficulties". This was written during the period when the New Age notion of leys transmitting some undefined power akin to positive or negative spiritual energy was all the rage. Many today regard this as having been an aberrant period of irrationality extolling barmy hogwash. The slightly less controversial stone-tape theory of buildings and places retaining images of past events in their fabric has similarly ebbed and flowed in its popularity, and Dom Robert had concluded that, 'I cannot avoid the impression that the presence of a Ley Line "tingles up" and keeps alive imprints from the past associations of the place'. He believed this place-inspired notion explained 'accident spots' and that expanding on his extolling dodgy primary leys he endorsed a geomantic corridor of malignant powers from Communist Russia supplying psychic venom to fuel our 1926 General Strike. [5]

His book also abounded with references from his childhood to a plethora of incidents associated with psychic happenings. His chronicling would possibly seem bizarre and overtly popular, but I was inclined to take all the contents generally at face value (though a ghost-written book might be expected to sensationalise), yet speculate on the wisdom or otherwise of his conclusions. Certainly there was no doubting his 100 per cent sincerity and solid Christian faith. I emphasised then that he revealed a thorough awareness that many 'possession' claimants actually required self-discipline rather than exorcism; psychological or medical treatment rather than ministering to. Pagans got short shrift and he claimed 'little devils' can move into houses used by witch groups, for spiritism [sic], gaming or as brothels!

I can't recall gambling or the sex trade being topics of conversation that day in 1977, but as the talk developed I found myself agreeing and disagreeing by turns, but well aware that involvement with occult occurrences may possibly rub off on to even the naïve and even the most cautious. In fact, when I paid a visit to the gents, he told me when I returned that he had carried out what he termed an 'antiseptic blessing' on the head made by Colin Robson which I had showed him and left sitting on the table, adding something to the effect of, "in case there was something there". It's rather comforting to know, actually.

As to retaining continuity with the pagan and pseudo-Celtic thread pursued to this point in this book, I noted that the wise Dom Robert argued in his book against the Church of England theologians who claimed exorcism (or as he preferred to term it 'healing and deliverance') to be irrational as a pagan practice by stating:

> 'Simply because an idea or attitude or belief was pagan has never automatically meant it was *wrong* ... The more we unearth the past and the more we study not only the pyramids but those great Bronze Age stone monuments that litter the countryside of the British Isles, the more we realize the ancient peoples were far from being unintelligent ... Here were people with considerable scientific knowledge who had no difficulty accepting the idea of non human minds and probably were capable of communicating telepathically with each other'.

Sprightly of mind and hardly doddering, he had, however, in his invitation to me drawn attention to his age – then 74 – and wrote, 'I am now an old man ... and am hoping to get on to the "other side" before too long. It will be interesting and exciting'. I cannot recall why, nor seem to have recorded the circumstances, but had reason not so long after my monograph appeared to ring Nashdom Abbey in the hopes of speaking to my exorcist friend. His abbot answered and announced he had bad tidings. Sadly, shortly before, Dom Robert had passed over. "It was a good death," the abbot assured me. "Pardon?" The abbot rephrased himself: "It was peaceful". End of story. Well, not quite. There was another sequel of sorts and I'll quote (almost verbatim) from my booklet:

> 'I have had two "dreams" associated with the [Hexham] heads since. One of these was simply of a strange face of a Celtic style in a local vicinity, though in clearer focus than my usual dreaming. The other stems from an admittance to my wife one night that I had turned on a light while going to the toilet as I felt a mild unease about the presence of the Robson and Craigie heads in the house, that being the night of 18/19 February 1979, and then while back asleep I suddenly "saw" Dom Robert's face in my sleeping mind and there was a tremendous "explosion" which woke me and left me with a feeling of well-being and that I had been blessed in some way and had no need to fear phenomena such as psychic attack'. [6]

To make it a trio of 'extras', seeking clues as to where I might find a decent picture of Dom Robert, I was helped by the current estates manager Lawrence May, who put me on to my monk friend's connection with stately house Cliveden, just up the road and which gained a notorious reputation. A few internet sites mentioned Dom Robert but I was particularly intrigued by one anonymous post which conspiracy buffs would love regarding Lord Astor, sex orgies and his chum Stephen Ward, a master occultist conjuring up 'weird spirits to visibly appear, which sound identical to those at Bilderberg ceremonies'. Hokum? No wonder Dom Robert was called to perform exorcisms at the huge estate and Ward's cottage, which 'contained the most satanic entities he had ever come across, including the spirits of several murdered [by Anthony Blunt] boys'. [7]

Deliverance in Hexham and Southampton

The fact that blessings were performed at the prime locations of this curious business makes for it being an interesting facet. In Hexham, according to former guide Betty Gibson, when members of the Robson family approached the abbey staff they not only sought identification of the idols but deliverance of some description. I have some confirmation of this although my source was neither present nor wholly reliable. Judith Coldfield, a sister formerly of 3 Rede Avenue recalled to me that, 'Someone came from the abbey. Nellie was R.C., but he did both houses. The Robsons were Church of England, but at No. 1 in the conjoined premises Mrs Dodd was **not** Catholic, but Anglican; it was her husband Isaac who was R.C. and the six children were brought up in that faith. To cast more doubts on the veracity of Judith's statements, Dodd family siblings Brian and Sylvia were insistent when I talked to them that there was neither a blessing nor deliverance at either house during their time there. However, after the Dodd family had been rehoused, Father Martin Deegan, of St Mary's, Hexham, performed a sanctifying rite of some order for the incoming tenants at No. 1.

The most recent house blessing related to the Hexham Heads was carried out around Easter 2011, again by Father Deegan, when incumbent tenant Mark Newton called upon the parish priest to again bless No. 1. The reason for this request was that Mark and his adoptive mother Margaret had been living in the house for three years and had never felt comfortable about the front bedroom. Neither of them would sleep there. Margaret was sleeping in the back bedroom and Mark downstairs. The priest not only blessed the 'haunted' bedroom – which was shunned by the family dog – but the whole of the upstairs, hall and living-room. Mark told me:

> "We like this house, we're still happy here. After the priest's blessing the atmosphere lifted, but I still don't like that bedroom. The priest said summat in Latin and splashed holy water around. He didn't believe in all this business, but still did it". [8]

Mark was unaware of any earlier blessings at either No. 1 or 3 Rede Avenue, but seemed cheered by the latest clerical intervention. As for Father Deegan he died shortly afterwards, of a heart attack aged 78 and by all accounts a highly-respected Irishman who had been taken to the bosom of the community. A fulsome obituary appeared in the *Hexham Courant*, but there was no mention whatsoever of deliverance. [9]

Meanwhile, the only evidence that Anne Ross felt sufficiently spooked that she felt the need to take the drastic step of seeking deliverance ministry comes from an account elicited by David Clarke in 1994. Describing the aftermath of the werewolf experiences and ridding herself of her collection of Celtic heads, she recalled

> "We got the exorcist in, Father Harrison, who is now the exorcist for the whole of Britain. He was in Wiltshire. He came in with the priest, our vicar, and he

looked at the heads and he said, "You must get rid of that one. You must get rid of them. They are drawing strength from each (an)other," and he put his hand on the Streetly [Staffs.] head, which is a deadly thing, but it had not been aggressive until these two came... and they seemed to gang up and their powers, the ones that had powers, kind of really increased and it was terrible and my neighbour, who is a spiritualist, and she didn't know about the heads, but she knew that there was evil and then she was told and she said to me, "Get rid of them. If you don't get rid of them you will die", and actually the day after we had them all taken away I nearly did, and I think she was right. If they had stayed I would have died'. [10]

INTERLUDE TWO
A PHENOMENOLOGICAL CORNUCOPIA
(or, weird shit happens)

Throughout my reinvestigation of the Hexham Heads puzzle I was bedevilled by all manner of strangeness. Fortean magic was afoot like some background static to the main thrust of following leads or interviewing either those involved (however peripherally) or experts in fields relevant to solving aspects of the overall riddle. Rather than ignore the untidy bits of marginal data or dump it in an appendix, on looking over the material it seemed better to place it here as it is essentially a looking-glass into the fantastical otherworld of phenomenological parallel reality/ies.

My son Ian and the oracular spirit of Bran

I start this catalogue of weirdness in my own home with my son Ian when he was aged around three. The heads sculpted by Colin Robson and Des Craigie were kept in the house and one day Ian came up to me and said, "Daddy, one of your heads spoke to me". I asked what it had said to him. "Can't remember". I urged him to think hard, but to no avail. Trying another tack, I asked which of the two had spoken. Again, "Can't remember". When it looked like there would be tears I desisted. I tried later and the next day, but again there was no recollection. But did this 20th Century episode represent the power of the Welsh Celtic king Bran echoing down the corridors of time? Bran was mortally wounded in battle by a poison dart in his foot so he ordered his followers to decapitate him and take his head back to Wales with them. They complied and his head remained uncorrupted and chattered away merrily as they carried on a marathon booze-up decade after decade without ceasing, until one idiot spoiled the party by opening a forbidden door and the sorrows of the world again beset Bran's companions like some monumental hangover. But Bran, still with the power of speech, instructed them to sober up and travel to England where they were to bury his head under what is now the Tower of London. What a tale he could have been telling my son. [1]

Which takes us back to the head cult, which may or may not have ever existed. At least classical writers testified to a severed head worship and Livy noted the custom of decorating human heads with gold and using them as drinking cups. I wonder if the Celts got a good head on their mead, just like Des and his pint of beer in Hexham RAFA Club?

Camera-shy idols

As related in Chapter Nine, after Anne Ross and an archaeologist friend found the Tigh na Cailliche shrine their immediate reaction was to photograph the stones outside, particularly the hag stone or Cailleach. In the interests of getting a better image, her companion unwisely moved the Cailleach's position. When he came to snap away both witnessed the heavy idol slide very slowly towards him, rolled forward and recalling the scary incident, Dr Ross said, "We could clearly see a rather baleful, malevolent face on top of it' and 'it was a very frightening moment'.

Forteans and paranormalists will not be surprised to learn that none of the photographs came out. Only when Anne Ross returned with the glen's guardian was it possible to obtain the genius loci's permission for suitable images. Similarly, when I tried to photograph the two Des Craigie demonstration heads in his son Nigel's possession, the one I would regard as a 'hag' proved difficult. As for the originals, when the late Hilary Evans, eminent author, seasoned paranormalist and actually a Hexham resident for 15 years in his early years, purchased a copy of my monograph *Tales of the Hexham Heads*, he asked humorously, 'Is it part of the mystery that nobody seems able to take a decent photograph of them – the ones in *Alpha* looked like tennis balls after our dog had finished with them . . .' Yet Dr David Clarke told me that when he visited fantasy fiction author Alan Garner at his home overshadowed by Alderley Edge, the writer showed him a splendidly perfect photograph of the Hexham Heads. Garner's work is steeped in mythology and it is my opinion that he represents modern shamanism in body and mind. [2] I recall when his book *Red Shift* was dramatised for television how the opening sequence briefly depicted 'Celtic heads' set in a rough stone wall: a small detail but it had a big impact on me.

One from the archives: one of the Heads photographed at Don Robins's home. (Anon)

No wonder the picture accompanying Don's *Alpha* article was rubbish. Even with a posse of snappers with professional training, including former teacher of the subject Paul Devereux, assembled to try conventional, infrared and kirlian photography at the session the results were uniformly abysmal. There were excellent conditions for lighting and display so perfect pictures were anticipated. For all three modes, when developed the results were blurred, ill-defined and overexposed; even the images taken with standard film. In his account of the pitiful end product, Don was left with a single explanation – the supernatural. For the scientist drew a parallel with how when paranormal phenomena such as UFOs, ghosts and anomalous animals is the subject of photography the images are invariably mediocre at best, if indeed the equipment does not jam, fail to focus, wind on or malfunction in some other way. Naturally after the abject failure of the project an exhaustive post-mortem was held; checks being made to cameras, films and darkroom processes. Don mused aloud how:

> 'It made me wonder why I had never seen photographs of the heads before. The only successful photographs seem to have been taken in the early stages of scientific examination. Was there a perfectly natural explanation that we had overlooked?' [3]

But in his haste to billet the bashful heads, it seems the search for explanations was forgotten.

The Borrowers are playing tricks with us all

If photographic images vanished or appeared blurred, tape-recordings involved in the conundrum fare no better. Nor did certain important items of evidence required for analysis. My own personal experience involved my answering Don Robins's request for a sliver from the head I had made by Des Craigie for him to compare with the samples already cut from the Hexham Heads, then in his possession. When I mailed Don to ask if he had any findings, he responded to say that my and the other material for testing had either been mislaid or somehow simply vanished. [4] Obviously not on the same scale of seriousness as the original heads entrusted to him having also disappeared into the void. But that's not all. Correspondence from that era is carefully filed alphabetically in boxes in our modified loft. The Robins archive is the only one missing. As it seems, so is he.

While chuckling as he told me that his autobiography *Exorcising Devils* was partially the work of a 'ghost writer', ghost banisher Dom Robert Petitpierre pointed out to me a mysterious aspect in which the original interviews for the book had disappeared and the whole project had to be begun all over again. And while on the subject of books, distributors Amazon announced a forthcoming one on English werewolf legends by another well-known ghost-hunter, the *Fortean Times* columnist Alan Murdie, being co-written with Victoria Amador. When my Parasearch director friend Dave Taylor contacted Alan he knew nothing about it and said there was no book deal, no Ms Amador or any intention to write any such work. All he could suggest was that it stemmed from discussions with Amberley Books during 2009, but werewolves were not mentioned and 'I am not planning a book on werewolves and never have been … Do let me know if I can help further; no need to fear the full moon'. [5]

Telephone blues

Telecommunications can be a sod at times, but calls involving research into the Hexham Heads mystery seemed particularly plagued by gremlins. All this was reminiscent of a television play broadcast in 1985 with strong fortean themes. [6] Seeing as Ken Campbell wrote and acted in it what was to be expected! Some cosmic joker seemed to be having fun with Julie Walters's character, Mavis, who played:

> ' … a sort of manic depressive one-parent family whose husband prefers the fa-

vours of his own sex. Miss Walters becomes obsessed with a telephone which is as neurotic as herself, lingers in the bedroom of a dwarf, cuts the lines in the exchange, but still has the woes of the world heaped upon her. Before switching off, one was constrained to believe that she deserved all her misfortune'. [7]

SUNDAY TELEVISION

BBC 2

10.5 Screen Two: Unfair Exchanges
starring Julie Walters
Written by KEN CAMPBELL
Mavis's plight will ring a bell in the heart of anyone who ever felt like murdering a telephone. Is some ghoulish mind behind the increasingly mysterious and sinister calls she gets? Is it madness or the system, or a joke that's bigger than all of us?
Julie Walters plays Mavis in her first major screen role since *Educating Rita*.
Danny .... GEORGE LAPHAM
Arthur .... DAVID RAPPAPORT
Ronnie ......ROBERT KINGSWELL
Phone poet...... BERT PARNABY
Tim Rickett .... KEN CAMPBELL
Band ....MUSICIANS' UNION
Music by
RUTH COLE and RICHARD KILGOUR
Designer DEREK DODD
Photography JOHN MCGLASHAN
Film editor ANGUS NEWTON
Produced by KENITH TRODD
Directed by GAVIN MILLAR
★ CEEFAX SUBTITLES

'I ring therefore I am' – Julie Walters meets the telephone
BBC2, 10.5 pm Screen Two: Unfair Exchanges

From a TV guide of January 1985 advertising the weird play which had me mesmerised and a nation baffled.

I have included that review as my recollection is rather hazy. I enjoy bizarre black comedy in that style and I found I had appended a note at the time to a contemporary TV guide page I had retained for such an event as this book. I had noted for posterity, 'During this she referred to a wooden object (musical instrument?) being made from a tree on a "ley-line". She rang a random number to jokingly-pissed ask, "I've got a question. I've got this dwarf here. Shall I fuck him?"'

Unfair Exchanges was anticipated by a radio play from the 1950s which featured a haunted telephone line. It was written by actor and writer Nigel Kneale, best known for his series of television dramas with Professor Bernard Quatermass (another link, as the name was plucked from the London telephone directory), being the central character. Kneale then created one of the most scary programmes seen on TV up until then, *The Stone Tape*, the inspiration for Don Robins's theories about stone being capable of storing data and images, with the capacity for the 'recording' to be 'played back'. [8]

Actually telephone usage is very rare for me in this era of universal emailing supremacy, but when I rang to quiz Hampshire author Sonia Smith about her extravagant claims (see next sub-section), there was a problem with the line when I uttered the word 'Priscilla'. The same happened with freelance writer Mike Hallowell, who only lives up the coast. Certainly the ghost in the machinery to trump these

Priscilla, Cleaner of the Uni

By PAUL SCREETON

It is not my habit to interview or quiz fellow authors regarding their craft or motives. I made an exception here (**HAMPSHIRE & THE NEW FOREST:** *STORIES OF THE SUPERNATURAL* **by SONIA SMITH. Countryside Books, £8.99**) because I was convinced Sonia Smith had not only fabricated her Southampton werewolf tale and substituted a cleaning woman for academic Anne Ross, but suspected a further seven tales in the slim volume were fiction masquerading as fact. Suspiciously, the book jacket neither claims it to be factual or fictional. Anyway, after some small talk about her apposite comment in the introduction where she said she hoped 'one day science will catch up and give us an answer' regarding the paranormal and we agreed that the likes of sceptical scientist Richard Wiseman (ironic name) are a new bogus priesthood, I then asked her to elaborate on her disclaimer in the introduction – 'I have used artistic licence in the writing of [the stories], to make them more readable, but all of the basic facts of the strange happenings are true' – as I suspected she had liberally peppered the book with porkies. She explained: "What I've written, it's all true. I'm not a journalistic writer so I express what I'm told through myself. I weave a story in my own way around what I was told. I listen to what people say and develop their character in my narratives. I try to give a flavour of who they were."

Fair enough. Actually she writes in what I guess is a Mills & Boonish way (actually never read one) but her book also reminded me of the tales and style utilised in Jeffrey Archer's short story collection *Twelve Red Herrings* (she's never read Archer).

Opening her book at random, I noted the chapter was entitled 'The Mistletoe Bough.' By coincidence, I'd read of a ballad of this name in the bath the previous day and recognised it as being a version of the urban legend Albert Jack had described. Briefly, a reluctant bride, wishing to delay as long as possible the consummation of her marriage, suggests hide and seek to postpone the dirty deed, secretes herself in a chest and suffocates. Smith (pictured) sets it in Bramshill

House, latterly a police college, but Jack pinpoints this and three other locations to which the myth is attached. Sonia told me she was unaware of other variants. When I tackled her on her mediocre phantom hitch-hiker effort, she cheerily told me she only writes about her native region and was aware "that one keeps repeating in the West Country."

I told her I enjoyed a couple of the tales, such as the railway ghost and his bag full of adders; also 'Sweet Fanny Adams', which explains how the saying associated with her refers in slang to meat containing no animal content. However, some stories are trivial to the point of banality such as 'The Devil's Hands' and 'Fairies at the Rufus Stone' (When Sonia told me she was a strong believer in the faery realm, I told her of the wood gnome I encountered in Carlisle).

Finally I got down to the nitty-gritty of my call. She acknowledged at the end of the first tale, 'The Werewolf of Southampton,' that she was aware of the media reportage of the macabre events which took place when archaeologist Dr Anne Ross took home two Celtic carved heads unearthed close to Hadrian's Wall and generally referred to as the Hexham Heads, but Sonia's almost parallel lines of script were about a university cleaner who found a werewolf manifested in her home (as occurred with the Feachems – Ross's husband is Richard Feachem and she then worked at Southampton University). If a story sounds more than coincidental and just too good to be true......

"Well, it's totally true in the sense it's as she [the cleaner] told it to me. I looked up about it, that these things have happened. Everything she said seemed to be true. I don't know whether she had read of it and her imagination ran wild. She seemed genuine and to believe it."

This was cleaner Priscilla Morgan (a pseudonym) and as I mentioned her name there was a phone malfunction, to both Sonia's and my bemusement. Sonia rang back immediately to say that because of confidentiality she would not give me 'Priscilla's' details, but promised to email her and pass on my phone number. Sonia sounded a pleasant, genuine person. However, still no word from the elusive 'Priscilla.'

* But even if Sonia Smith fabricated the cleaner – when the Anne Ross story was established and verifiable – it still has folkloric relevance as amounting to a bizarre representation of ostension. Fact or fiction? I'll leave it to you. Read the book and decide.
** (Image courtesy of Countryside Books)

How I reviewed Sonia Smith's book *Hampshire & The New Forest: Stories of the Supernatural.*

was an interrupted call in April while I was chatting merrily with archaeologist Dr Jill Eyers, when I decided to see if she was a fellow fortean. I got as far as asking: "Have you heard of Charles Fort?" when the line went dead, her voice had vanished and crackling sounds began. When I rang back she was equally bemused and not used to phone malfunction at her end. Curiously, the sound had become crystal clear, as if we were only feet away instead of 200 miles. [9] There have been other cases, but my wife makes the most zealous call centre employee look work-shy and never has any problems with phonecalls. Another similar anomaly was sufficiently unusual to warrant a mention when Sylvia Ritson commented:

> "I read your appeal/letter in the *Courant* [out loud] to my daughter and son's girlfriend. Suddenly the TV went awry. It kept changing volume. Kept going up to the maximum. It's never done that before or since" [10]

From the telephone to television to automobile elctronics. When Dr Don Robins was about to start his journey back to Middlesex from Southampton University after being loaned the Heads, he switched on the car ignition to find all the dashboard circuitry was dead. After a brief fiddle with the fuse-box the car sprang to life. Accepting this may have been coincidental, Don also admitted making a fast and apprehensive journey back home. [11]

Another instance which seemed sufficiently significant to warrant recording centred upon the Mouselow stones, which featured earlier. They were in transit back to Buxton Museum after being displayed at a Glossop exhibition and were being stored temporarily at a local house in 1985 when a number of inexplicable electrical faults are said to have occurred, including a power failure and computers malfunctioning. [12]

Werewolf graduates to teach cleaner a lesson

The aforementioned Sonia Smith, 'Priscilla' and her scary monster amount, I guess, to folkloric ostension or more likely poetic licence. The good folk of Southampton wait centuries for a werewolf and then two come along. A year ago I reviewed a book by Sonia and speaking to her expressed scepticism at her veracity. [13] (see reproduction of review article) Sonia simply promised to email her informant and pass on my phone number. Still waiting for the call (or have the telecom elves blocked it ...). [14]

Spontaneous human combustion (well, not quite)

This round-up of miscellaneous items may seem to have been a rag-bag with relevance, but it covers many of the key bases of phenomena. This was echoed at the close of my interview with museum director Lindsay Allason-Jones, the attendee at UnCon 2011 who had stood up and challenged remarks about the Hexham Heads made by speakers Andy Roberts and David Clarke. The dialogue went like this:

'**Paul**: Are you a real committed fortean?

LIindsay: Erm, I have subscribed to *Fortean Times* for many years. Um, due to the fact that it always kept me abreast of the latest thinking. And because we used to get a lot of enquiries at the museum, and a lot of them were very fringe. And we used to say that the only enquiries we hadn't had at the museum were spontaneous human combustion and Guatemalan goatsuckers. Everything else that has been in *Fortean Times*, we have had brought in quite seriously into the museum. The Hexham heads, to me, is just one of thousands of weirdnesses that I have been expected to comment upon over the years!

Paul: That's a big disappointment, because we were rather expecting at the end to film a chupacabra here...

Lindsay: Well, that would have been really interesting, but as it is we're down to the, er... In fact at one point one of my colleagues actually managed to set fire to his sleeve while he was taking a photograph, and as the computer expert doused the flames, he said "We are now down to the Guatemalan goat-sucker". So we saw everything. We had people saying they had been members of the Ninth Legion, we had crop circles all around – you name it, we had it! So to me, these were just another...

Paul: Another curiosity.

Lindsay: It was a normal day in the life of the Museum of Antiquities, yes.' [15]

Having afforded two-thirds of the book to delineating the events in question and placing them in historical context, I feel I have established that here is a multi-faceted mystery worthy of a non-fictional Sherlock Holmes. But before attempting to come to any preliminary conclusions, we need to consider the plethora of theories – sometimes conflicting and overlapping – and aspects which make up the puzzle. In a similar situation with her book on broadly the same area of investigation, *Mind Monsters* author Jenny Randles wrote:

> 'Let us start with the recognition that there seems to be three key elements in the experiencing of *monster reality*. These are the place where the event occurs, the person who is at the root of the experience and the state of consciousness'. [1]

My analysis, too, concentrates on the genius loci angle and its relevance (Rede Avenue and Dr Ross's heads collection); the individuals who appear to be the root cause (Des Craigie and Anne Ross); and his/her state of consciousness (Craigie in trickster mode, Nellie Dodd fatigued and Ross with a history of psychism and werewolf fantasising). But surely Jenny has forgotten something – there's an elephant in the room, or rather the 'mind' monsters themselves and the forms they take! Hence Chapter Sixteen examines the parapsychological theories and also something of the neurological or 'all in the mind' dimension, having dealt with place in Chapter Fourteen and another important aspect, the negative nature of the head image as applied by human expectancy in Chapter Fifteen.

Having firstly established what went on from 1971 onwards, it's now 40 years on and time to examine the current thinking as it might apply to the component parts of the puzzle from the viewpoints of various 'ologies' involved. With no axe to grind, no academic reputation to guard and no peer-reviewed paper to write to secure a university tenureship/sinecure, I can sift the evidence with a dispassionate eye and a breezy style and demeanour. There's still some fascinating material to come, including a juicy sex angle, and several bombshells in the Colin Robson at 52 interview. Well, let's keep on truckin'.

PART THREE

The source of the weresheep encounter and abbatior presence rumour? A 500-year-old stone carving in Hexham Abbey. (Paul Screeton)

CHAPTER FOURTEEN
GENIUS LOCI & PLACES OF POWER

Genius loci or anima loci represents the traditional type of worldview and empathy with landscape which is all too rarely recognised by modern culture nor experienced at first hand by 21st Century humankind. It is numinous but it is not unreachable. Many countryfolk are so steeped in its influence that they instinctively follow the seasons and react to the subtleties of the earth energies around them. They can predict the weather and forecast the behaviour of all living things within their geographical domain. This bonding with place and recognition of spiritual dimensions needs no reappraisal as it is eternal, yet forever changing in subtle ways.

Although bored by uninspiring schooling, beaten down by materialistic employment, conditioned by brain-washing politicians and numbed by dumbed-down broadcasting, most exist in a limbo state of apathy, robbed of the ability to form original thoughts or act independently. But those still with any semblance of cognitive ability can experience the presence of a spiritual diorama. Geomantic author Nigel Pennick favours the Latin term anima loci (place soul) over genius loci (spirit of place), but as the latter term is more widely known and used, if not entirely understood, I'll stick with it. Nigel defines the word 'spirit' as having two connected 'but distinct meanings: firstly, a sense or character; and secondly, a discarnate, supernatural entity or being, probably with its own consciousness and personality. In describing the character of a place, [genius loci] has elements of both these meanings unified in a place and perceived by the human consciousness as a totality'. [1] For further reading on the political ramifications of anima loci I recommend a booklet by Nigel [2] and for the female/Mother Nature aspect of the earth spirit, a lavishly-illustrated 'art' book by John Michell. [3]

And he's climbing a stairway to heaven (Oh, you are awe-ful!)

An optional term is numen loci, ascribed by the Lutheran scholar of comparative religion Rudolf Otto to sacred places that he names a 'numen' and from which the term 'numinosity' derives. As a theologian with an interest in the spooky quality of places selected by mankind as holy or sacred, he identified an early indicator in the Bible. Citing Genesis 28 where Jacob sleeps with his head on a specific stone and has a visionary dream where he witnesses angels on a ladder to Heaven and a presence he assumes to be God, Otto argued this had to be 'awe-ful'. [4] Jacob had concluded, 'How fearful is this place! This is none other than the house of Elohim …' and erected in upright position the stone he used as a pillow. Locally, near where I live there is a spot known popularly as Jacob's Ladder in the magical ravine Castle Eden Dene, where deer and voles roam. Are such places with this terminology significant and perhaps sacred?

This numinosity of place can apply to geographical features large and small, but for each their form has been specifically determined by 'spirit' rather than mundane geophysical forces. I was taught all about mountain uplift and erosion for 'A' level; what was not in the textbooks was how subtle earth currents were also influencing landscape structuring. Take Glastonbury Tor, for instance. It still takes my breath away each time I approach it, especially if anew from a different direction. I was similarly awestruck when suddenly encountering St Paul's Cathedral as I mounted the summit of a steep bank and saw it through an early Sunday summer morning haze. It was almost an epiphany. That was a religious site, but the railway viaduct at Ribblehead on the Settle-Carlisle line similarly blew me away as we drove around a bend to be confronted this magnificent monument to blood, sweat, tears and a secular master-piece signifying man's ability to challenge any natural obstacle. No wonder this temple to Mammon has attracted as much folklore as the most holy religious sites. [5]

But the earth spirit does not recognise the high and mighty, a navvy is the equal of a bishop, there's no social nor hierarchical boundaries, she also knows no higher authority.

Although 'genius loci' is still the preferred term used by earth mysterians (also known as geomants, neo-antiquarians and ley-hunters) and 'window area' by ufologists and paranormalists, it seems that recently geographers and other 'soft sciences' academics interested in ghosts and haunted places have jumped on the bandwagon and are reacting to what Roger Luckhurst has identified as a 'spectral turn' in the humanities and social sciences. [6] As always, where amateur esotero-geographers such as John Michell, Anthony Roberts, Paul Devereux, Nigel Pennick, Jimmy Goddard, Philip Heselton, Chris Street, Adam Stout and myself have blazed a pioneering trail, academe is trying to catch up and cash in, just as it took a post-war generation of 'lunatic fringers' to lay/ley the ground for more enlightened ar-chaeologists to discover terrain-oblivious lines (a ley by any other name) and ritual landscapes (some of us called this hermetic topography) which were under their noses while their superiors were too busy organising their student-slaves to grub about in muddy trenches and up their own arses passing port around the high table.

So for those seekers after wisdom who recognise this influence of locale, it is but another step on the ladder to enlightenment and as a Gnostic this is my goal. I honestly feel that by immersing myself in the study of the events surrounding the land and its tenants at one end of Rede Avenue, Hexham, I am be-ing spiritually nurtured. Sounds soppy and New Agey put like that, but if you've bought this book and read this far you'll doubtless empathise.

Although the earth spirit has been here for aeons, it is fragile and can be easily dislocated. I will argue here that the Hexham Heads – whatever their provenance – when moved, disturbed some vulnerable speck in the psychic fabric and upset the equilibrium on several levels and allowed a portal to open and release a daimonic reality hybrid and interfere with the electrical field to the extent that the family next door experienced the phenomenon known as poltergeist activity. Also that this simple act had generated a warp in the time continuum whereby the carved head industry of 2,000 years previously inspired a concrete plant worker and later a schoolboy in the 20th Century to follow suit via a subliminal level.

Also, as a Gnostic, it follows that though nominally also Christian, I feel no deep commitment to any religion, a human impulse which as the atheists keep lecturing us, led to corruption, overt materialism and an intercessionary priesthood to save us from thinking for ourselves. That said, Dr Anne Ross sug-gested the Rede Avenue district harboured the remains of a pagan shrine site, so who am I to argue? That aspect is under scrutiny as I write, but Tir na Nog can wait.

Anyone passing No. 1 and 3 Rede Avenue would not give them a second glance. As might be expected of houses built by the local council in the 1930s they have been modernised since the events which gave these solid, brick-built households a degree of notoriety. After a long period of lying empty a new tenant moved in late in 2011 and if my negative description of the garden is out of date I apologise. Once it was full of blossoms and providing fresh produce for the table. Des Craigie's father was a keen gardener and as is traditional in North-East England took pride in his leeks. After he died the garden was allowed to return to nature and so when new tenants moved in it was Colin Robson who was tidying the garden when he found the first of the pair of Hexham Heads. But today the garden looks neglected and anonymous. It certainly does not have any air of significance or sacredness; it puts a damper on any expectancy that a genius loci seeks to be recognised, that the location shouts out, "look at me, can't you see my interdimensionality, look, here's a fracture in the space/time continuum where the geological transients are activated and the Gods visit periodically as is their wont during seasonal perambulations". Or is it just what it looks like; mundane, disregarded and with all the charisma of a World War II bombsite.

Put on my blue suede shoes (secular pilgrims)

As yet the garden and any genius loci has yet to attract 'pilgrims' excepting we four '*Heads!*bangers' and the Southampton werewolf territory has been redeveloped and unrecognisable. But it is a human impulse to seek genii loci; it is why tourism began as far back as Roman times. Why we have Justice Secretary Kenneth Clarke and his wife 'monument bashing' (the phrase relating to the 'shed bashing' he organised for his school's railway society and I also did around loco depots) and Marc Cohn writing the song *Walking in Memphis* about seeing the ghost of Elvis walk through the gates of Graceland. These secular shrines are latter-day places of power just as influential as Lourdes and Mecca. I went through a phase of making umpteen visits to northern megalithic monuments along with John Watson and sundry companions. I, too, fell under the spell not only of these often wild places but previously the bewitching allure of Alfred Watkins and *The Old Straight Track*, still a thriving pursuit whereby Nick Stead recently made a pilgrimage to photograph the **very** bedroom where editor Philip Heselton printed the **first** issue of *The Ley Hunter* magazine (which incidentally I subsequently edited, 1969-1976).

Yet lack of evidence for a shrine does not constitute there not having been one. Because she was the 'superstar' scholar much has been made of the possibility of a pagan shrine at this spot in Hexham despite her notion being highly-subjective and wholly unsubstantiated. If it were to be proven correct it would trump the whole catalogue of minor events which are in themselves anecdotal and speculative.

The Celts were notorious for their sacrificial victim bog burials and the immediate area under discussion is marked old maps as being known as Bogacres; suggestive perhaps of a plethora of springs on what is a stepped plateau between steep slopes which otherwise could have been conducive to good drainage. Yet the name suggests that underlying strata mitigated against gainful land usage and we can assume the acres were boggy! To the Iron Age people such water-logged locations were liminal and sacred, places for deposition, sacrifice and where springs emerged it was believed they sprang from the underworld to join the mundane plane. Hence such places were revered and marked by shrines. If findings elsewhere are reliable indicators, then such a brackish site could be expected to be worth exploring for wooden or stone human or animal figures or actual bodily remains. As for shrines or temples, it was the practice to set aside specific locations to serve as such. No doubt the priesthood had criteria for selecting the appropriate sacred temenos. Perhaps they used a sixth sense or primitive dowsing equipment. When a structure was built, in Britain it was usually square and of timber with a ditch to enclose it , although circular examples have been found. Could something similar have existed in the Rede Avenue vicinity? Only large-scale excavation is likely to prove Anne Ross right or wrong.

But, of course, a genius loci is impotent without human interaction. The spirit world may be largely unseen, but its existence is unproductive without human intervention. Without an observer it may as well not exist. Yet all indications are that the Hexham Heads would have preferred to be left well alone once created. That's why they would turn of their own volition to face the place from which they had been taken. An urge to be reunited with the place where they had acted as guardians for the resident genius loci.

No prizes for best-kept garden, but this spot has been a place of pilgrimage for those wishing to pay their respects to the site where the Hexham Heads were discovered. (Paul Screeton)

Yes, that find spot. The Robson brothers showed me it and said that the Hexham Heads were on the ground in undergrowth, their mother has said they were two and half feet deep in the earth, whereas sister Judith gave me a depth of four or more feet. When I asked Nigel Craigie his opinion, he replied that he had heard "they were found on the surface in the garden where my granddad had been a keen gardener", but after I mentioned Judith's claim, he seemed momentarily non-plussed before conceding magnanimously that, "if she says they were buried that deep, I wouldn't cast doubt on it". Yet after I questioned why anyone should dig so deep, Nigel referred unnecessarily to being from farming stock, but, "I'm more inclined they were in the back of the hedgerow or near the surface".

But if this is a special place worthy of being bestowed as having genius loci status, where is the 'weird shit'? Best to start with what you know yourself. So, early in the investigation I was standing at the corner of Rede Avenue while Stu was being filmed talking about genius loci aspects. They say, name something and you summon it! At this very point I distinctly heard the sound of a canid panting, as if it was an Alsatian or such bothered by summer heat (it was actually a chilly March day). When I looked around there was nothing there. And before any Hexham folk reading this point out that Mark Newton often looked after a German shepherd called Sheba, I know the dog and it was not present. Subse-

If there really is a residual resident evil in the vicinity of Rede Avenue, 200 yards down the hill on Allen Drive, at the corner with Maidens Walk, there is a garden, one of whose guardians is a Pan-like grotesque. Resident Lee Teasdale (pictured with his sons Joss Carruthers, left, and Daniel Teasdale) told me he is an advocate of feng-shui and has always protected apotropaically all houses he's owned. "If anything gets past the gargoyle there's a foo-dog at the front door to stop it", he observed. He'd moved in from Gateshead two years previously and knew nothing of Rede Avenue's reputation.

quently Stu suggested I experienced an aural hallucination; encountered an invisible black dog ; it amounted to the *genius loci* spirit warning me off; or I mistook the sound of invisible men in flapping white coats coming to take me away. With friends like this … But seriously, it's maybe a small matter, but following the night of the were-sheep, the Dodd family's healthy pet dog died.

Next door, the Robsons's budgie also met its demise at the time, and as there was poltergeist activity, which has been associated with weak electrical fields and deaths of small creatures, perhaps the Hexham Heads were to blame. In *Poltergeist! A Study on Destructive Haunting*, Colin Wilson records an incident where, 'When the two pet goldfish died, a [poltergeist] "voice" claimed it had electrocuted them by accident (which if true, seems to confirm that poltergeists use some form of electrical energy)'. [7] For good measure, there's even an element of nominative determinism here – the budgie was called Sparky. Not only that, but when I spoke to Colin and Leslie Robson in 1977 they told me they buried Sparky at the spot where they found the Heads and one subsequent winter a solitary flower bloomed over the spot and seemed to glow, while one night around midnight a bright light hovered over the location a short distance above the ground.

Prior to the Hexham Heads discovery in 1971 there is no indication whatsoever of paranormal activity at Nos. 1 and 3. Des Craigie's father had been tenant for 30 years and Nigel Craigie told me:

> "Certainly from our family's point of view there was nothing that we experienced, nothing while my family lived there. I sometimes stayed with my grandfather overnight. As I say, I'm not aware of anything happening. I'm sure if anything had it would have been known in the family. My grandfather was a keen gardener. I'd have thought he might have disturbed things had there been anything there for quite a while. Or if there had been a shrine maybe he'd have come across it in the course of digging a leek trench". [8]

As for the actual bricks and mortar nitty-gritty, I summoned the help of Clerk to Hexham Town Council Derick Tiffin and his colleague Colin Dallison. Emails originated from Derick, who initiated the co-operation of various local historians, but it was Colin who supplied the bare facts. These are that following slum clearance, permission was granted to build 60 council houses at Bog Acres. Not surprisingly with a name like that the district was enterprisingly renamed Round Close in 1934. Another development in renaming occurred in 1974 when Round Close was split into four, utilising the names of regional rivers: Allen Drive, Chirdon Crescent, Derwent Road, Nent Grove and Rede Avenue (whose houses are believed to have been built in 1936). Colin found it implausible that stones from a purported abbey could have been used in the construction of Nos. 1 & 3 Rede Avenue, as some internet post had misinformed. Nothing to interest archaeologists was found at Bog Acres during construction, although what may be the remains of mediaeval buildings were found; a consequence being that the builders, Grady, were barred by Tynedale District Council from building all over the Kitty Frisk estate in the 1960s because of stones found when constructing 2 Edgewood. Nor was anything of importance found in 1993 when the abbatoir was demolished and Pescott Court built.

Wraiths thin on the ground in Hexham

There is a school a few hundred yards to the west of Rede Avenue, and current tenant at No. 1 Mark Newton had a macabre tale to tell:

> "It was formerly a grammar school with old buildings. There was a story that a young male teacher was molesting kids. He was supposed to have hanged himself in the school. Maybe it was just to scare kids from trying to go in after school hours. I remember we used to dare ourselves to go in. I can't remember if any ever did. I only got as far as the building. The caretaker, Harry Ferrol, had two big dogs. They went in one day and came back whimpering. It always had a reputation for being haunted". [9]

Hexham Abbey's haunted Night Stair.

Of course, co-investigator Stu Ferrol's father was that caretaker and they lived in a house attached to the premises. His father did indeed have two dogs, Newfoundlands, which he would take into the empty school with him to do his final check before locking up, sometimes accompanied by Stu and his mother. Stu recalled:

> "One of our dogs, the older one, a female, used to always make for the exit closest to the Bogacres Farm buildings. She would then sit and whinge for the duration of the time we spent there. She never went looking for the other dog or us; it didn't matter also which door we entered the school at she would still make for that one exit. Her crying was a bit more than just simply wanting to be let out, it was a panicky sort of cry, as if desperate to get to, or away from, something. The exit she went to was at the end of the corridor which the ex-caretaker's dog froze in, looking down toward the exit, hackles up. I don't think his dog would go into the school after that but that could be a bit of added folklore. [10]

Additionally, Stu Ferrol told me of a separate hanging from a tree in the school grounds of a man who was living next door to George Watson, who for a short period had custody of the Heads. There is no evidence of correlation.

I also asked Mark about other Hexham hauntings and was not surprised to hear of ghostly monks at the abbey. According to Mark, one has been seen several times on the Night Stair, walking down it and who stops, stands and stares at people. Also a monk has been reported pushing people in the crypt and to add a really unlikely aspect, Mark claimed some clergymen at the abbey he had spoken to would not venture into the crypt during the hours of darkness. One other location being the House of Correction, now governed by English Heritage and not open to the public owing to its state of deterioration. According to Mark: 'Moans and groans have been heard and the sound of chains rattling'. There's also The Grapes' groping ghost.

Whores' babies born only to be snuffed out?

The sound of a baby's crying was reported by Stu Ferrol in his first letter to me in 2002 and we've subsequently discussed this since, whereby summarised it amounts to his hearing it from the former family bungalow around 2am to 3am over a 5-6-year period from the direction of nearby Rede Avenue. If this were to be confirmed by a separate source it could be assumed to be paranormal and not a real infant; even associated with the Romano-British period. With Maiden's Walk just down the hillside, could there have been a shrine here where Celtic women came to give birth or even a Roman villa complex, either for a similar purpose or even more carnal purposes? If the former, might the Hexham Heads have been two-thirds of a representative maiden-mother-crone trio (one of the extant pair has always remained unchallenged as a witch/hag/crone representation) and if we accept Des Craigie's claim, he said he made three. Alternatively, it is known that during this post-Iron Age period rural brothels were run by the occupying forces and infanticide was practised, whereby bodies analysed from Yewden, Bucks., have been found having allowed 38 to 40 weeks of gestation, which is around the normal times of birth. Evidence points to the disposal of unwanted newborns, their being of no great moral concern to the callous Romans, but at least saving the life of a mother may have been so, particularly a lucrative nubile whore. No wonder the pitiful cries of a slaughtered infant might echo down the corridors of time to haunt Hexham. [11]

As with the Hexham Heads poser and Lindsay Allason-Jones fielding regular press inquiries, Dr Jill Eyers, director of consultancy Chiltern Archaeology, was reported as observing, "Even now, a year after the initial press attention, every other day I'm getting inquiries about this story. It seems that everyone is intrigued by this puzzle". She added that further research consolidated her brothel theory. But as always there's an equal and opposite opinion, this time from Brett Thorn, keeper of archaeology at the Buckinghamshire County Museum, who favoured a mother goddess cult and the site being a shrine-cum-maternity-unit and "the large number of babies who are buried there could be natural stillbirths, or children who died in labour". [12] Whichever way, it could explain the crying.

Intrigued, I rang Jill and had a friendly half-hour of wide-ranging conversation, but I'll stick to the essentials, particularly the controversial brothel theory and the supernatural. Jill recalled:

> "I worked on the villa site a lot. I was in the valley where it is for three years. It has a nice atmosphere, so tranquil. A brothel is not what you would associate it with. The infant corpses were excavated in 1912 and when I came across them I realised they must have been killed deliberately. The more research I've done the more evidence I've collected. I'm a carefree person, but after seeing them, depression hit me and for three nights I couldn't sleep. Just so <u>many</u> babies. It was a radical theory to put forward and for such a sleepy vicinity, and Lady Hambleden in her manor up the road – I've had tea with her. But the babies were definitely killed in a brothel". [13]

As for Brett Thorn, Jill knows him well and "he's a naughty boy". She gave her reasons, but realised she was talking to a journalist liable to quote her and stir it – as if I would – making her sound uncomplimentary and provocative. So, there I draw a veil of confidentiality. But, you ask, what about babies crying?

> "I never heard anything while I was in the valley. I used to chat to the locals in the pub. It was never mention and when you're there awhile you would hear of anything like that going on".

Dead end? No supernatural? No shrine? Jill reassured me, "There's still plenty to be discovered, so don't let that put you off".

Flimsy as the baby crying aspect is, there is an intriguing footnote to the US Goatman speculation, whereby a prime spot for hearing the call of this manimal is a location known as Crybaby Bridge, in Maryland. Motorists stopping late at night report hearing Goatman's shrill baying. Conversely the sound has been attributed to an 'infant ghost' as the bridge reportedly got its name because a young mother drowned her newborn under it.

Or, of course, the sounds in Hexham and Prince George's County could have been made by those cousins of wolves – foxes on the prowl – or maybe even a werewolf.

The beast with two backs
Had I any corroborative evidence for the following episodes in this already complex investigation they would have formed part of my examination of manimals. As it is, I have consigned it to the realm of ostension and the wider concept of cultural identity. It resembles a possible Hexham meme [14] (an oft-derided term, one which when used can usually be substituted for a more specific term and is championed by that sceptic Richard Dawkins and paranormal U-turner Susan Blackmore) but seems appropriate as defining echoes emanating from 1 Rede Avenue to the pubs and clubs of the greater Hexham consciousness.

One of the four responses to my original appeal for information in the *Hexham Courant* elicited a phone call from a 58-year-old who has lived in the east end of Hexham all his life, Barry Scott. He began by telling me he and his friends had been discussing my letter while drinking in the Ex-Servicemen's Club, They thought the Hexham Heads had been made by a quarryman. But the conversation became more intriguing when we got talking about the events in Rede Avenue and the weresheep experience. Barry certainly had a novel take on the encounter:

> "These people I was drinking with are all local characters. They all know the story. It's about the slaughterhouse there. People went in [broke in] at night to steal meat. One man had a sheep on his back. That's what they seen [from 1 Rede Avenue]. He was carrying it on his back".

How the purported sheep stealer could have been spotted by Nellie Dodd from upstairs at No. 1 Rede Avenue. (Paul Screeton)

We discussed the Dodds, whose home was almost directly opposite the abbatoir, having experienced this at night – probably when over-tired – and the tale had become warped to involve a hallucinatory sheep-cum-human in the bedroom. Sleep deprivation does strange things. "That's the craic," said Barry, "The slaughterhouse was still there in 1972". I asked if he could name the man with the sheep on his back. "Yes," he said, "I know him. I'm not telling you his name. He's 73 years old now and wouldn't appreciate it. Quite a few had stolen from there". [15] Interviewed four days later, Barry's tale found no sympathy when I posed his claim to the Dodd siblings Brian and Sylvia. In addition to their home not being with a direct line of vision from the bedroom where the beast appeared, Brian argued that it was physically impossible for a man to scale the wall and the sheep could only have been alive. Pouring more cold water on Barry's scenario. Brian related that Hexham was noted for a "bar-room lawyer" brand of storyteller; Sylvia adding, "What Hexham people don't know, they make up". But maybe it is irrelevant whether the event which Barry described truly happened. From a folklorist's point of view it has its own significance; particularly as it represents ostension, i.e., a described event is based upon an earlier account. It is not essential that it represents fact following fiction, for, assuming the weresheep encounter inside the Dodd household is basically true as described, the Hexham Heads tale has long since taken on all the trappings of folklore, aura of daimonic reality intervention and the hype and hyperbole of misinformation. There is even an element of credibility to Barry's tale, in that it could have occurred (despite No. 1 Rede Avenue not directly overlooking the slaughterhouse, but a street **was** visible from upstairs, and objections regarding the wall and if it was a carcass and not alive, the body could have been thrown over the wall and then retrieved. So, if Nellie Dodd had looked out and witnessed a felony she would have seen a sheep's body and the head of a man carrying it – a weresheep! So it does have its own inner logic and consistency of sorts.

By developing an account which had already taken on a life of its own through media attention, commentators' plagiarism and distortion and my intervention, perhaps Barry thought he would hoax me. I was later to find Des Craigie was a master at playing pranks so maybe it fits a certain Hexham stereotype. Journalists are always wary of anyone contacting them unbidden, suspicious of a hidden agenda, but here Barry was responding to my appeal. If he was telling a porky about the sheep it was a good one. But if a jape, what had he to gain, except maybe share with his cronies in the club how he thought he had fooled the investigator. But on a deeper level a myth can select its teller and manipulate him into exteriorising it by couching it in his own way. As a likely yarn-spinner, Barry we salute you!

'To Hexham wi' you an' ye'r whussel!'

Towns make capital out of any local legend, as with Lincoln's Imp, Coventry's Lady Godiva, Nottingham's Robin Hood and Edinburgh's Greyfriars Bobby, however implausible or debunked. Hexham has its riots and a battle and little else apart from the Hexham Heads. But any happening which strikes a chord to give identity to a place will find a resonance among local people and help create a shared identity. Actually, I had recognised this trait decades ago when in the summing-up to my book on Hartlepool's notorious monkey-hanging legend I wrote:

> 'It is a fallacy of conventional scholarship to distinguish between these aspects with rigorous discipline and distinction. For folklore is the psychic life of a people and cannot be separated artificially from shared events. Legends may seem like lies but they always have an element of truth. Even when exaggeration and embellishment are applied, even to the extent of deliberate falsification and invention, such "lies" of a people are not wholly gratuitous. They refer to some strata of communal reality where underlying fears, deficiencies, desires and dreams require exorcising or compensating. Their falsity makes them just as real; their power makes them come true'.

Slaughterhouse Four

This particular strand of warped reality was to take another twist when Mark Newton, revealed that a were-sheep's form was seen in the slaughterhouse. On my first of several encounters with Mark he mentioned his association with the abbatoir and its legend and this account of his forms an amalgam of various comments he made to me:

> "Me and my friends would hang around the slaughterhouse during the school holidays. We helped the drivers with deliveries to butchers. I was about 13 then [d.o.b., 25 August 1969]. It was said to be haunted by a half-man, half-sheep. The haunting was the talk of the slaughterhouse then. All the workers knew about it. People there didn't stay long. The story may have been made up to keep us kids away".

Yet despite his caveat, Mark assured me there was substance to his assertion and a creature or at least a ghostly phantom had been witnessed by the manager of the company, whose Christian name was Hilton, but the surname escaped him. Mark claimed:

> "He saw a dark shape in the slaughterhouse where the carcasses were hanging. If there was a call-out he was the only one with a key and this sighting was at night. It was half-man, half-sheep. It scared the hell out of him and he's a big man. After that he wouldn't go back without someone else or with a torch. He was the only one to see it. This was in the 1980s".

Shades of poltergeist phenomena – to boot!

This was not the only supernatural aspect to the abbatoir. Mark told me:

> "There was a changing-room where the workers changed from their civvies to working clothes. You didn't want blood and what have you on good stuff. Only one man had the keys to the changing-room, yet there were constant mix-ups of boots. Shoes put in lockers would appear outside, all mixed up. And this was in daytime".

It seems the slaughterhouse became commercially unviable during the 1990s, perhaps because of the cost of conforming to strict Euro hygiene regulations or some other reason. The land was sold for the building of a halfway house for the homeless hoping to get a council house. At the risk of labelling them unsavoury, Mark claimed the Pescott House residents include problem drinkers and drug addicts, requiring the constant presence of security guards.

On the first time I met Mark I mentioned I had spoken to Barry Scott the previous day and when Mark said he knew him, I asked if Barry could have been making mischief. Mark assured me with, "No, he wouldn't have been pulling your leg". Coincidentally, Barry's daughter Claire was a neighbour, living at No. 5 Rede Avenue. Small world! In fact, in circular fashion, in a bid to find Hilton's surname, I rang my new contact Barry to find he was unaware of any weresheep sighting inside the abbatoir, but promised to make inquiries on my behalf. As good as his word, Barry rang back the next day and as I was out left a message to the effect that the manager's name was Hilton Stonehouse. His informant believed the manager had moved near Gateshead, but "had passed away". There was another blow when I rang Barry a few days later to learn he had "spoken to two lads who knew him and they said he never mentioned any ghost or creature in the slaughterhouse and both said he's definitely dead".

Undeterred, I was then given another possible witness or someone who could flesh out the rumour of the phantom manimal, Maurice Dobson, manager of the abbatoir when it closed. Upon making further inquiries I discovered he suffered dementia; so a second dead end. But I then received the name of yet another possible contact, a man who ran the office called Lance Whale. When I rang Barry for the ump-teenth time, he told me Whale, too, had passed away. However, he supplied me with the name of a butcher who had worked at the slaughterhouse, Cliff Eels. To cut a long story short, although he was no in the phone directory nor on the electoral roll I had a hunch he lived in Haydon Bridge so caught a train there and went in the first pub I came to, the Railway Inn, where apparently I had just missed him. However, one Keith Alexander gave me his address and directions, so off I went. His wife welcomed me inside and when I said I'd just missed Cliff in the pub I put my foot in it as she exclaimed, "Oh no, he wouldn't have been in there!" She contacted him and we spoke; the outcome being total bemuse-ment and a denial of any knowledge of the weresheep aspect. Another wild-goose chase and a bit of a shaggy-dog story, but I was sure there was some relevance if only I could find it.

That image Barry had implanted of a man with a carcass over his shoulders harked back to something antediluvian and I pictured in my mind's eye primitive cavemen miming a hunting scene with the war-riors draped in skins and the tribal shaman wearing antlers or a pair of horns as depicted in the famous cave art image of the late Palaeolithic era Pyrennean 'Sorceror of Trois Freres, all moving in imitation of their quarry. The image also reminded me of the 21st Century spectacle of singer Lady GaGa in an

A comparison of Henri Breuil's image of a prehistoric shaman as drawn at the dawn of hu-mankind and Lady GaGa flaunting a dress of animal flesh for a photoshoot at the twilight of civilisation as we know it. She told chat show host Ellen DeGeneres, "I live halfway be-tween reality and fantasy" – very shamanic.

outfit which took the shaman's animal skin ceremony a stage further and revealed the meat beneath. Never mind her half-hearted statements that the steak dress and matching accessories was a symbolic statement about her not being "a piece of meat" and/or criticism of US military policy on gays, this is an artist from a burlesque background. Successful performers of that art form go deep into themselves and express contact with other dimensions in their actions. The ensemble was judged the most powerful fashion statement of 2010 by *Time* magazine but it was pure theatre. [16]

So, if this sheep business had some archetypal relevance in Hexham there had to be an antecedent. There was. Confirmation that my time had not been entirely wasted was exonerated by the image of just such a beast with two backs larceny in the abbey as a stone carving from around 1500AD. The guide I consulted describes it as 'crude', along with a man playing bagpipes, a fox preaching to geese and other figures. They can be found in the north choir aisle at the base of Prior Rowland Leschmann's tomb in the chantry chapel. My faith in Barrry Scott's seeming leg-pull had paid off – or at least I felt my sleuthing had not been entirely wasted.

Lo! Behold a rural wolf panic

From sheep to wolves, their natural predators. For all the historical description available, its local nature and the beast being vulpine, the Wolf of Allendale tale has never excited me. Not even the fact that damned data recorder Charles Fort covered it in his book *Lo!* nor that compatriot Stu Ferrol had celebrated its centenary in the pages of *Fortean Times*. [14] I admit I have reacted like the celebrity cur of the Haydon Hounds, Monarch:

> 'The wisedog was put on what was supposed to be the trail of the wolf. But, if there weren't any wolf, who can blame a celebrated bloodhound for not smelling something that wasn't?' [15]

Nor am I sure it was or wasn't. All in all, however, there was a mystery: deprivation of livestock, which in a more modern age would have been associated with a mutilation epidemic; public reaction constituted a social panic; and there was already an escaped immature wolf at loose and witness inconsistencies, culminating in a similar but older wolf being killed on a railway line. The redoubtable Fort could conclude prosaically that the pet owner's denial of responsibility was the reaction of one dodging responsibility for compensation claims. And so the furore subsided, but Stu points out sightings of the beast came close to habitation and one was recorded in Cock Wood, less than a mile from Bogacres and where when we were filming there was a sudden tempest.

One of my keen correspondents, David Taylor, drew my attention to the Tynedale church at Gunnerton, near Hexham, which is dedicated to St Christopher. Before his Westernised reinvention as patron saint of travellers, this guy was famously cynocephalic and iconography of him as such stretches from Russia to Ireland, with a Greek Orthodox monastery reluctant to show visitors a dog's tooth of the celebrated manimal. But there is a distinction to be made between cynocephali and werewolves as the former have the heads of dogs and not wolves. Thus no consideration of Ancient Egypt's Anubis nor dog-headed extraterrestrials. [16]

The coldest of UFO 'hot spots'

If the 'window area' paradigm were to have any relevance regarding Hexham, the various elements studied by paranormalists and ufologists should show a marked frequency above average. In fact, the opposite is the case, particularly in comparison with parts of the Pennine chain farther south. For UFO events in Hexhamshire, forget it. Stu Ferrol checked the local archives with scant mention and Dr Peter

McCue, author of *Zones of Strangeness: An Examination of Paranormal and UFO Hot Spots*, informed me during a long chat on the phone that Hexham does not figure in his discoveries of abnormally active locations.

Stu's mother did, however, once spot a large red UFO out of the kitchen window while her husband was school caretaker and it seemed to be directly above the prominent bell tower to the west of Rede Avenue. Apparently she was so unnerved she screamed and dropped a plate. The aerial object reduced in size and zipped away. There were several witnesses and it made news in the local paper. It could have been the same sighting which freaked out a woman taxi passenger who bolted from the scene at nearby Slaley. No other reports were even this substantial.

When American UFO researcher John A. Keel unveiled his concept of 'window areas' his home audience was massively hostile and the vehicle for this revolutionary idea, *Operation Trojan Horse*, sold a mere 2,000 copies in the US. The book was – and still is – highly influential in the UK and Western Europe. His main points were that the UFO enigma had always existed; that UFO denizens were ultra-terrestrials interacting with us through geophysical gateways and maybe influencing and even controlling us; the menacing Men in Black are parahuman elementals; that contact is concentrated around the 'window areas', where geological conditions cause electromagnetic effects which prove conducive to manifestation of alien encounters and earthlights misidentified as extraterrestrial craft. The stages by which Keel came to these breathtaking assumptions is not explained, so maybe it can all be put down to inspiration.

In contrast, a similar but more comprehensive concept came from the assiduity of two Canadian scientists, Michael Persinger and Gyslaine Lafreniere, who studied and diligently mapped UFO and fortean events to analyse distribution for geographical and monthly peaks of activity. The clusters which were found showed a similarity to Keel's 'window areas'. Their hypothesis was explained in a book entitled *Space-Time Transients and Unusual Events*. (17) Their data consistently pointed towards seismic-related sources and the transients of the title are localised electrical columns associated with tectonic stress in a geological fracture. This model is hard science-based, provides rational explanations for much of the UFO and phenomenological data and does not require any paranormal speculation, this adding up to the best blueprint for the enigma so far and unrivalled since its inception in the mid-1970s. For the purpose of my book, although Hexham is almost bereft of flying saucer phenomena (hence no discussion of 'flap' or wave zones), it does have the Rede Avenue poltergeist behaviour and possible shrine as data for fault line association, flimsy though it is. Perhaps the very paucity is the direction to look?

Where's Charlie Dimmock when you need her?

There's an intriguing phrase in *Messengers of Deception* where Jacques Vallee writes of 'silent agents walking among us unseen, placing social time-bombs at strategic spiritual locations'. He was speculating within a ufological context, but he had stressed the folkloric dimension in his books and it is not wholly fantastical to concede that the Hexham Heads – whatever their genesis – have, as Dr Ross suspects, been beacons urging further examination of the discovery site. I think maybe someone should take up a spade and if the archaeologists are reluctant, simply get a dowser to see if there is a structure and if so hire a gravedigger to moonlight (full moon optional) and dig a trench to verify or otherwise speculation. If there's nothing, think of the potential for prize-winning leeks!

FAMILY CURSED BY HUMPTY DUMPTY

'By SANDRO MONETTI

THE CURSE of Humpty Dumpty has shattered a family's life.

Since Michael White found the ancient, egg-shaped carving in his garden, his wife Alison has been hit by a crippling illness and his children have seen ghosts in their bedroom.

Horrible

The devoted dad's business has also collapsed in financial ruin.

Now Michael, 43, is selling his home and auctioning the spooky stone relic.

"I can't wait to get rid of that

HAUNTED: Alison and Michael with the ancient stone carving

Spooky relic brings years of bad luck

horrible thing," he said yesterday.

Michael has been told by experts that the smiling head was almost certainly made by ancient Celts.

He believes it was cursed in connection with ancient rituals held on a site known as Druid's Altar near his home in Bingley, West Yorks.

"I found it five years ago stuck in the roots of a giant sycamore tree," he added. "Since then, nothing has gone right."

So his 14th century home goes on sale next week for £210,000.

The head — kept in his garage wrapped in oily rags — will be auctioned at Retford, Notts, today where it is expected to fetch up to £300.

Auctioneer Nigel Smith said: "I can't imagine who would want a cursed head, but I hope it sells."

CHAPTER 15
'CURSED' HEADS: ASPECTS OF MISFORTUNE

If I were to say I was no more – nor no less – superstitious than the next person, that would be a lie. I have a very mild form of obsessive-compulsive disorder where each time I suppress one aspect another pops up, but it's under control. Only recently have I taken the heads made by Des Craigie and Colin Robson 'on tour' as rail enthusiasts say and I admit to fearing the worst 30 years ago when I took them to be professionally photographed (as depicted here on the front cover) at my workplace. My trepidation was misplaced, as have been subsequent forays with them. Incidentally, the photograph of two heads being held by me has been used to illustrate numerous books and articles over the years via the Fortean Picture Library, into whose domain I have transferred the copyright, and often been used willy-nilly. Latest unofficial sighting has been the website of Los Angeles band Hexham Heads – leader Ken Ramos being amused that they were my hands. This abuse and consequent lack of remuneration is niggling, but so is the presumption given that these heads made by Des and Colin are being passed off mistakenly as the original Hexham Heads. This distortion of the truth has led thousands worldwide to have been conned by a myth not of my making.

But again I'm digressing. On a serious level let's consider instances where the carved head phenomenon has been associated with bad luck - even death. The term 'cursed' has become popular in this context both for the tabloid press and writers and speakers at conferences. The word itself sounds charged with malevolence, but how does it stand up to scrutiny when applied to ancient (and modern) carved heads? And what of those owning examples as curiosities or for study purposes?

The head-butcher, the baker, the antiques dealer
Talk about the devil being in the detail. It was only after reading David Clarke's interview with Anne Ross for the umpteenth time that the significance of her anecdote about a Hampshire head struck home. Previously in this book the assumption had been that the Rose Road haunting was associated specifically with the Hexham Heads. Perversely, here Anne Ross seems to suggest an alternative cause, just to confuse matters. She told Dave Clarke of a stone head built into a wall at what had been for a long period a baker's shop, but when taken over by an antiques dealer who naturally had an interest in such things, upon inquiring about his property he was told the head 'should never be moved'. So what did he do? Moved it, by taking it out of the wall for Dr Ross to examine it at her leisure. For a number of days it resided in her study. For what happened next, I have cobbled together two versions from Dave Clarke's interview because the transcript and the published version in *Twilight of the Celtic Gods* differ. Here's the hybrid:

"One story that I have never told people is the one about the Winchester head in the baker's shop. Now this was interesting because there was this little head built into the side of this very old baker's shop which had been bought by an antiques dealer which had the tradition that the head should never be moved, but he agreed that the only way to date it was to take it out because you can't just from the mask. But anyway he took it out of the wall and I had it for a number of days and the first thing that happened was the house became haunted ... and there were these terrible footsteps about and everything went wrong ... things were moved in the antiques shop and in the end we gave it back ... and I felt terrible as I was instrumental in having the thing taken out of the wall. The local tradition was connected with the ghost".

This is ambiguous. I assume she means her home in Southampton, but I suppose it just could mean residential quarters attached to the shop. If the former she's associating the werewolf with a cursed Winchester head rather than the Hexham Heads.

'Little Mannie' caused wee problem

A particularly controversial artefact, dubbed a 'god dolly' by pioneer collector and exhibitor Sidney Jackson, and nicknamed 'Little Mannie' by its Manchester University museum curators, has been described as both a carving and sculpture. Anne Ross mentioned it in conversation with David Clarke and he subsequently included it in his doctoral thesis. I'm justifying its inclusion here as much from a 'toilet humour' angle as Dave's categorisation due to the stories and lore which it has attracted and parallels with elements surrounding heads in the native British tradition. Five inches high, the stone carving came to light during the 1960s in the cellar of the Conservative Club in Hollingworth, a village north of Glossop. Though coming from the High Peak district with its enduring tradition of pagan continuity, the strange figurine has been the focus of paranormal phenomena. It seems local historians had been aware of its existence for many years and a story linked to its discovery tells how it and another broken statuette depicting a female deity were found amid candleholders and chicken bones, leading to its association with witchcraft. One assertion is that these were theatrical props to form a circle and make him seem more macabre when exhibited at the turn of the last century. Recent opinion argues that its provenance as African, not Celtic, and its nature as being as a fetish object from Sierra Leone rather than Wild Boar Fell. [1]

As is the wont of museums faced with unconventional exhibits, Little Mannie currently resides in the Mancunian museum's reserve store with other puzzling idols. He's not a pretty sight whatsoever, with large lentoid eyes and huge nostrils. There are truncated arms, too, giving the appearance of a man/hippopotamus hybrid creature look.

My reference to lavatorial jokiness pertains to John Prag, the museum's Keeper of Antiquities, who was taking it to be examined by experts in London. When he answered the call of nature he had an embarrassing experience. He told journalist Kevin Ludden, "When I went to zip my flies up,

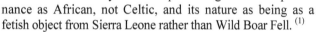

Little Mannie: blamed for archaeologist's embarrassing wardrobe malfunction.

they just fell apart. I couldn't believe it". Dr Prag was not the only member of staff to be victim to Little Mannie's mischief and mishaps had led some staff to refuse to handle the ugly artefact. The vile-looking creation had been blamed for a series of misfortunes:

- Dr Prag's car was broken into hours before he took Little Mannie to London's National Gallery.
- After photographing Little Mannie, an employee who had never had a motoring accident had his caravanette scraped down one side that night and the same happened to the other side the following day.
- Another staff member preparing Little Mannie for exhibition split his head open on a door.
- A researcher who had been studying Little Mannie was pushing her child when its buggy inexplicably fell to pieces.

Dr Prag, 49, concluded:

> "He does look truly malevolent. Perhaps the gods are taking revenge on those who have taken him out of his natural environment. I treat him with respect".[2]

But not everyone who came into contact with Little Mannie was phased by its reputation. Historian Tony Ward, who obtained the curio for the museum collection, was quoted as saying, "The stories of its 'influence' amuse me. I carried it in my jacket pocket for a couple of weeks, but I have seen people react to it".

Back with Anne Ross, she seamlessly moved from discussing the Winchester head to Little Mannie, noting similar stories pertained. Having previously suggested it is of 'considerable antiquity' and possibly Celtic in origin, she told Dave:

> "I don't think it is Celtic at all. I wouldn't be surprised if it's from Africa. I know from Patsy where it was found, but it sounds to me more like witchcraft. I don't know that it is from Africa but it is certainly a very nasty little thing. I can't stand it. John [Prag] had had a terrible time with it. He doesn't like it at all and has blamed it for a lot of things ... and we have had a lot of accidents with heads. In fact, a lot of my colleagues wouldn't drive stone heads from one place to another".

Sidney Jackson compared Little Mannie to a tiny, hermaphrodite 'god dolly' excavated from beneath a Bronze Age Somerset Levels trackway in 1966; Anne Ross initially thought it Celtic but changed her mind; then came the traveller's souvenir curio from a few centuries ago and Dark Continent origin. When Tony Ward collected it from its discovery in a club's dingy cellar, the finder described it as "just the sort of thing grandfather used to make". Shades of Hexham's Des Craigie and relatively modern manufacture.

'Back-seat drivers' with murderous intent

The next contenders in the 'Celtic Mr or Mrs Nastiest' nominations are the Bron-y-Garth heads. We left Anne Ross telling Dave Clarke of downright refusals to transport stone heads by car. Dr Ross then in the interview relates her own traumatic experience of taking to London these two small Welsh quartz sandstone carvings, found near a spring at the small village near Offa's Dyke on the Welsh border with Shropshire. Local people had remembered them positioned upon a wall before they were unearthed in a garden in 1964. Both heads were ball-shaped and around 19cm. However, one was janiform (having opposing faces) while the other was more traditionally skull-like with deep holes resembling eye-sockets. The owner had agreed Dr Ross could borrow them and take the pair for examination at the British Museum, so she had her husband Dick prepared for the journey. She recalled to Dave:

> "It was a beautiful day, sunshine and clear sky, and as we carried them down the garden path from the house to go to the car there was a most almighty clap of thunder and a terrible thunderstorm and we had three accidents on the way home in the car in which we were very nearly killed. The brakes failed on one occasion".

Echoing experience with the Hexham Heads, both Anne Ross and Sidney Jackson agreed the skull-faced Welsh head had an 'evil expression', which both blamed upon its purported homicidal tendency.

The fall and rise of Humpty Dumpty

A carved head which needs little introduction is 'Humpty Dumpty', an ovoid sandstone creation which has featured in the media and whose present owner used it to illustrate a talk and displayed him at the 2011 *Fortean Times* UnConvention. At 24cm in height and bearing a cartoonish human face, the well-worn artefact was unearthed in the grounds of Ryshworth Hall, a 16th Century mansion at Crossflatts, Bingley, West Yorkshire. Substantially different from the traditional strain of archaic heads which pro-liferate in that region, it has a triangular nose with tiny nostrils, pronounced mouth with the upper lip divided into two arcs suggestive of an attempt to give it a quizzical look (others have suggested smiling or sneering) and prominent eyebrows above drilled holes for eyes. House owner Michael White was using a mechanical digger to clear vegetation when he dug up a giant sycamore tree in the grounds, in whose roots he found the carved head lying face down. This was 1984 or 1985 and he cleaned his ac-quisition to reveal its facial features. According to Mr White a string of bad luck followed over subse-quent years, beginning with a member of a local history group who borrowed it for verification, telling its finder he should shun involvement with the curio. Asked by a journalist to comment on this, Mr White said:

> "He would not elaborate on it. He said a guy who was the curator in a museum where he had been to verify about this head had himself had bad health which he had put down to these heads, and he said 'tell the gentleman concerned that he is better off not having anything to do with this head'. Well, I don't believe in ghosts and bad luck like that, and I wanted to keep it. It's an artefact I found at the house and I wanted it to stay with the house. However, the guy who had the head verified for us died shortly afterwards so we didn't get any more informa-tion from him". [3]

A friend of the Whites was also loaned the artefact and experienced bankruptcy, illness and moved away from the area. Upon the head's return he regained his health and seemingly wealth. Mr White's wife Alison refused to have the find in the house so it largely remained in the garage, except for the bad-luck pal's tenure. Nevertheless, the husband and wife, then aged respectively 43 and 34, became beset with misfortune and mishaps, with health deteriorating and financial problems. At this point both the Grade II listed eight-bedroom house and the troublesome head were pit up for sale. A story in the *Yorkshire Evening Post* caught the attention of newsdesks at a couple of national tabloids and the 'cursed head' aspect was played up for all it was worth. [4]

The lurid account in the *Daily Star* had business collapse and crippling illness, with the added details of the head being wrapped in oily rags in the garage, the children seeing ghosts in their bedroom and most bizarrely that Michael White had been told Humpty Dumpty was almost certainly Celtic and he believed 'it was cursed in connection with ancient rituals held on a site known as Druid's Altar [revered rock outcrop] near his home'. [5] The version in *Today* included the sacred site heritage aspect, death of an 'antiques expert' who had advised the couple to get rid of the artefact dying 'shortly after', central-heating boiler bursting and flooding the kitchen, while adding that Alison had developed myalgic encephalomyelitis, forcing her to quit her job in PR and being involved in a car crash costing £1,000 in damage. [6] The editor of a small magazine published in Sunderland, hence *Wear Wolf*, condensed the *Today* piece and in the following issue carried a fascinating letter from current custodian Andy Roberts where he relates that day after he and David Clarke bought the head, 'I went down with a mystery virus [and] had a serious motor-bike accident within days and someone was/is trying to sue me for something I wrote in *UFO Brigantia*'. Andy was the mag's publisher/editor. [7]

Humpty Dumpty was sold by Henry Spencer & Sons in Retford, Nottinghamshire, on 14 November 1990 and auctioneer Nigel Smith was reported as saying, "I can't imagine who would want a cursed head, but I hope it sells". It did sell. David Clarke and Andy Roberts were there and bought it for £180; lower than the Whites' expectation of £300 upwards.

Later developments elicited the information that Alison had encountered a phantom, too, in the form of a disembodied hand at the top of the staircase one night and which vanished when she turned on a light. She also said the children, Samantha, aged eight, and Victoria, aged six, reported multiple ghostly sightings in their room, "They say it has been a dog, a man, a boy and a woman. And they say these people come and talk to them". They then moved the youngsters away from that room and the staircase, both of which they connected with a 'queer feeling'. On seeing the Whites depicted outside their home, my eye was immediately drawn to the doorway and what appear in the photocopy to be guardian heads on either side. If such, then they were not doing their job, the haunting was fiction or the images are not of apotropaic embellishments.

After having sold Humpty Dumpty, the Whites' fortunes picked up and a year on the *Bradford Telegraph & Argus* reported that Michael had found a well-aid job as a travelling shower door engineer (not the same as running your own building firm, Ryshworth Property Developments) and Alison had started a teacher-training course (not as prestigious as being a high-flyer with Marks & Spencer), but the girls had got over the scary haunting. Mr White was also quoted as believing the run of misfortune had been transferred to the new owner 'who dismissed the talk of a curse', going on to say Andy had contacted him to say 'he had been laid low with an unknown illness'. [8] In a letter to me Andy thought the Whites 'pulled the wool' over the journalist's eyes to get a free advert to sell the house, which was still on the market for £210,000. Concluding, Andy wrote, 'The head is even as I write giving me a glance that says "just you wait Mr Sceptical pants".' [9]

The auction catalogue described it as 'probably Celtic period' and the Whites ruminating about human sacrifices and druids, but I'm sure Dave and Andy only saw it as a modern trophy with a colourful background: a talking point, if not a talking head. And if it had been able to speak it might have told how it had been made by a carpenter living in part of Rysworth Hall seven years before the Whites moved in. Rather in the manner of Des Craigie's intervention, following interest in the Press, Halifax woman Jean Jones contacted a local newspaper to reveal (or claim, knowing the template for 'Celtic' carvings) it had been crafted by her late father, William Hodgson, in 1978. Again, as with Des, it had been created to amuse a child, or rather in this case his grandchildren. It had apparently been buried as a joke to amuse them, saying it would be discovered hundreds of years hence. She told a reporter, "He'll be sitting on his cloud rocking with laughter".

Doubtless he would also be amused by H. Dumpty being carried around like the head of Bran, such as his entertaining the forteans at UnCon 2011. In an act of ostension mirroring Nancy Craigie back in the 1950s, the 'Ant & Dec' of forteana, Andy Roberts and David Clarke introduced silver paper to their 'ventriloquist's dummy'. Dave told me:

> 'We simply put the paper in the eyes for fun; we brought the head on stage at the end of the talk and hoped the silvery glint from the paper would make it look eerie. During the lunch break we put the head on display in the cafe and it quickly became the centre of attention, with a queue of people all wanting to touch it (or not touch it), be photographed with it etc'. [10]

A member of the audience, Steve Jones (a pagan Yorkshireman, so not to be confused with more famous namesakes) made an online comment about Humpty Dumpty, recalling picking him up for closer inspection:

> 'It is a good carving with attention having been made to putting in eyebrows, nostrils and lips on the face. Five minutes after putting it down, I found 5p on the floor (yes, I am mean enough to pick it up). I was then invited to take part in a documentary being filmed about the Hexham Heads as they wanted me to explain my "Deck of cards" theory of entities. [That's Graham and Stu] We shot it briefly in the green room. I then spent a wonderful afternoon listening to talks and watch the by turns funny, sad, and downright bizarre film about Ken Campbell's ventriloquist dolls. [yes, the Bran/H. Dumpty aspect is there] On the way home I popped into a pub for a pint and promptly won £5 on a quiz machine....' [11]

Dreadful coincidence, or ...?

Briefly, I'll mention a carved human head of ambiguous origin found in a garden at Marple, on the western edge of the Peak District, during the 1960s. Its finder, Robert Woodward, subsequently gave it to a friend as a 'house-warming' gift when they settled in Scotland. The friends were member of a witches' coven and delighted with the present and used it in their rites. Mr Woodward continued:

> "However, they immediately began to experience an extraordinary succession of 'bad luck'. The head was very soon blamed and became once again a garden ornament. They suffered financial catastrophe, two miscarriages of much-wanted foetuses, partial failure of the house (necessitating living in a caravan in the garden for a long time), business collapse, family split-ups, etc. Finally they pleaded with me to take the head away, attributing all their problems to its aura of menace and 'undoubted evil'. But before they would let me put it in the boot of my car for the journey back to Northwich they absolutely insisted on wrapping it around with a number of talismans of Hebrew, Christian and non-Christian origin. They then wrapped it up completely to prevent any of their spells being moved during the journey.
>
> Not very long after this incident the pan-Am aircraft exploded over southern Dumfriesshire and scattered huge pieces of wreckage over a very wide area. Some large pieces fell directly into the garden of my friend's house, which was completely surrounded by pieces of personal property and pieces of shattered human beings. Their house, when the pattern of wreckage was finally plotted, was found to lie exactly on the centre of gravity [sic] of the site. They suffered

appalling trauma as a result of the Lockerbie crash and they are still far from being recovered from the shock of what happened that night". [12]

Provenance irrelevance theory

A good deal of the first part of this book dealt with how from purportedly being 1,800-year-old artefacts made by Iron Age head-hunters and assumed to be such by the most prominent archaeologist in that field of research, and endorsed by the authorities at a top Northern university museum, the intervention and potential embarrassment of a semi-skilled worker having claimed to have made them more like a mere 18 years previously, saw an abrupt volteface whereby archaeologists became wary of applying dating to artefacts and geologists got into a contretemps while getting their petrological knickers in a twist. A most extraordinary, amusing and undignified display. What seemed to get forgotten in all this academic hoo-hah and kneejerk uncertainty was the paranormal dimension to it. Another area of lurking discomfiture.

Fellow head fetishists and co-authors of that modern classic *Twilight of the Celtic Gods*, David Clarke and Andy Roberts bought, as I've related, a head of definite dubious origin at auction with no expectancy that it was either Iron Age nor 'cursed', and I'm sure they had been amused rather than aggrieved to learn in advance that it was made only 13 years before the sale:

> 'In fact, the actual age of the "cursed head" [Humpty Dumpty, aka The Druid's Head] and indeed all the others we have investigated has no bearing on the subsequent development of the stories, but tells us a great deal about how strange beliefs and superstitions develop often from mundane beginnings. The crucial factor is not the heads themselves but what people **believe** about their power – as important a factor today as it would have been 2,000 years ago'.

Dave reiterated his viewpoint for Graham's film *Heads!*:

> "All this suggests that the actual artefacts themselves and the age of them is totally irrelevant; that the one key factor are the people involved and what they invest, in terms of belief, into a solid object. So I think that it's irrelevant whether it's Celtic or whether – in the case of the Hexham Heads – by a child messing around with a block of clay. I think that once people have got the idea that there's some kind of weird, supernatural presence invested in that object, that becomes reality in its own right". (13)

Despite confusing the roles of Colin Robson and Des Craigie this, of course, is an opinion straight out of the soft sciences and reflects Dave's ufological interest, where as an interested observer I watched over the decades the emphasis shift from extraterrestrial contact expectancy to sociopsychological analysis whereby ufonauts dwelt not in outer space but the mind's inner space; or at least that became the U.K. and European model (whereas paranoid Americans largely see UFOs as a physical threat to security). In other words, not how carved heads came to be around, but what the individual projects upon and thinks of them.

This is nothing new. As far back as 1982, after having sent the celebrated author, showman and shaman Tony 'Doc' Shiels a copy of my *Tales of the Hexham Heads*, he replied with a fascinating letter on the subject. Among his observations was an example of his wise counsel which is both succinct and prescient:

'I really don't think it matters too much when the heads were made, or who made them, the things <u>worked</u> and that's what matters'.

Which is quite the same as Dave's analysis. Both would agree age and craftsmanship were irrelevant but Dave sees the observer imbuing his or her thought **upon** the stone, whereas Doc sees the stone itself as imbued **already** with thought.

Lindsay Allason-Jones had also developed a strong opinion on the Heads provenance:

"What I do find interesting about the Hexham Heads scenario is how over the years many people have not wanted to give up the mystery, even faced with a solid piece of analysis. I think that's very interesting psychologically! I think that it's very interesting that so many people got sucked into a sort of Celtic twilight of their own imagining when it comes to these heads. People were seeing and imagining things which I think shows a very interesting power of suggestion from an artefact. And I am not saying that they didn't see those things, but I'm not entirely sure that they can entirely blame the heads for that!" [14]

CHAPTER SIXTEEN
THE PARANORMAL & PSYCHOLOGY

Looking for answers in this chapter, the trail leads from images and sounds embedded in stone through personal physical contact to the brain and mind. Disclosure is rendered through the process of making the opaque known by way of considering relevant aspects of the comprehensive consideration of conflicts and interpretations, each overlapping the next in the manner of playing patience – which we all recognise as a virtue in the context of character – and, in fact, one of the theories here is named 'deck of cards'.

Competing hypotheses may be anathema to the favourer of quick-fix Occam's razor, but the true drama is found in the detective assessing the character and motivation in the rogues' gallery that is competing theories and the most and least likely solutions to aspects of the overall mystery. It would seem the entities or monsters dwell in many places, in town and country, wild forests and rational minds; they originate from primeval times to visitation from a distant extraterrestrial future, as products of the collective psyche of social panic to deliberate construction by dabblers in occult ritual; and whether they be the product of the Devil's evil machinations or the result of human foibles, mostly they are indicative of human mischief or folly.

The territory is unclear and it is neither all down to dwellers of the liminal borderlands with a set geographical hinterland nor the popular catch-all solution that it's 'all in the mind' and thus can be easily dismissed or treated in woolly fashion. There are many dangers in dealing at any level with this commonwealth, but the greatest is taking ourselves too seriously and relying on rationality, for all explanations are but myths.

Stone Tape theory
I aired my misgivings regarding the Stone Tape theory in Chapter Seven, but recognition has to be given that it has its attractions. Those who have been beguiled by the conjecture range from the bold/flaky (Tom Lethbridge) to the obsessive (Don Robins), taking in along the spectrum the innovative Nigel Kneale, the archival David Taylor and earnest James Burke.

I remain unconvinced but hopefully ambivalent. Therefore there's little point in reiterating the points made earlier, but I should briefly remind readers this concept is based upon the supposed ability of quartz or similar crystals used in building or carvings to store coded energy containing complex place-memory and images from the distant past and the ability to retrieve this by exciting the stone electronically.

**Nigel Kneale: a tribute collage to the stone tape theory man,
who even had a stamp issued in his honour!**

Nigel Kneale, as mentioned previously, fictionalised this process, while also on television James Burke bravely attempted to retrieve sounds of the past from stones at Dorset's magnificent but ruined Corfe Castle. Commenting upon *The Burke Special* broadcast which aired some time in 1973, dowser Tom Graves said he had heard nothing more of the intriguing process whereby researchers claimed that they could distinguish fragments of human speech and other recognisable sounds, considering a hoax, but then dismissing it as not what the ardent Burke would perpetrate, despite, in my eyes, Burke dressing as if he had stumbled out of a torture dungeon porno movie set in his butch black bondage gear.

In 1976, in a *Nationwide* broadcast it was again mentioned in such a manner as to suggest viewer familiarity with the theory. As mentioned earlier, Anne Ross and Jenny Robson appeared with roving reporter Luke Casey, who began by discussing how the head was a powerful symbol for the Celts and compared it to the place in iconography that the cross holds for Christians. Luke's introductory purple prose poem continued:

> "It represented all the great deep, dark and dreadful things of man's nature. It
> was an avenging, insatiable god-figure in which good and evil were mixed up.

All destiny was there. This ghastly deity wasn't just a head; it was a severed head. The Romans were no great believers in having a dog and barking yourself, so they employed Celtic mercenaries to man the fortifications and discourage the Scottish drift south. These Celts brought their religions with them. They varied from tribe to tribe, but had in common the head. Prisoners taken in battle were disembowelled in front of the many shrines; and the severed heads of the bravest and wisest were kept as a gruesome talisman. The gods themselves were heads of stone, and if there's any truth in the old stone tape theory, what more likely receptacle could there be to store up the awesome memory of those savage times? Those cold impassive eyes must have soaked up death like blotting paper".

Not having yet got my hands on a copy of the broadcast, though there does seem to be a copy extant, all I can do in the interim is refer to how paraphrasing in *Fortean Times* magazine mentions that Luke contibued by speculating that psychics could somehow activate such stone tapes to activate and revive those frozen fears and barbarity. Editor Bob Rickard, before resuming the transcript as quoted in Chapter One, noted there was no evidence to link the theory and the Feachems' werewolf experience. Bob also suggested the beheadings and literal gut wrenching be ignored. After Luke pondered a stone tape 'action reply' the TV narrative takes over where I mentioned it in Chapter One.

Earlier, the maverick archaeologist and freethinker T.C. (Tom) Lethbridge wrote many books on 'fringe' subjects between 1957 and 1972 and deeply influenced my thinking and that of many others with open minds. He distinguished between ordinary ghosts such as spirits of the departed and what he labelled 'ghouls', and while endorsing a form of stone tape premise, envisaged these as negative and destructive stored extreme emotions. All haunting and sighting of nature spirits were also dependent on the individual's personal 'psyche-field' and its interaction with landscape features where the earth's energies have concentrations of power. Hence not only 'window areas' but cancer clusters (despite medical profession and staisticians'protestation). The same concept was believed by the committee which produced the document *Exorcism: The Report of a Commission Convened by The Bishop of Exeter* with my friend Dom Robert Petitpierre as its editor. For the reasons given above, the findings stressed 'positive thinking' and recommended that 'the blessing of a new home is not an irrelevant activity', and nor was Dom Robert's touching my Colin Robson head (see next sub-section).

The premier piece of historical scholarship done on the stone tape theory is an erudite cobweb-dusting of archival material going back to the mid-19th century by Parasearch director David Taylor. This is certainly an eye-opener for those who believe Nigel Kneale invented the doctrine as some fictional conceit and are blithely unaware of psychometry. As Lethbridge chose to divide haunting into 'ghost' and 'ghoul', Dave chooses spiritist and mechanistic. [1] I see the split as between 'ancestors' and 'immortals'; 'deaders' as Hayley Mills's simple character in *Sky West and Crooked* would describe the former and 'archetypes' as psychoanalyst Carl G. Jung would name the latter. One fading whilst the other remains eternal; one decaying with the other renewing.

So it seems walls maybe <u>do</u> have ears – for those that would hear and believe.

Psychic influence transference theory

As a 'spin-off' to the stone-tape theory, I present the putative influence transference theory. I'm not really convinced and it smacks of silly superstition on a playground level. A game of tag but with a sinister twist. But such notions doubtless have some basis, even if it is no more than a crude folk belief. Folklorist Dr David Clarke's investigations in South Yorkshire certainly give substance to this notion.

When I interviewed him for the film *Heads!*, Dave related:

> "There's lots of stories where you've got a group of five people and only two see the thing even though they're all looking at the same landscape or whatever. So I think the fact that he [Dick Feachem] didn't see anything is not all that significant. I've come across lots of similar stories just in South Yorkshire, in the ghostlore of this area, where it's like the ability to see a ghost is on touch in that somebody who's got the sight can touch somebody else and give them the ability to see spirits. That's something I've heard of several times. So the fact that he didn't see something may be simply that he didn't handle the heads, or wasn't touched by somebody who had handled the heads". [2]

Er, if his wife Anne had undoubtedly handled the Heads, there must have been marital contact? The children both saw the zooform. Whatever: to move on.

As a folklorist myself well aware of the power of transmission of myths among common interest social groups, this internet posting is yet another example of the extraordinary influence that one *Nationwide* broadcast had (can anyone name any other sequence from the show? No!). Here's what Dominic Brayne posted to an internet group:

> 'I recall, when growing up in the 1970s, that the teatime TV show *Nationwide* on UK BBC ran a story about the discovery of some Celtic stone heads. The story then descended into true *Tales of the Unexpected* territory when they announced that there was a curse on any who touched the heads, when they would be visited by a werewolf. There then followed (allegedly) a bloodcurdling tale of a boy who had the misfortune to touch one in a museum and upon his return from school was confronted by a werewolf in his empty house. The tale terrified our whole school and for weeks no one would go home after school on their own, irrespective of the fact that as far as I can tell none of us had ever seen a Celtic head. The strange thing is, talking about it years later, we could all remember the story but none can recall actually seeing it on TV – so did *Nationwide* run this tale, and do others remember it?" [3]

Daimonic reality theory

If I was selecting the ten most influential books for the fortean canon, I feel an outside chance would allow *Daimonic Reality*, by Patrick Harpur, entry. [4] It is cogently-argued, diverse yet structured. There will never be a simple, satisfactory unified theory for fortean events, but Harpur is another questing soul making a stab at the holy grail. Addressing phenomena, he observes that 'if these strange visitations have any purpose at all, it is to subvert the same modern worldview that discredits them'. Just as I re-engaged myself with the Hexham Heads brainteaser , Patrick, already a believer, decided to re-examine general fortean data within a framework; to present it to himself as much as to others. He noted that fellow seekers were largely unaware of a precedent to their view, an historical context for the very evidence of their own eyes and senses, and to provide this was partly what his book aimed to provide this was partly his book's aim. Daimonic reality certainly resonates with the paraphysicality of genius loci, giving substance to the events at Nos. 1 & 3 Rede Avenue; its archetypes give form to the werewolf and genii cucullati; and thirdly he engages the blurred area between fact and fiction popularly known as urban myths which in my book encompasses the accretion of misinformation since 1971/2 and the deeper level of the Heads in the Hexham psyche.

I cannot improve on the review of Harpur's classic which I wrote in 1994 and here is an extract to explain his neo-fortean viewpoint:

'The daimons of the title here embrace all apparitional figures: including fairies, angels, souls and aliens; flexibly changing form to suit their eras, i.e. cultural tracking, as abstractions or preferably remaining personified. . Archetypal personages going back from Jung to the Gnostic/Hermetic/Neoplatonic tradition of philosophy. The Neoplatonists described the world of gods and daimons as anima mundi (soul of the world) and Harpur reckons this has the advantage over the collective unconscious as a root metaphor as it returns us to the idea of soul instead of psyche; reintroducing the idea of an objective ensouled world 'out there'. Particular places are where we are more likely to encounter the unseen order of things. Lights hang over prehistoric sites while military bases, power stations and reservoirs attract hovering UFOs because these are the shrines of our modern secular culture, becoming a shadow display of hi-tech alien 'spacecraft' to mirror our technological preoccupations. At such places the laws of time and space, matter and causality seem attenuated: caravan sites and trailer parks being in that luminal area between town and countryside are specially prey to UFOs and strange creatures which particularly favour boundaries. The greater transparency at certain sacred sites has led to the ufological, and broader, term 'window areas'. Paradoxically they straddle many borders, such as that between fact and fiction. Harpur concludes the section with a discussion of urban myths, seeing them as also spanning the gap between fact and fiction; ambiguous and using the friend-of-a-friend convention to distance us from the alleged event.

After the collective unconscious and anima mundi, he constructs a third model, that of imagination, for making intelligible the nature of daimonic reality. Primary imagination is here defined as encountering the sacred; secondary imagination is recreative and evaluating, making from the human condition art or at a personal level being therapeutic.

Not only is a rather complex theory of models made to make sense (he could have included other models such as Mercurius or faery, but as all forteans will understand, daimonic phenomena cannot, by definition, be explained (for explanations are images and myths anyway). Daimonic reality is a self-coined metaphor to empasise the power of the models examined. However, after taking the reader through such topics as missing time, scars, strokes, near-death experiences, stigmata, changelings, midwifery, alien sex, Bigfoot, supernatural food, satanic child abuse and bogus social workers, shamanism with Doc Shiels and Arthur Shuttlewood, John Keel's quest, soul and body, he ends the book with two instructive examples of successful descents into the Underworld – 'now more that ever the most appropriate spatial metaphor for daimonic reality'. These visits involve greys and C. G. Jung.

For a book that is arguing that its subject matter cannot be explained and that soul resists spirit's wish to find single underlying principles, Harpur has come as close as anyone so far to produce a unifying theory for the great diversity of subject matter loosely labelled paranormal/supernatural/mythological and folkloric. Naturally the author sees the paradox, aware that the book's perspective is partial and incomplete. Nevertheless it is a remarkable *tour de force*'. [5]

The publicity department must have sent the author a copy of my review for Patrick wrote a brief, flattering letter in response:

> 'Dear Paul – Many thanks for the handsome review: you're the only reviewer (incl. *Sunday Times*, *Literary Review*, *Independent*, etc,) who seems (a) to have actually read the book I wrote rather than the one they imagined I wrote! And (b) to have grasped what I was driving at so that's encouraging at least … '

Only during re-reading *Daimonic Reality* recently did I realise werewolves and vampires escape inclusion and analysis, while Patrick cover black dogs and sister Merrily's ABCs.

'Deck of cards' theory

As discussed in Chapter Ten, two distinct 'species' of hooded entity exist and researcher Steve Jones pondered why there were differences not only in size, but some were distinguished by glowing red eyes, although he attributed this to a recognition of observers' fear. Well aware of the great regional variety among folklore spirits and also the shape-shifting capacity which was itself prevalent among many of the denizens of the faerie realm, a theory looked set to coalesce. In an article for the magazine *Folklore Frontiers*, Steve wrote:

> 'It began to wonder whether the appearance depended upon the observer. I came to the conclusion that there are a series of archetypes like a deck of cards in our minds and when we encounter these type of entity the mind shuffles the deck and deals a card so that one person may see a large hooded shape, another a small one, another a black dog, etc. [6]

Thus Nellie Dodd reported a were-sheep and the Feachem family witnessed a werewolf, where the stimulus was likely identical: a shape-shifting entity umbilically attached to the Hexham Heads. But let Steve continue:

> 'The Owlman of Mawnan may be another version; sightings of this creature were first reported in the 1970s. The last sighting was investigated by Jon Downes in his book *The Owlman And Others,* which was seen by a 14-year-old boy Gavin and his girlfriend. Gavin is a pseudonym for a person who subsequently went on to become fairly well known in scientific circles and doesn't want his name associated with the subject as it still scares him recalling it. He saw a half-man, half-bird figure about eight-feet tall with glowing red eyes.

> One of the [hooded entities] sightings reported to myself was of a seven-foot tall, black-cloaked figure seen in the car park at Stonehenge by some Americans as they drove away from the site. They thought it was someone dressed up to thrill the tourists until it vanished! I was giving a talk at the *Fortean Times* UnConvention in 2002 on the subject of "Hooded Entities" and mentioned this tale. A gorgeous woman sitting on the front row got excited and at the end revealed that she had been there with her mother the day before and had seen the same thing; her mother had seen nothing and thought she was lying. The girl, who was a model for *Vogue*, was going to give me more details, but sadly I was unable to speak to her afterwards, so don't have any more details than what she said at the talk'.

When I heard about Steve's talk I thought he had hit upon something original, but later when re-reading *Needles of Stone* realised others had made the connection already. This was a ground-breaking and controversial (for dowsers) book by Tom Graves, who I first met during the heyday of earth mysteries enthusiasm. In it he tells a relevant tale from the professional life of a psychiatric social worker friend who had to deal with the aftermath of a student group's joke conjuration atop a burial mound after finding an ancient gramarye of spells. They wanted to see if anything would happen. It did. Tom recalls:

> 'My friend wasn't able to get a precise description from the students of what suddenly appeared on top of the barrow, since its appearance was slightly different for each of them. (This is a characteristic of "guardians" and many other kinds of "thought-forms"). As one of them put it, it was like a horror-movie monster, but it seemed to them to be very real, and right in front of them'. [7]

Similar but diluted. More size/colour/clothing/hairiness/detail differences, rather than werewolf/ vampire/Big Foot/black dog/Gyles Brandreth.

This is not dissimilar to 'distinctive categories' of entities which author Paul Devereux delineated in his ghostlore analysis, where he listed such spectral figures in the landscape as white ladies, black monks, phantom hitch-hikers, black dogs (culturally tracked to anomalous big cats), and so on. But he was perplexed by a stretch of country road, the B4068, which produced three separate types of haunting, whereas no other road in the vicinity produced a single report of paranormal activity. Also his suggestion that 'people see what they know' gives a fresh twist to the deck of cards theory in that it points towards expectancy and conformity (Anne Ross's childhood werewolf obsession and Nellie Dodd's sheep familiarity). Paul concluded that he was 'pretty sure that genuine apparitions were indeed hallucinations – a fusion of subjective and objective qualities', while being bemused that 'they be place-related hallucinations', i.e. location specific. [8]

Paul Devereux leapt to the defence of Michael Persinger when his university tenureship was in doubt, having experienced personally what has been cruelly described as 'The Dungeon' where participants are not stripped and whipped but wired to what critics have dismissively dubbed his 'god helmet', whereby it is claimed that by activating the brain's temporal lobes mystical experiences can be induced, thus relegating the Almighty to the infinitely insignificant. Without entering that debate here (for I assure the reader I can speak with some authority and personal experience, as described elsewhere), what I will say is I do not think temporal lobe epilepsy (as it is commonly, wrongly and crudely described) has any relevance to the subject in hand. That said, Dr Persinger and his colleague Gyslaine Lafreniere wrote a classic book all forteans should read, as I have done several times, but forgot they also touched upon this topic in *Space-Time Transients and Strange Events*. The passage I'm about to quote is interesting for drawing attention to 'stored images' (redolent of the stone tape theory in another context) and visual expectations (as in cultural conditioning). So from a controversial apparatus we have:

> 'With this unnatural stimulation of the memory areas in the brain, the person could vividly and emotionally experience his stored images; he could richly perceive the nightmares and crude monsters normally suppressed from consciousness except during dreams. A human being, under this condition, could experience a "waking nightmare" of fear-inducing stimuli. They would seem quite real, quite material, for there would be no reason for the person to think otherwise.
>
> Consequently, what the person sees could be shaped by his expectations, when he heard or imagined or seen in movies. Each person might perceive the same

stimulus in different ways. Where one person sees a globular UFO with men inside, another person might see a metallic ship. When one person sees a giant,
beastly humanoid with fangs, another might see it with a hideous, wolf-like face.
There could be combinations of animals in the monsters seen. Examples of these
instances have been reported'. [9]

Thus the creatures seen in Hexham and Southampton could easily be one and the same but perceived differently, without recourse to rurality of location or childhood dreams; nor for that matter the cine-matic-style werewolf description given my by Anne Ross's son Richard.

Control system theory

Worth a paragraph if only for completeness, the control system theory is probably relevant but has drawbacks such as lacking a feasible coherence and has more than a whiff of conspiracy about it. On the plus side it leans towards the unified theory grail seeking. John Keel termed it the Eighth Tower, concealed but it could be a specific device in a set location and still functioning today. Far-fetched, but it mirrors such notions as science-fiction Matrix series; the Gnostics' Demiurge and his acolytes; Jungian archetypes; the ancients' gods; Christians' saints, Harpur's daimonic reality; Downes' zoo-forms; and as the Fall of Man continues its relentless anti-evolutionary deterioration towards the gutter of entropy, celebs. Just as one reviewer suspected a chapter I wrote on man-made global warming to be a spoof, you can never be sure if Keel had his tongue in his cheek, but as with celebrity culture individuals his control system theory has proven ultimately fleeting and the most easily disposable explanation.

Tulpas: the thinking man's thoughtform?

Among the motley collection of books donated by my grammar school's old boys was a neglected copy of Alexandra David-Neel's *With Mystics & Magicians in Tibet.* [10] I borrowed it and gave it a rare ex-cursion from shelf life and found the book wholly different from other traveller's tales , already drawn to the supernatural. The writer, born in France in 1868 and living to be 101, drew upon 14 years living in and around Tibet. Immersed in native culture, she was convinced of its people's psychic achieve-ments and occult skills. Alert readers will have recognised the author's name: just as Marianne Faithfull is synonymous with a Mars Bar and Sting equals tantric sex, Dame Alexandra (opposite) signals tul-pas. But just as those salacious rumours are modern myths, so the Tibetan tulpa thoughtform maybe belongs in a category alongside its country cousin the Abominable Snowman as it was known in my childhood, or yeti, to give it the local terminology.

The paranormal investigator and author Kevin McClure, in a three-paragraph filler for his ground-breaking but shortlived magazine *Common Ground*, rather dismissively commented:

> 'Tulpas take up only five pages of a 288-page book. She describes them as "magic forms generated by a powerful concentration of thought', and while she does claim to have created one herself, in the form of a monk, which was once seen, briefly, by an unnamed independent witness, she admits that, '"I only relate what I have heard from people, whom in other circumstances, I have found trustworthy, but they may have deluded themselves in all sincerity". If ever we hope to be taken seriously we are going to have to stop taking snippets of anecdote out of context and quoting them like established facts'. [11]

Cryptozoologist Richard Freeman has also spread doubt upon the tulpa myth which now thrives among New Age adherents and Eastern mysticism followers, having had a Buddhist friend explain that the

tulpa has a long folklore pedigree, but as with Christianity absorbing paganism, Buddhism co-opted this belief. The more cynical suggest inspiration from Madame Blavatsky and see David-Neel's long life as an explorer as having accounts highly dramatised much in the spirit of T Lobsang Rampa, the plumber from Plympton, Devon – not Tibet. Richard also discusses the Loch Ness Monster and the Rev Dr Donald Ormand's efforts to exorcise it in its thoughtform guise. [12]

If the deliberate – or involuntary – creation of tulpas in the form of weresheep or werewolf sounds far-fetched, there's a 'true' account of a fabled wolf's manifestation. Born Violet Mary Firth, but known publically by her pen-name Dion Fortune, the occultist describes how she inadvertently created a monstrous, snarling wolf from herself. As she had been brooding over some betrayal and revenge, doubtless strong emotions played a role in this exteriorising, plus the fact her meditation had led her into the realms of myth, specifically the Fenris wolf, a demonic form which devoured Odin in Norse folklore. The account can be found in her most widely read work, *Psychic Self-Defence*, where after learning her housemates had been troubled by wolves in their dreams, with some difficulty she reabsorbed the thoughtform.

The publisher of this book, too, has had a novel take on tulpa creation. In *The Owlman and Others*, Jon Downes stresses he is using 'pure conjecture' when creating his own scenario in which he imagines Doc Shiels, having just read John Keel's classic *The Mothman Prophecies* about a winged apparition in West Virginia, inventing a similar beast. After the copycat Cornish 'hoax' sighting, Doc found he had set in motion a sequence of events whereby others began witnessing the spoof zooform, Jon wrote:

'Perhaps this very act of creation helped form a tulpa which then got out of hand. If so, then I suspect that Tony was as surprised as anyone else when other people started to report sightings of the creature'. [13]

Thus there is a strong link with the provenance irrelevance theory which Doc alerted me to in 1982.

By her own admittance, Anne Ross is on record as having as a youngster been obsessed with werewolves. So it is quite plausible that either she inadvertently created a tulpic werewolf or the Hexham Heads somehow fed off her subconscious and did the job themselves with the co-operation of some interdimensional spirit which took on the zooform guise. As for Hexham, I strongly suspect the genius loci of lower Rede Avenue was equally capable if the circumstances configured correctly to equally create something similar, but in that case a more rural farm animal hybrid. Colin's school artwork, discovery of the Heads and the storm may have combined to create a perfect circumstance whereby these elements coalesced and a fraught family situation of illness, tiredness and anxiety were sufficient catalytic motivation for a nightmarish thoughtform to manifest.

As for Sonia Smith – casting aside my 99% certainty her account is pure fiction – what **if** 'Priscilla' the cleaner exists? Just assuming so for a moment, she would have been sharing a place of employment with Dr Ross and could have heard about the shenanigans at 6 Rose Road. More precisely, what if Anne Ross had left the Hexham Heads on her desk and 'Priscilla' gave them the once over with here duster and out of curiosity picked them up for closer inspection? That would link with the influence transference theory. Just maybe Sonia's story has some substance. Or am I just helping fiction appear as fact when every molecule in my brain tells me she was fibbing (but she sounded too posh to lie!).

Arguably the best article written on thoughtforms is also the most thorough, penetrating and non-academic on a particular guise. My late friend author John Michell submitted the piece, 'Satanic curses: Bogus social workers and demonic abductors', for my magazine, *Folklore Frontiers* as a reaction to his heartfelt concern at the fear this moral panic had induced in the nation's psyche. [14] The piece was both detailed and balanced, highlighting the consistencies, irrationalities and the quasi-materiality of imitative borderland creatures which 'derived their existence to some extent from the *night side of nature*'. He also drew a parallel with the Men in Black, sinister beings masquerading as bureaucrats, intimidating UFO witnesses from the 1950s onwards. As with bogus social workers they betrayed all the trappings of bureaucracy, giving warnings or disinformation. Both being essentially alien functionaries, neither group did anyone physical harm; more significantly out of more than 200 BSW incidents during 1990, in no single instance was a child found to have been molested nor abducted, yet this and the attendant satanic child abuse scare saw parents and family kin arrested and jailed without a shred of evidence. The title of Middlesbrough M.P. Stuart Bell's book on the Cleveland scandal caught the mood and the underlying truth perfectly, *When Salem Came to the Boro*, [15] while satirical magazine *Viz* lampooned the affair with a 'Bottom Inspectors' strip. Meanwhile, the real social workers continued to abuse their sweeping powers, which became the envy of police forces throughout the land. [16]

Altered states of consciousness

An altered state of consciousness (ASC) should not be confused with fantasy thinking, day dreaming or wishful thinking. It is a *portmanteau* term for experiences beyond the norm: not everyday humdrum existence, but a realm where the mind introduces new vistas, concepts and experiences. The causes and effects are legion and range from the involuntary epileptic fit to circumstances involving sleep deprivation, through triggered out-of-body experience or a mystical vision, to the barometer of drug experimentation from getting bladdered on a Saturday night and convincing no-one but yourself that the fellow inebriate at the bar is the beshtest friend you've ever had to a bad trip on acid or heroin withdrawal.

If the mind is powerful enough either singly or working in group fashion to create tulpas or summon a servant of the Devil through a black magic ritual, what is its capacity for such creation – visually or even physically – when semi-conscious, either before or after sleep or when the body is physically exhausted or becoming dissociative as a result of travel fatigue.

The events in Southampton were too complex and long-lived to consider hallucination as a repetitive factor, but it could possibly apply to the nightmarish nocturnal even at Hexham's No. 1 Rede Avenue. Fatigue has certainly played a role in many otherwise extraordinary fortean cases and Andy Roberts's forensic demolition of the Todmorden 'UFO abduction' of P.C. Alan Godfrey with its combination of tiredness and misidentification springs to mind. But to cite a more mundane but closer to home case, a dentist had extracted one of my troublesome teeth, but by the late evening it had refused to clot and cease bleeding, resulting in a surgery opening at 10pm to stitch my gum. Told to go home and sit upright until 2am, around 1pm the combination of loss of blood, trauma and general torpor caused me to hallucinate. An eerie blue entity began slowly forming at floor level close to my chair. Its features were basically of human dimensions and I got the impression it was distinctly elemental and quasi-corporeal. Before it completed its formation I literally threw in the blood-stained towel and headed for bed. I must be one of the few parents and grandparents who have been able to honestly tell children there really is a tooth fairy. Also it was a *bona fide* hallucination: nothing more, nothing less, nothing else.

So what if Nellie Dodd experienced an ASC? Factors which suggest a high likelihood of fatigue, even with constantly dealing with the domestic demands of a family of six children and a husband, would be the lateness of the experience, between 1am and 2am; a sick, fractious child; the claim that Brian and his brother had been annoying one another; inclement weather; and the dog playing up. Obviously there had to be a disruption of her circadian rhythm and stress from maternal concern and maybe familial friction. In such a fraught situation she could have been susceptible to an ASC. With or without the dubious slaughterhouse sheep carcass theft scenario implied by Barry Scott, she could have experienced either a hypnagogic or hypnopompic dream/hallucination, but if there is an iota of credibility to her seeing a man outside with a sheep on his back, in her state of mind that could have transferred itself mentally to her more immediate surroundings in the bedroom. Trouble is, the young Brian was aware of the presence, felt it touch him, even if he didn't witness its form. Then again, the husband, Isaac, appeared in the bedroom but saw nothing of the phantasm. Was it all Mrs Dodd's false but seemingly real memory of an encounter with daimonic reality? Whichever way the experience is viewed, it has entered the annals of the anomalous, does not succumb to easy analysis and is an intriguing topic for forteans to mull over for years to come.

**Des Craigie's home from home: Royal Air Forces Association
Hexham Branch & Club. (Paul Screeton)**

CHAPTER 17
SUBURBAN SHAMAN, er, DES CRAIGIE?

Remember back in Chapter Ten local Hexham historian Stan Beckensall suspecting me of supporting a shamanic slant on antiquarian matters. Well, sir, here's why! All societies in their own way have shamen or shamenesses, so Stanley would expect me to introduce the topic here, and I do so with pride. So far the only commentator on the Hexham Heads that I have previously found to have made such an association was author Ian Wilson, who in personal correspondence with Anne Ross put it to the scholar that her 'bedroom invader' could have been the spirit of a Celtic shaman in ghost form; rather spoiling his paranormalist argument by invoking 'a pre-Christian witch-doctor who might have assumed a wolf's head in a manner seen in some prehistoric cave-painting'. Trouble is, cave artwork is Palaeolithic era (32,000 to 11,000 years ago) and if genuine the heads accumulated in the Southampton home dated from the Romano-British period (150BC to 450AD).

Prankster! Or more of a shamanic Trickster?
If Des Craigie is – as I will demonstrate – a prankster on a small scale, I will also argue that he may well constitute a Trickster on a cosmic scale. Not only that, my thesis suggests the man who claimed to have made the Hexham Heads in his lunch-break could have gained some semblance of shamanism through a serious illness and that where he lived played a major role in his life. If 3 Rede Avenue constituted a genius loci then perhaps he had 'chosen' status and was influenced by whatever god visited the site seasonally. There's an anecdote of him throwing a referee's shoes down a well and the sports arbiter almost following. Likely the intercession of his team-mates saved Des from further trouble and the soccer umpire from visiting Hades. But tricksters are there to break rules and challenging an authority figure such as a 'ref' - out of the comfort zone of the pitch - was in varying measures impromptu, disruptive, foolhardy and amusing, but pertinent to the sacred – the well. You didn't mess with Des.

Certainly Des ticked several of the boxes for being a bona fide trickster figure: fundamentally ambiguous and anomalous - his claim is far from universally believed; an inverter of situations – the amateur versus the experts; time and space has no boundaries – modern pitted against ancient; and messenger and/or imitator of the gods – well he seems to have been under the influence of some mischievous tutelage when rebelling against of all people the umpiring referee when he transgressed a sporting boundary.

During early 2011, in an attempt to gain some further insight into Des Craigie, I rang his son Nigel at home to establish a rounder portrait of his father. In essence, much of Des's leisure time and pursuits revolved around Hexham RAFA (Royal Air Forces Association) Club. During World War II, Des had served as RAF ground crew, mainly driving munitions trucks in Burma and later Indo-China. Nigel commented, "I don't think he fired a shot in anger". [1] It was while serving in the Far East, Des survived a bout of malaria. If severe this can be a life and death matter and perhaps if so Des underwent a form of medical crisis during which he was in a sense resurrected. Such a critical situation can often single out an individual, whereby it is not the doctors' intervention but the gods who save the patient and mark him or her as special.

Des Craigie, son Nigel and daughter Nancy, for whom he claimed he made the Hexham Heads. Provenance of the photograph is lost in the mists of time, but the Readers's Digest book still exists.

A keen sportsman, as a footballer Des played not only for the RAFA Club but Hexhamshire in the Saturday league for Shaftoe Leaders. For the RAFA, he also played cricket and in his later years Crown green bowls. After his wife died he even baked scones and entered them competitively. But gardening was his greatest hobby and despite the constraints of the Rede Avenue garden he had a trench of leeks and showed his finest specimens at the annual RAFA Club horticultural show. He remained a staunch member until he had a stroke. And if all this detail seems extraneous, it is background to portraying a man who was seriously doubted by some as the maker of the Hexham Heads and there is evidence he could get up to monkey business. Forteans will be well aware of the trickster element in shamanic activity and it is hard not to suspect somewhere lurking in this mystery is that mischievous streak of leading others astray.

Stu Ferrol had already told me his father Harry had played football with Des , who then had a reputation as a practical joker. On the occasion of his 78th birthday, Harry recalled:

> "I knew Des when we played football together. He was always playing about, messing with our kits, like if we had a certain sized bottoms he'd swap them around with someone a completely different size and that kind of thing, always playing pranks. I also worked with him for about five months during the Fifties at Alco in Hexham where we made fence-posts. We used to get those concrete posts by the side of the railways and we had to pull the wires out, carefully, so they didn't snap. But you'd always hear Des's going 'twang!' because he'd snapped the bugger. He was always as daft as a brush." [2]

"When will three meet again?" The demonstration batch of heads Des made together for the first time since 1977 together with Colin Robson's head. (Paul Screeton)

I mentioned these recollections of minor japes when they played football together and Nigel chuckled as he recalled his father playing a game at Allendale and his team was none too pleased with the adjudicating, so Des threw the referee's boots down a well. Nigel added, "The ref almost went down as well". Then there was the fancy-dress contest at the club:

> "My dad dressed as a tramp. He looked quite the part. I was only four or five at the time. He won and afterwards went to a neighbour's and fooled her. Then with her in on the joke, they went to another neighbour's, completely hood-winked her and got inside the house for a cup of tea, and it was only after half-an-hour they revealed it was him. He certainly had a sense of humour".

And crafty with it. Typical trickster behaviour.

One major aspect of trickster behaviour is shape-shifting; to transform himself into a tramp and fool those he knew intimately would be worthy of a knighted thespian. Discussing tricksterism, Patrick Harpur voiced his opinion that hoaxes involve not only exposure of some flaw in society (in Des's play-acting it would be the unequal distribution of wealth and status), but betray a sinister aspect – 'they like to play god behind the scenes'. I found Des a believable interviewee, but learning of the tramp episode made me extremely dubious.

Also, forteans are well aware that if there's a mystery, ostension will kick in to both copy the original and create the beginning of a mythology and often add fresh facets. Hence the meteorological explanation for corn circles followed by the 'flying saucer nests' before the human art stampede which followed the ragged confessions of Douglas Bower and David Chorley, much in the manner of Des coming on the scene.

Earlier 'Piltdown Man' challenged the notion of Darwinism even down to a crude representation of a cricket bat beside the hybrid man-ape skeleton. Anne Ross said the Hexham Heads were Celtic so Des said they were modern. Hoaxers enjoy upsetting a rationalist view with a totally contrary one and it's usually in a socio-cultural context.

If a song or film is a hit someone claims the tune or script was stolen from them or if recipe makes millions some opportunist will claim to have been the originator. Hence Des has been suspected of fraudulently claiming to be the maker of the Heads, either as a simple prank or a shyster seeking financial gain, whereas he protested that he came forward only to set the record straight that they were modern and his handiwork.

Trickster operates on various levels. He's an archetype who dwells at a deep level in the collective unconscious, but from there the influence can be awesome. Representing only a tiny part of any individual human, once connected to the matrix of humanity the archetype within grows from subhuman to superhuman. Des may have had humble jobs and lived a mundane life, but malaria and suburban shamanism guaranteed him at least a small footnote in history.

My journey through contacting people associated with the epic Hexham Heads adventure and having read so much misinformation and watching new mythology accruing has led me to the conclusion that it is not easy to identify deception, hoaxes or downright fraud. No wonder so many experienced authors shunned the approaches to tackle this topic in book form. Similarly ethnographers have shunned trickster material as irrational and too damn weird. As a folklorist I can appreciate the vexation felt in this aspect of research, but I see it as adding, rather than subtracting, from a study where patience is a virtue and ambiguity a bedfellow.

28 Prior Terrace
Hexham
NE46 3EY
Tel · Hexham 604385

Dear Mr Screeton,

Many thanks for the "booklet" you sent me, my family & I thoroughly enjoyed reading it, and thought it was very good and pretty accurate. I also saw the article in the evening chronicle

Like yourself I would be interested in knowing where the original "heads" went to. Someone must know but is keeping very quiet.

I haven't really anything of further interest apart from a phone call I had a while ago from a friend of Alan gardeners who wished to have a talk with me if he came sometime to Hexham. I have enclosed a P.O. for £1·30p for a further 2 copies of the "Tales of Hexham Heads".

I hope to hear from you if you receive any further information on this subject.

Thanking You

Yours Faithfully

Desmond Craigie

Everything associated with Des was intriguing. He wrote me this letter in 1980. I think it safe to assume the Alan Gardener (sic) refers to the author Alan Garner. Nigel was unaware of the great man visiting. But did he?

CHAPTER EIGHTEEN
BEDROOM INVADERS

The phrase 'he's a beast in the bedroom' does not necessarily necessitate physical lycanthropy. What goes on behind the bedroom door is normally private, but the media has already been privy to experiences as described in this book, but we all understand that this is normally a private space and not to be overstepped. That there is a well-understood boundary point where transgression is forbidden. So if the interloper be a werewolf or a more bizarre were-sheep, then it has to signify that something is happening which is far from out of the ordinary. The presence of the zooform at No. 1 Rede Avenue may not sound as scary as that in Southampton, but it seems to have terrified Nellie Dodd more than the werewolf did Anne Ross. Nakedness and the sheer primal nature and expected threatening feral menace of a werewolf puts it in a predatory league far beyond a sheep with a human head. Whichever way, there can be no ignoring the bedroom location, inherent sexual intimidation and perhaps also forbidden attraction, depending on the experience and his/her current psychological situation, and even ability to have been involved in the beast's presence and perhaps creation. I must say I am an adherent of Jungian psychoanalysis and his concept of archetypes, seeing Sigmund Freud as obsessed with sex and dismissive of occultism. Freud was, in fact, born with a caul (membrane covering a newborn's head immediately after birth), believed to be the sign of latent lycanthropy, and as early as 1906 was extolling Johann Weyer's 1563 book of werewolves and himself published a paper in 1914 entitled 'Wolf Man'. But it took longer for the sexual connotations of wolves to reach a mass market, as with Neil Jordan's film of the Angela Carter story *A Company of Wolves*, apparently a 'feverishly Freudian' reinterpretation of the Little Red Riding Hood story, and according to author Bob Curran, which 'brought the concept of the werewolf, now with a simmering sexuality, to the fore in public imagination once again for a time'. Actually, that was 1984, and Bob was referring back to the Hammer horror classic of 1961, *Curse of the Werewolf*, starring an actor who was born to play the role of a werewolf – Oliver Reed.

While on the topic of films, a small detail, but not without significance, lies in the description Anne Ross's son Richard gave me in 2011. Recalling the wolfman in his bedroom doorway as a child, he was adamant the ears were prominent: large and pointed. Look at any wolf and its ears are triangular and rather stubby. This seems to mitigate against a true hybrid and points towards a cinematic origination, hence ostension, leading to a cultural rather than cryptozoolgical explanation. But there's the small matter of Richard's very young age at the time. Would a child aged under ten have seen and been influenced by 'X'-rated werewolf films? Or was the manifestation the thoughtform from an adult? And here's another more general puzzler. How is it that werewolf films have no literary heritage, unlike creations such as Dracula and Frankenstein's monster? They were shunned even by the greatest writer in that genre, Edgar Allan Poe, who was at the pinnacle of his career when he crafted the horror story classic *Berenice*. Should it be assumed this was where Anne Ross got the inspiration for her daughter's name? I doubt whether Isaac Dodd nor Dick Feachem resembled Oliver Reed, although Peter Underwood described Dick as burly. Remember the zooform passed ethereally through the former and the latter heard but never saw the wolfman. This chapter considers the possibility of family psychosexual dynamics and the maiden/mother/crone timeless triumvirate of the ages of womanhood.

'Maid and Mother, and Crone that's grown old'

Before separating the three stages of a woman's life for individual attention, it is worth looking at these in a religio-folkloric way. Applied to the wolfman personae, the first stage subdivides into the infant with the werewolf as morality tale cautioning not to speak to strangers, accept sweets or go to see his non-existent puppies, for it will be a paedophile on the loose and on the pull. By adolescence, girls are bombarded with 'wolf whistles' (seen as flattering one's esteem or sexual harassment) and predatory comments, usually in the context of pack animal immorality instinct and brotherhood rapine. The MILF (Mother I would Like to Fuck) aspect here is a woman with experience and who 'is obviously up for it' as she's proven her fitness to breed. For an example of the crone as seen from that pack animal mentality, look no further than the behaviour of lecherous football players acting as a single entity, boasting of 'spit-roasting' women and with the most dire example being serial Jekyll and Hyde wife-cheater Wayne Rooney, lured by the dubious charms of a slapper known as 'Auld Gran'.

When teens think they're becoming hairy monsters (and that's just the girls)

It would be futile to try to attempt a comparison between Berenice Feachem's encounters with the werewolf and those of folkloric Little Red Riding Hood (dating from Perrault's *Contes* of 1697 and made famous after its 1812 inclusion in the Grimm Brothers' collected fairy tales), for there is no moral or assault involved. Anyway, Berenice was 15 years old, the age where parapsychologists' favourite explanation is that much poltergeist phenomena is triggered by the presence of puberty-age teenagers, particularly girls with their menstrual periods beginning. However, my research has shown that age and gender of those affected to be statistically irrelevant. It sounded like a good lead to me that the poltergeist incidents in Hexham could be attached to the two Robson daughters, but Wendy was 23 at the time and on her honeymoon, while Judith was 18 and consequently a woman. There were four daughters next door, but nothing untoward went on before or after the weresheep incident in the night-time. In Southampton, there was no incidence mentioned of polt-style activity and anyway how many homes have menstruating daughters without attracting the cameras from *Most Haunted* or have three ceramic mallard flying off the wall?

Yet books such as Curtis Jobling's *Wereworld: Rise of the Wolf* assume youngsters have become accustomed to the notion that puberty triggers special powers and both adolescent boys and girls struggle with physical changes such as putting on 'puppy fat' and increased hairiness, particularly the pubic triangle, plus the testosterone fuelling aggression and mood swings. There is now a huge market for those 11+ fantasy novels, which is the best place for were animals. But it is salutary to realise such life-forms can also intrude in the everyday lives of ordinary folk. Meanwhile, the scientific killjoys are out to dehumanise polt behaviour by renaming it 'recurrent spontaneous psychokinesis' or obfuscate and neuter it further by applying the simple initials 'RSPK'.

MILF attraction and matriarchs

The only mother in this saga who I have met is Des Craigie's second wife, Jean, a friendly, good-looking woman, but as pointed out earlier, definitely behaved like an alpha female. Pictures of Anne Ross show a confident, hugely-attractive natural redhead and it is telling that until I reminded him from

Was Anne Ross naked when she jumped out of bed? She says the room was unnaturally cold, but she received the heads during a summer. In preference to seeking a horror movie shot of a naked woman confronting a devil, I'm reproducing this 1674 picture from Jean de La Fontaine's *Nouveaux Contes,* in which I'm in good company: *The Witch on the Wall* sheela-na-gig author Jorgen Andersen did so, too. It shows a demon repulsed by a woman lifting up her skirt. I doubt that upon confronting the werewolf Anne Ross recalled the practice of anasyrma, the displaying of genitalia to curse evil spirits, whereby her bare loins would have been seen as an affront to this devilish emissary from some ungodly plane of existence. Whatever, it seemed to have met its match like the folkloric account of a Roman army fleeing at the sight of fellow redhead Boudicca displaying her genitalia as her followers confronted them.

his own transcript that Dick Feachem had been present at the interview with Anne Ross, Dave Clarke had forgotten her husband had been present. OK, so it was Dr Ross who was primary witness, but he was a fellow archaeologist and heard the wolfman moving around. At the Dodd household the were-sheep 'passed through' husband Isaac as if <u>he</u> was invisible and none of the media quotes him nor the 'head' of the Robson household.

Despite Anne Ross exuding authority, by her own admission the collection of heads and werewolf's presence was sufficiently stressful to threaten the physical breakdown of her family. Perhaps there were already other stresses in the marriage weakening the fabric of the family dynamic. Maybe it had its genesis with an aspect from her childhood. In 1994 she told David Clarke:

> "There were werewolves in the old Irish tales, there is no difficulty about Celtic werewolves and there are tales of wolves. I've had experiences with supernatural wolves myself when I was a child, so whether that is valid I don't know, but I discovered that the whole area was once moor which was inhabited by wolves".

In an exaggerated reflection of Anne Ross's childhood attraction to wolves and study of werewolves, author Adam Douglas records a case of a woman who had an obsession with wolves, leading to her dreaming of them constantly, becoming troubled by urges towards bestiality, lesbianism and adultery, culminating in her following her uncontrollable impulses by tearing off her clothes during a family get-together, and in front of her shocked mother adopting the mating position of a she-wolf. Not put off by her bestial *alter ego*, the next day the husband happily copulated with his wife only for her to cause more surprise by growling for two hours while scratching and gnawing at the marital bed. She told psychiatrists she was possessed by the Devil. These modern-day equivalents of mediaeval witchfinders diagnosed 'chronic pseudoneurotic schizophrenia'. A layman would adduce werewolf delusion syndrome. The unsympathetic – barking mad! [1]

It is tempting to speculate that somehow the carved heads and concomitant wolfman were able to feed off family stresses and Anne's Ross's mental state. Her interests and occupation could have bred fantasising and allow legend and myth to be attracted to her as if she were a magnet. Some people seek to make legends real as with groups who hold vigils, congregating at a location on the anniversary of an event in the hopes of witnessing a re-enactment. For others this ostension – a term used by folklorists to explain myth resurfacing in the present – is involuntary. In her study *Mind Monsters*, Jenny Randles describes this process as 'a kind of cultural predisposition to make legend come true'. Unlikely as it is, maybe Dr Ross got a vicarious thrill from wish-fulfilment made flesh.

It is in just such a situation that a bedroom invader could manifest, particularly the seductive succubi or incubi, which particularly prey upon solitary spouses whose partner is absent or who is frustrated. On the other hand it has to be said that as a unit, the Feachems hardly fit the dysfunctional family stereotype. As mentioned, currently Dr Ross is in her late eighties and suffering dementia, while son Richard acts as a carer. A small but telling detail is that although he acknowledged to me that Berenice was his step-sister, all references to her were to "my sister".

Yet the strain on family life shows the enormous pressure they must all have been enduring. This could apply to an observation by Carol and Dinah Mack on bedroom behaviour by succubi and incubi, 'Marriage itself can be threatened by subversive species who engender animosity between couples'. The writers also regard many demons as driven by instinct and 'many are only hypostatisations of desire'. And of specific interest here, 'Yet to see where Desire can lead, follow the furry, fanged creature heading towards Lust with his usual fiendish verve'. [2]

In addition to having seemingly made her professional career a hobby, or vice versa, Dr Ross seemed steeped in Celtic lore to an obsessive extent. From personal contact with certain individuals, I have found such a narrow focus unhealthy to their best interests and sometimes a recipe for disaster. However, her son assured me she never went as far as to embrace paganism as a practising adherent, and her calling for a house exorcism via her vicar suggests a pragmatic Anglicanism. A passage from John Keel, who greatly influenced me and many other forteans' worldview, may have relevance here:

> 'Controversial religious texts dating beck two thousand years tell how Christ
> ordered his followers to stone a pitiful beggar. They were taken aback but
> obeyed, and as their stones fell upon the wretch he slowly turned into a loath-
> some hairy beast with fiery red eyes, having been the devil in guise'. [3]

As Gnostic Christian myself, I do not recognise the passage. Nevertheless, it put the notion in my mind that Anne Ross had dabbled sufficiently to allow the Devil (or emissary) to come down to Hampshire. No doubt a Palestinian stoning was the equivalent of a present-day exorcism.

Trotters 'n' lightning

Nellie Dodd's tale of a were-sheep as a bedroom visitor is probably unique. Consequently there are no comparisons – or at least only very superficial. One aspect which came to mind is a report of a gigantic pig-like zooform from Hampshire, at a church in Andover and on a Christmas Eve, 1171. If accounts are in any way trustworthy it was running around the altar as a bolt of lightning struck the priest from within the church. More fortean events from 1577 involved churches, lightning and a black dog, primarily centred upon Bungay, Suffolk. My point is simply to allude to a tradition of electrical storms connected to supernatural creatures.

Applying the MILF theory to a hybrid sheep-man might seem to border on the desperate, despite a man 'sowing his wild oats' as being akin to a jack-the-lad and 'ram' (an epithet worn with pride, yet a woman in the same circumstance would have in earlier days been referred to as a 'good-time girl' or in today's parlance unfairly as a 'slag' or 'slut'). Anyway, as noted, protective spirits figure prominently in this study, and Pan (meaning 'all' and 'everything') was a guardian of flocks and patron of shepherds, who offered him lamb (ironically), milk and honey. Perhaps not Pan himself, but the fecund Mrs Dodd could have been visited by a demon which manifested as a satyr, those shaggy, goat-like beings associated with bacchanalian orgies. Whatever, when Nellie screamed, that at least signified Pan-ic!

CHAPTER NINETEEN
PSYCHIC BACKLASH?

A national newspaper succinctly described it as 'Monstermind'. This perfectly encapsulated the *raison d' etre* for the attempt at an invocation of aquatic serpent-dragons throughout the world by the Psychic Seven International (P-S-I), a team organised by Tony 'Doc' Shiels in early 1977 of seven professional psychics. Their collective intention succeeded beyond their wildest surrealistic dreams and the global experiment raised monsters in Britain, the US and USSR over three days beginning with Imbolc, the last day of January. Unfortunately five members of the original P-S-I group succumbed to 'psychic backlash' as Doc described it. In his monster-raising account/autobiography *Monstrum! A Wizard's Tale* he asks rhetorically:

> 'Can dragon-raising seriously damage you health, or do we put it down to coinci-
> dence? I think it all has to do with the fact that, one way or another, we have to
> pay for what we get. Our success was costly'. [1]

Thus he prepared for phase two with both trepidation and some new P-S-I members and a concentration of efforts on the Loch Ness Monster. The result was a Doc picture on the cover of the *Daily Mirror* for 9 June 1977. However, the euphoria was tempered by a backlash to Doc and members of his family, where illness or injuries to him and daughters were added to by 'a devil's dozen of other unpleasant things, all happened in July or August ... There was something thumb-prickingly nasty in the air, to be sure'. For a period Doc called a halt to invocational activities. Then in 1982 he successfully raised a series of Irish lough dragons and gave me the exclusive story for my magazine *The Shaman*. [2]

Unfortunately we were not in touch until after Doc's backlash period or else I could have provided a more personal account, as he was a prolific correspondent. Our first contact was him buying a copy of *Tales of the Hexham Heads* in 1982. However, the topic did arise when as the patriarch of what *The Sun* tagged 'THE WEIRDEST FAMILY IN THE LAND', he had something to say about a fellow Gaelic, but a matriarch, Anne Ross.

In his first letter after buying the booklet he described it as 'great stuff', and then lexilinked a couple of participants' names, particularly Craigie seeming to have a Gaelic link with stone. Briefly, lexilinking is seeing significance in nomenclature similarities using all manner of connections and is to normal wordplay what synchronicity is to coincidence: i.e. a subtle but significant cosmic influence at work. Being a trickster I'm not sure Doc's attribution of it to an A. J. Bell is true, but he Charles Fort, James Joyce and surrealists utilised lexilinking. But does it really reveal hidden meanings?

May 4th,'82.   3 Vale View, Ponsanooth,
                                                Truro, Cornwall.

Dear Paul,

Sorry for the lateness of this reply... I've been up to my eyes in
all manner of things! Many thanks for the 'Tales'... great stuff!

I well remember Luke Casey's piece on 'Nationwide', and I've thought
about the heads many times. I was very interested in the names of two
of the principal characters involved... Craigie and Dodd... which
'lexilink' to two people I know, who encountered a strange 'lynx-like'
beastie in Ballyvourney, Co.MMMM Cork, in August 1980, Seamus Creagh
(pronounced 'Craig', Gaelic for 'stone') and Pauline Dodds (a significant
name to ley hunters). Robin and Robson could mean something, too.

The idea of certain ball games originating from the 'head cult' of
the Celts is of great interest. The Celts were great ones for gelding
their enemies, too... so there's a possible origin for games with
rather smaller balls! I'm not being flippant, it's all part of the
fertility game, and I've very recently been researching the ancient
versions of golf (another Celtic game) which has amazing 'earth
mystery' connections... a truly shamanic game... should be played by
all serious ley hunters!

The were-wolf, ram or goat is a powerful image, and I'm particularly
impressed by the fact that it had its effect on Anne Ross, of all
people. Have you seen the book she did with Ronald Sheridan, GROTESQUES
& GARGOYLES (David & Charles)? She may have been obsessed with 'heads'
when researching the book and getting involved with the Hexham horror.
I really don't think it matters too much when the heads were made, or
who made them, the things worked and that's what matters.

I'm being nagged... have to chop some wood, etc etc... so I'll write
another longer letter soon. I'm amazed that you remember my stuff from
IT days... and, yes, we must exchange notes on present day shamanism.

                                         Keep smiling,

P.S. Do you have any weird
tales with golfing
connections?   Doc Shiels
P.P.S.
Sorry this was so rushed!

**The letter to the author where Tony discusses elements of the mystery, including lexilink-
ing and Anne Ross putting herself in psychic peril.**

Back with the letter, Doc also mentioned seeing the *Nationwide* broadcast, what I have called provenance irrelevance theory and significantly that Anne Ross 'may have been obsessed with "heads" when researching the book and getting involved with the Hexham horror'. That book being *Grotesques and Gargoyles* written with Robert Sheridan [3], but was Doc pointing to her letting her enthusiasm become obsessive and leading towards a dark place? [4] I would suggest so.

Anne's boast of *an da sheeladh*

As for Dr Ross herself, despite the formidable scholarship she was not averse to parading her unacademic belief in her own psychic powers. She was happy to reveal the werewolf visitation to the family home and verbose on the matter for the *Nationwide* broadcast. A more personal insight into her second-sight comes from the interview she gave Dave Clarke in 1994, saying:

> "Well you might say Anne Ross might feel something psychic, because I have got quite a lot of psychic powers inherited, so you might say that was something I was bringing out of them [her collection of heads]".

Later in the interview she returned to her psychism, and specifically referring to the arrival in Southampton of the Hexham Heads, she recalled:

> "But as soon as I opened the box, and I'm not given to this really although I do see ghosts and I do have inherited psychic tendencies, I mean my mother had quite a lot of second-sight and I have quite a lot myself, but when I am working on my work I am very objective. I don't deny these things, but I'm very objective".

And to close her adventures with carved idols she returned to the topic:

> "I do believe there are more things, but they don't worry me because I know I can't explain them and I don't think anybody can. Maybe one day they may be explained and I think until then you've just got to accept them. You know, animals see things, my cats see things, not regularly but they do see ghosts. Dick was very level-headed and not given to seeing ghosts and having psychic experiences. He's a very practical Norman Frenchman who has never seen a ghost in his life and is not really much given to thinking about them". [5]

Anne Ross was well aware that the territory she was exploring was not just on the physical plane of judging the age of artefacts, but that her study material belonged to the supernatural realm. Hence she was tangling with all manner of other aspects, including that espoused by the trickster archetype (whom she met manifest in a mild degree in her 'nemesis', Des Craigie) and his domain.

George P Hansen warned in his book *The Trickster and the Paranormal* of personal destabilisation, loss of critical judgement (including 'trickster-induced irrationality'), ruined careers and wrecked marriages. [6]

Well, Anne experienced most of those, particularly doubts over her analysis of the Hexham Heads and admitted her fears for the fabric of her family and even her own life unless she divested herself of the collection of idols.

Relics that spooked a boffin

By Journal Reporter

ONE OF BRITAIN'S top Celtic archaeologists got more than she bargained for when she was sent carvings a Hexham labourer claimed were his lunchtime artworks.

Yesterday, Newcastle-born scholar Dr. Anne Ross, aged 46, of Southampton, said: "First I woke up one night and the air was freezing cold — the way people say it goes when ghosts are about. I felt really frightened.

"Then I saw this shape moving towards the door. It was like an animal standing on its hind legs. It was half-human, half beast, like a werewolf.

"A few days later I got the same feeling when I was in my study, although I saw nothing. Other members of my family, including my daughter and young son, felt most uncomfortable. They also heard and saw things."

The two roughly carved heads were found two years ago in a garden in Rede Avenue, Hexham. They were thought to be Celtic religious symbols, and were sent by Newcastle Museum to Dr. Ross, at Southampton University for identification.

Moulded

But then Mr. Desmond Craigie, aged 55, of Prior Terrace, Hexham, claimed he had made them only 18 years before.

He said: "I made them for my daughter. I was working at an artificial stone firm and simply moulded the mixture and roughly carved the face."

Dr. Ross said: "We had full tests carried out and it seems unlikely that they were made recently. Analysis showed that they were carved from a local rock.

"Of course the analysis could be wrong. I intend to come North and see Mr. Craigie, and examine the area where the find were made."

Another mystery surrounds the two heads. Shortly after they were found a nextdoor neighbour saw a figure similar to Dr. Ross's description. Mother of six, Mrs. Ellen Dodds, aged 44, was moved to another council house because she had been badly frightened.

Dr. Ross said: "I cannot explain it, but there is something evil there. In May, I became ill, and then asked for the heads to be sent back.

"Immediately, I recovered and all my family agree that afterwards they felt very relieved—as if a weight had been removed from their shoulders."

Where it all began to go wrong. How *The Journal* (Newcastle upon Tyne) reported the Southampton werewolf.

If I suspected Anne Ross maybe brought her dementia on herself, got too close to occult matters and was a bit of a raver, I have gained some insight into her later private life via parapsychologist Keith Hardiman, who became interested in the Heads after reading my piece in *The Unexplained*. Now semi-retired after practising as a psychotherapist, and working as a computer systems engineer, he currently pursues his interest in consciousness studies and extraordinary experiences. He contacted me with regard to his continuing fascination with the Hexham mystery and intrigued me by revealing having met Dr Ross on two or three occasions. Prompted to tell more, he revealed that these involved Saturday night get-togethers at the home of his friend Dennis Bailey in Lysia Street, Fulham, London, around 1981 to 1983. Dennis was a colleague of Keith's wife Anne, when they worked at Charing Cross Hospital, and was a member of the Order of the Cubic Stone, and admired Aleister 'The Great Beast - 666' Crowley and The Golden Dawn. Keith explained:

> 'As for the "parties", these small informal affairs were attended by people who in my mind at the time, me being a Northern lad, seemed to be a mix of the eccentric Bohemian and academic types, i.e. a high priestess of the local witches coven with her partner a transgender male named Della, a couple of Crowleyites, a member of the occult order OTO, to name a few. Dr Ross would arrive with John, who was a lecturer at Goldsmiths College. My impression of her was favourable, not at all like certain academics who appeared narcissistic and remote; she was warm and pleasant when approached without being flirtatious or forward and seemed genuinely interested in the experiences of other guests and never uttered a condescending remark about these people. Her knowledge of Celtic research and archaeology was formidable, which was understandable. However, she did mention her deep interest in other people's pathworkings into the inner imaginal realms. To the best of my knowledge, Dr Ross never practised or was involved in any magical ceremony. However, she was curious about pagan ritual and I would be surprised if she didn't take part in some aspect of ritual paganism as I'm sure she was well acquainted with Caitlin Matthews, who practises Celtic shamanism. I did not know about the weresheep in the area adjacent to the Heads. These stories, real or not, seem to imprint themselves on the environment and are picked up by people sensitive to it. The figure seen by Anne and her daughter and son seems to be a nightmarish pagan figure; something that a person steeped in the rites and rituals of ancient Celtic people might project from their subconscious on to the local environment. There were no untoward goings on at these meet-ups and these seemed more like a meeting of curious minds as far as I am aware; no familiarity of a sexual nature took place there'. [7]

Another of my researchers dug up several interesting and surprising leads about the Ross/Feachem family, but which have no direct bearing on the book's subject matter – except one. And it made me laugh. Apparently Dick Feachem for a period restyled himself Richard deFeachem. This chimes with Anne Ross's remark in 1994 to David Clarke about his pride in having Norman ancestry. Was this a shared in-joke? A piss-take at his expense?

More seriously, as discussed earlier, another archaeologist who devoted his life to stone heads was museum curator Sidney Jackson. David Clarke reported:

> 'One story heard on a number of occasions during fieldwork in West Yorkshire linked Jackson's sudden death directly to his "obsession" with Celtic stone heads, the suggestion being that this had brought about fatal consequences for his health. This type of urban legend was perhaps influenced by horror fiction and the stories surrounding other famous curses like that surrounding the opening of the tomb of Tutankamen, which has been a well-known tradition in popular books of the supernatural since the 1920s'. [8]

Best to be forewarned....

CHAPTER TWENTY
COLIN ROBSON AT 52 (TALES OF THE UNEXPLAINED)

The actual filmed interview with Hexham Heads finder Colin Robson could not have been simpler. Only Graham Williamson and I arrived at the family man's home on the green in the pretty rural village of Ovington in April 2012. Graham set up two cameras, one on Colin, the other upon myself, and we had a friendly chat about the events as Colin remembered them. An easy-going, plain-speaking sort of guy, the results of the conversation were not, however, so straightforward. After an hour and a half, with a break for tea or coffee, I was left in no doubt that the myth which the mystery had become had now added several new puzzling aspects, and rather than unravel problematic points, had made the whole matter more opaque. Readers who have been paying close attention will note how several aspects previously taken at face value are bluntly contradicted, particularly Colin's vehement denial that the Heads were returned to the family from the Museum of Antiquities. So here's a condensed version of all the pertinent points. [1]

Paul: Firstly, Colin, can you tell me about the day you and Les found the heads, in your own words?

Colin: Well, like I say, I was eleven years old. It was a long time ago. But as I recall, we were both out in the garden that day, and we were just digging around as children do, pulling some weeds out of the garden. I started to dig a hole for some reason . As far as I can remember, I got about eighteen inches, two foot down. And I came across a head. 'Course, being a young boy, I was all excited, I was shouting me brother, "I've found a head!" So we dug a bit more, he was adamant that he wanted to find one, and subsequently he came across one as well. Er, I believe I found what they call the 'boy', and Les found what later become known as the 'witch'. The girl. And that one had like, quartz... a little, like, quartz in its eye. They were about that size. [*He indicated with his fingers something maybe a little bit bigger than a cricket ball.*]

Paul: Were they heavy?

Colin: They weren't heavy-heavy, but they were... you know, you can imagine if you picked a stone up that size, it would be the same sort of feel as picking a large stone up.

Paul: How would you compare them, then? What sort of size? A sort of tennis ball, golf ball, or...

Colin: No, there's been a lot of things said about them that I've heard over the years, but I would have said... yeah, like a cricket ball   sort of a size, and probably weight as well. They were slightly heavier than a cricket ball, I would have said.

Paul: You see, the thing is that there seems to be a lot of mythology grown up around this. For instance, one account says that Les was sort of watching you from upstairs, another one says you two were throwing stones at one another...

Colin: No, that's certainly not true!

Paul: Another story says that your mother was watching you two argue, and she gave Les a plastic spade to dig with. Is any of that true?

Colin: No, there's none of that true because at the time that we found the heads me and Les were the only two in the house. We used to come home from school, I think we used to get home about half past three in them days, and me mother was always at work and so was me father. Me and Les would let ourselves in from school, and we'd entertain ourselves by putting the telly on, listening to music, or in this case deciding to dig.

At this point Colin told he was surprised to find me in the garden, but not really shocked as he's had many others enter the garden and ask similar questions. He told me Leslie found the second Head six inches deeper in the hole.

Colin: We carried on digging after that for about another foot to see if there was any more and there wasn't. Obviously then we lost interest.

Paul: Exactly where in the garden were they?

Colin: When you came out me back door they were in me back garden. There was a hedge that went right the way along the back of the garden. Probably about five and a half feet of privet hedge. So actually right at the side of the hedge next to the washing pole.

I then introduced the subject of the discovery date, mentioning discrepancies, including Colin's own declaration of February 1972 to Myles Hodnett and latterly sister Wendy's pinpointing it to her April/ May honeymoon in 1971. In a nutshell, Colin pointed to his youth and was a little embarrassed when he said:

Colin: You know, every story I've ever read afterwards, it's always said 1972. In my own mind, was always 1972, but it could have been 1971.

Paul: Well, in the book I wrote I put down February 1972. And everyone's quoted that afterwards... So we'll move to the next bit. Having sculpted a head when you were at school. Were the heads which you and Les found sculpted or carved, have you any idea? Or is it so long ago?

Colin: I would say that they were a stone that had been carved. That would be my opinion, you know, what I remember. Because I haven't seen them since 1972. They were taken away and I haven't seen them since.

Paul: Can we come around now to the business about the sort of odd things that happened after the heads' discovery? How soon was it after you and Les dug them up that strange things happened to the

family?

Colin: We took them next door to a Mrs Dodd, our next door neighbour, and we were very friendly with her and her whole family. There was quite a few of them, the Dodds! We took the heads next door to her to see what she thought of them. So we actually took the heads into her house. We never, ever took them in our house.

Paul: They weren't inside the house?

Colin: Yes. They were inside our house later on, but not at the time. With me mother being out of the house, we took them to Mrs. Dodd. And she suggested we take them out to Hexham Abbey, to see what they thought of them. Which we did.
Paul: Straight away?

Colin: Straight away. From them being at Mrs Dodd's house.

Paul: And who touched them there.

Colin: Mrs Dodd, me and Les were the only ones that had touched them until then. We took them down to Hexham Abbey -it must have been about half past four in the afternoon. On the way down we called into the [place] where me mother was the manageress at the time, and we told her we were on our way to Hexham Abbey and what had happened. And me mother just went "Ah well, off you go." Boys will be boys. I don't think she was too interested, to be honest. And we took them there – I mean, I don't know for definite, as I say, I was very young, but I would say they were in Hexham Abbey for three to four days before we got word to go and get them back. In that time, that was when we woke up one night, I remember we woke up one night to hear some terrible screams. We realised it was coming from next door and we thought it was some sort of trouble. I remember me mam and me dad getting up, and the whole household was up. And we went next door and Nellie, as they called her, Nellie Dodd, and one of her young daughters – don't recall which one, I think it was young Carol – and they were in a real state and they said they'd seen this half man, half wolf sort of idea. Half man, half beast. That was the first of the weird goings-on as far as the...

Paul: Can I just – can I just interrupt here, you said half-wolf...

Colin: Well, she described – that's what she described it to us at the time...

Paul: You see, Brian and Sylvia were adamant that she said that it was half sheep.

Colin: I think I have heard that said, but it is maybe ... as I said, it might have been that, I was a very young boy. But definitely, certainly she said it was human on the bottom side, and the top half was animal.

Paul: Yes. So what happened then?

Colin: Like I say, I think it was three to four days later, possibly longer, when we got the heads back from Hexham Abbey. They said that they thought they were very old. But that's just what they told us. We took them home and just a couple of days later strange things seemed to be happening in the house. There was like a presence in the house as soon as the heads came in the house. Me mam used to have a – like a big glass display cabinet in the house that she kept ornaments in and suchlike. They were put in there... basically just put in there as ornaments, silly as it seems. And we would come down in the morning and the heads would always be turned round, facing the other way, usually facing towards where we actually found them. We tried different things – I didn't try anything personally, I was obviously a young boy, but I remember me mam and me dad turning them right around to face away from where they were usually facing, and in the morning we'd come down and they'd always be facing the same way. I think me father, being... you know, he just didn't believe in anything, he said that somebody was coming down during the night and tampering with them, so different things were set up to ensure no-one was going in the room to do this, i.e. the door locked during the night so no-one could get in, and they were still turned round. Taps would mysteriously turn themselves on in the middle of the night. You would wake up in the middle of the night and you would just hear water running, you would go downstairs and the taps would be full on. One instance, there was a mirror that we used to have, an old mirror that we used to have hanging to the left of the cooker. Now, if it had fallen off the wall during the night it would have fallen on the bench. There was such a clatter me mum came downstairs and the mirror was actually lying on the frying pan which had been left on the cooker. Which, you know, the law of gravity says can't happen. But the mirror wasn't broken. That was the funny thing, the mirror should have been broken, should have shattered. It wasn't even cracked. Another time there was an, erm... there was a picture fell on top of one of me sisters – I'm not sure which one it was, to be honest. And the glass was shattered all over the bed. That could have been a natural phenomenon. There was... Frankly the most frightening thing I recall was, there was about ten people in me mam's living room one night, and this must have been a good couple of years after we found the heads, I would say. Definitely over a year. And she had some little coloured bottles.

[*He indicated the size of one with his hands, about as big as a hotel shampoo sample.*]

Colin: And she had a little bric-a-brac on the wall, and there was about four or five of them. And I'd seen this with me own eyes, and everyone else witnessed it –they actually jumped off one wall. They didn't just fall onto the floor, they actually jumped off one wall and hit the other wall. And I'll never forget that as long as I live. I've seen that. I know there's something out there, I know there was something strange about these heads, because I've seen that with my own eyes and I'll never, ever forget it, even though I was a young boy. I seen it go from one wall to the other – it's like something you see in a film. And I seen it with me own eyes, and it was unbelievable.

Paul: So you reckon it was a poltergeist infestation of some sort?

Colin: Well, something like that. All I can say is we never seen anything in the house, we never had any strange events happening until we took the heads in the house.

Paul: Can I just go back to the abbey visit? Who did you see first, do you recall?

Colin: Hmm. We just went there and we found a local priest or whatever and he took them from us.

Paul: You see, a woman called Betty Gibson got in touch with me – have you ever heard of her? [*Colin shook his head.*] She told me that you saw a verger, who took them from you, passed them to her...

Colin: Well, this could be right, could be right.

Paul: ...who kept them in her house for two to three weeks, then passed them to Professor Charles Bailey, who was teaching her at evening class in Hexham. He then passed them to the Newcastle Museum of Antiquities, where they were displayed.

Colin: As far as I'm aware, you know, they were in the Newcastle Museum of Antiquities for a while, but that was after we had them back from the abbey, as far as I'm aware.

Paul: So they came back from the abbey... er, three or four days later?

Colin: The thing is, as I recall, after the heads were found and all this nonsense started going on, I was visiting – I opened the door to find ITV, I think it was *Look North* at the time? Peter Moth was one of them, and they interviewed us, and they interviewed me – I'd love to see the archives of it, because it would be such a laugh! And I was standing there, this little boy with me parka coat on, and I actually had the head that I'd made. Everybody always wondered why I made it, and I don't know why I made it, but I made it for –

Here I interrupted to find out more about the TV interview

Colin: I was nervous. He then took the heads away and that's the last I seen of the original heads. Peter Moth took the heads away and we heard they were at the Newcastle Museum of Antiquities.

Paul: So this business of what Betty Gibson told me...

Colin: I just can't understand why anybody would have them in their house: I took them to the abbey and I remember me and me brother both went down to the Abbey and they had them in a glass display cabinet for a few days.

Paul: Oh, in the Abbey?

Colin: In Hexham Abbey itself. That's where we took them and that's where they were.

Left baffled, I moved the conversation on to the head Colin sculpted at school.

Colin: What happened was, we were all at school, and we were asked to make a clay pot sort of thing. I made a clay head, that's all that happened. I made a head and it wasn't long, within six weeks of making the head and bringing it in from school, that I found the Hexham Heads.

Paul: Did you feel, when you made the head at school – 'cause I remember when we had the conversation about it, you said it came second in a competition, and the master who was judging it said something about, "It's a horrible thing..." Can you think back to why, if other people were making pots and things, you thought that a head was the better thing you could do?

Colin: I don't know. I just started off with a bit of clay I'd never done clay stuff, but I'd imagine everyone starts off rolling it into a ball to start with. And I just made this head. But it was the way it turned out; when I found the heads it was just so uncanny as to how it looked, especially the female one. Which was strange. But that's as far as I can say. I don't know why I made the head and I don't know why I made it the style I did.

Paul: You do know where the head is now, don't you?

Colin: I don't. I would love to see it again, but I don't know where it is.

Paul: Er, I've got it.

Colin: Have you? Oh, right!

Paul: You gave it to me.

Colin: What, when I was very young? Oh, right!

Paul: When I met you in 1977, I was completely taken aback when I was talking to you about it, you said, "Do you want it?" I said, "Yes, I'd love to." And you went in the house and you brought it out and you gave it to me.

I then turned to strange tales associated with the garden following the Heads discovery.

Paul: Can we talk about the garden? The budgie Sparky who seemed to sort of pass away during this business, the strange flower in the garden, and the light above it. Also if there was any sounds of babies crying can you sort of add that into it. So my question is, as well as what went on in the house, there were strange things going on in the garden at this time, weren't there, Colin?

Colin: Well, what I can remember is, I know not long after we dug the heads up this flower appeared, and it would be almost luminous. It was almost as if there was a spotlight on it. When you went out – there was no light there, you couldn't see the flower. When you went back indoors, when you looked outdoors, it looked like this flower was glowing somehow. Now, strange... there was strange noises coming out from the back garden and it sounded something like... you know, it could have been a cat, I don't know. But it sounded like a baby crying. We used to get that kind of stuff.

Paul: How long did it go on for, this sound sort of like a baby crying?

Colin: This went on for years, not just weeks. We never heard those noises before we found the heads. It was just a normal run of the street – you know, run-of-the-mill street. The most you would hear was the odd argument up the street when someone was drunk or whatever. But I was a young boy. And my opinion was that there was something unearthly the day we unearthed the heads, rather than just the heads. That's my opinion.

Paul: I've read both the articles Myles Hodnett wrote in *Tynedale Life* – and met him – he quotes you as saying that there had been a Celtic burial ground at Rede Avenue. Can you tell me who told you?

Colin: Ah... I believe it was somebody from the University of er... Antiquities, I think. Definitely somebody who was in the house one day, somebody to do with, you know...

Paul: Ah yes, I heard this about a visit from somebody from the university. What was the purpose of that visit?

Colin: I think it's when the heads were actually in there, I think they came to see us, because I think that was the first instance of us seeing this Dr. Anne Ross, who was the next person who wanted to look at the heads. And I think they'd been in touch with her or whatever, and she wanted to look at them herself, and that was the next stage.

Paul: That was another thing I'd like to establish. Did Anne Ross – she said she thought there might have been a shrine at Rede Avenue, and that she would like to visit it. Did she ever actually physically visit it?

Colin: As far as I know she did actually come to my house, yes. I don't think I was actually in at the time, but I do think she came to the house. I believe – I believe that's what my mam said, that she did arrive one day.

Paul: Did she speak to Ellen Dodd as well, do you know?

Colin: I believe she did, yes. I might be wrong.

Paul: Moving on a bit – when all this was going on in the house, I mean, it must have been very scary. Was there ever any talk about exorcism in the family?

Colin: No. But me mum did, I think, get the local priest from the Abbey to come up and bless the house. He came up and he blessed it. And I know Mrs. Dodd next door got her... they were Catholics and we were Protestants, and they got their house exorcised.

Paul: I heard from one of the accounts that the person who did the blessing at your house, even though Mr. Dodd I know was a Protestant, I know Nellie was a Catholic and the children were brought up as Catholics, but she allowed the clergyman who did it at number three to also do it at number one. Is this – do you remember that?

Colin: No, no, I don't remember that.

Paul: This one, this is one of the accounts where I've got no reason to doubt that.

Colin: I don't know. Probably. Sounds possible.

I then mentioned the werewolf described by Anne Ross and family members.

Colin: Personally, I don't believe in werewolves. I would think that it's one of the stupidest things you could ever believe in, in my opinion. All that I'm saying is that I witnessed things with me own eyes in Rede Avenue, which... I'm not surprised she saw something in her house. Now, Mrs. Dodd saw the same sort of thing, obviously. And I heard the screams, and I saw the state of the woman and her daughter after it happened. And there was – you know, there was no other reason for it. So it was pretty obvious that she had seen something horrible. So did this Dr. Anne Ross. I personally never seen this sort of a wolf figure. All I seen was things moving around in the house, and things getting turned on and really strange – you know, strange sort of things. But I never seen anything like that. I'm not to say that she didn't see it. All I say is that I do believe she had our heads in her own house at the time, so I do believe something would have happened. I do believe there'll be stuff that'll happen wherever the heads are now. You know, the heads are my property, but I wouldn't want them back in the house. I take a lot of frightening. But those things... I really wouldn't want to sleep in the same room as those two things!

Here I told Colin I'd had no trouble sleeping in the same room as his and Des's head. I also mentioned Dom Robert's blessing and my visit to the Craigie home. Colin said he wished I had brought Des's head with me for comparison. I explained I had travelled with some trepidation that as his mother had claimed I promised to return Colin's head, I had erred on the side of caution and left both at home. Another point raised was the family move from June Crescent to Rede Avenue was simply it had three and not two bedrooms.

Paul: Right then, the Heads were in Southampton and Anne Ross wanted them out.

Colin: That's what we were told.

Paul: And they came back to Newcastle. Now, I'm told that arrangements were made by a Dr. Smith there to return them, and they were returned to your family. They were then...

Colin: No, that's not true. The heads... from Peter Moth taking them away from our house, they've never ever been back to our house.

Paul: But...
Colin: That is stonewalled [*sic*] fact.

Paul: But I have a cutting that said when they were returned to your mother she loaned them to someone called George Watson.

Colin: No.

Paul: Part of your family, I think, George Watson.

Colin: I've got an uncle called George Watson, that's who they'll be talking about. Me mother's brother, who's passed away now as well, they were never ever loaned to my uncle George.

Paul: You see, there was – there was a piece in the paper that said that George Watson had them, that his wife took exception to them because there was a strange smell in the house, that they were returned to your mother, and your mother's quoted in this story – now, if I... [had thought] there was going to be an argument about that I would have brought it...

Colin: Okay. I'm not going to argue about that. If that happened I don't know nothing about that. As far as I'm aware the heads were never brought back to the house. After Peter Moth took them, they went from here to there to the other one, but they never came back here. Me uncle Geordie, he lived in Cheshire, it's been sixteen years since I went down there, to be honest.

Paul: It said he was in Allen Drive, and he...

Colin: No, he never...

Paul: ..your mother was quoted in this story as saying she didn't want them but she would bury them in the place the lads had found them.

Colin: Well, the only George Watson in my family is me <u>U</u>ncle George. We used to call him Uncle Geordie. He's lived in Cheshire ever since he met his wife, who he met in the war. He was actually on the beaches in Dunkirk. And later on, after getting out of the war he became a policeman in Cheshire, and that's where he lived all his life until he died. He never lived on Allen Drive. So I'm a bit mystified by that one.

Paul: Well, the way I see it is that George Watson had them three or four days, and we've tried... I've left notes, I've knocked on the door... she doesn't want anything to do... Doreen Turner, who's George Watson's daughter in Allen Drive, is that correct?

Colin: Oh, you're talking about... I see where you're coming from now. You're not talking about me Uncle George here. You're talking about... there was a George Watson, he had a daughter called Doreen...

Paul: His wife was called Doreen as well?

Colin: I believe she was, yes. But they never ever had anything to do with them heads. I don't know where that's come from, because they weren't part of our family. They weren't related to us. I don't know why they would ever have the heads, quite honestly. Seems a bit strange, because they were just someone who lived at the end of our street. I don't see why they would want them. Unless it's something that I've never ever heard of – knowing my father, whether he said to George, "Have 'em in your house for a couple of days, see if anything happens!" I don't know. Certainly I've never been told anything about that.

Paul: Well – heh! – I know that journalists can make a hell of a mess of stories in the paper, so I'm not going to argue with you about that...

Colin: I don't believe it's worth you looking into that bit because I don't believe there's any truth to that at all. As I have stated right the way through me interview here, I was a small boy when it happened. Now obviously I wouldn't be told everything that was going on among the adults as far as the heads were concerned. But as far as I'm aware, and me mother's never said anything to the contrary over the years when we talked about the heads, from Peter Moth getting the heads I've always been told that we never ever seen them again. That's what I've been told. I know I certainly haven't.

Paul: So as far as you're concerned they went to the museum, and if they sent them down... they were obviously in Southampton. As far as you're concerned they might never have left Southampton? You see, the bit I'm coming to is that...

Colin: The last I heard is that they were in Southampton. That's the last I ever heard of the heads.

Next I briefly brought Colin up to date with how Don Robins took custodianship of the Heads and then moved on to an area with which Colin had some involvement and strong opinions, Des Craigie and his challenge to the Celtic origin of the Heads.

Colin: I've always believed that he was a liar for the simple reason that... I mean, there was television coverage, there was a lot of newspaper coverage at the time, I mean, I was a young lad at the time but from where I was sitting it just looked like he thought there was gonna be something in it and he wanted to get his finger in the pie. Personally, that's what I think. I can't see why anyone would make a horrible stone effigy like that for their three-year-old or four-year-old child or whatever she was or he was, to play with. It just doesn't make any sense. I don't think it ever will make any sense to me. I don't believe that he made them, that's probably why I called him a liar, because I think he is a liar. And I'll always say that.

Paul: You're not alone...

Colin: I don't think he ever got anything out of it. I've never got anything out of it apart from years of people coming asking me where I found them, sort of thing! I've got nothing against him, but I think that's why he first said it, though. And I think once he'd said it he couldn't back down from what he'd said..

Paul: I've done a bit of background and he was a hell of a prankster.

Colin: Yeah, from what I've heard. But personally if it had been the other way round and Mr Craigie had found them and I was the man who'd made them, say, for instance, I think I'd have gone round and spoke to Mr Craigie myself. Do you know what I mean? I wouldn't have went to the papers and said "That's a load of rubbish because I made them, blah-de-blah". You know, we all sort of knew each other in Hexham. I didn't know Mr. Craigie very well, I knew his father better than him, before him. We used to call him Old Mr. Craigie. And he was a very pleasant, very nice old man. Personally, had it been me, as I said, I'd have went to Desmond Craigie and said, "Look, these heads that all the fuss is about? I actually made them." You know? I think that's the way I'd have come across. And I think, personally, that if he had made them, that's the way he'd have came to me. Never understood that.

Paul: And also he made them for his daughter Nancy to play with, she put bits of – or so he said - she put bits of Penguin biscuit wrappers in the eyes, but you said they were buried two foot down. I mean, that garden had to have been dug over and dug over by his father, it had to have been. He grew leeks!

Colin: It had to have been, because when we moved in... I mean, from what I recall, when we moved in that house there was roses in the back garden. There was a border round and you could always see it had been looked after, I remember Old Mr. Craigie used to love his garden. He was never out of the garden. He would have found those heads, you know what I mean? He had to. He was for always digging his garden, and weeding, and cutting his grass, and god knows what. He had a marvellous garden.

Paul: Yeah, but how did you find the heads, then? I mean, if he'd been digging all these holes and that sort of thing, how did you find them?

Colin: I don't know. It's either luck or fate or whatever you want to call it, but I dug –maybe I dug deeper than he ever dug, and I found the heads, and that's it. But like I say, it definitely had to be eighteen inches to two foot down, what I dug for the first one, and the other once was maybe six inches below that. So they weren't actually on the surface, you know? So it's quite possible that he's dug over the top of them many a time when he's been turning his garden over. I don't know. All I know is that I found them and we're sitting here talking about it!

Paul: Right! While you had the heads, we know Nellie Dodd touched them. Did you show anybody else them, around the estate? Neighbours?

Colin: No. No, we didn't take them to the houses or anything. One or two of the neighbours came in to look at them while they were in our house, whether they handled them or not, I don't know.

Paul: Now then, I heard a fascinating story to do with the slaughterhouse. A man called Barry Scott, do you know him, by any chance?

Colin: I do know him. Lot of years since I've seen him, but I do know him.

Paul: Barry Scott rang me up after I had a piece in the *Courant* asking for information. And he said that what he reckoned happened was that on the night of the weresheep incident, Nellie Dodd looked out of the window...   [*Colin starts creasing up.*]   ...saw one of the naughty lads going up the road who had been over the wall in the slaughterhouse who had pinched a carcass of a sheep, and the sheep was on his back...   [*Colin is now laughing out loud.*]   ...so this hybrid creature of a man and sheep was somebody walking up the road with a dead sheep on his back. Would you like to comment, perhaps?

Colin: Well, you know, very interesting tale, I suppose. But absolutely rubbish, because she seen the weresheep or whatever you like to call it in her bedroom. So that obviously cannot be true. But yes, very well-thought-out.

I explained that Barry swore it happened and the thief was a 73-year-old well known to him. Colin continued to pour scorn on the scenario.

Colin: Nellie Dodd and her family were a bit like me and my family at the time, we were very streetwise. It wasn't a horrible place to live. We were all good friends. Believe me, if we'd have saw anything like that gannin' up the street, we would have laughed. We certainly wouldn't have screamed like Nellie and them did. You know, this thing was actually in her bedroom, as she told us.

Paul: Was Nellie working? I'm asking because Marie, the child, was ill, if she'd had a hard day at work she might have been stressed.

Colin: I believe Nellie worked at the time. I don't know where, but I don't think she worked long hours. And I'm sure that day she'd been home with Marie. I mean, as far as I'm aware. I think Marie got sent home from school at the time, as I remember.

Paul: On the night when this incident happened next door, Brian and Sylvia told me that it was a particularly wretched night, and the windows had blown open and all that. Can you remember if it was a particularly stormy night?

Colin: I honestly don't recall that. I just remember waking up, being a young boy, and hearing me mam and dad saying there's something wrong next door and hearing all the screams. Yeah, I think it was windy, but it wasn't particularly cold out. I have heard my mother quoted as saying she heard a crash before the screams, but I just remember speaking to Nellie, who was the salt of the earth, she wasn't the type to make things up. And I just remember seeing her face, and seeing the little one's face, and I knew that they'd seen something. And it wasn't nice. You know, that's my total opinion of it.

Here I have deleted Colin's confirmation that the Dodds's dog and Robsons's budgie died shortly after the weresheep incident, but he put these down to natural causes, although confirming the luminous flower was over where Sparky was buried. I then raised the apparitional weresheep in the slaughterhouse and high staff turnover, neither aspects of which Colin was aware, but led to information to bolster the genius loci interpretation.

Colin: I certainly wouldn't have wanted to work there. I can imagine it would be quite eerie. But really I think the whole area around Rede Avenue, right up to the end of my street, there was quite a few reports of people seeing things in their house. It wasn't just us and it wasn't just Nellie next door, my mam told me there was quite a few people down that street that she said had seen some things moving themselves.

Paul: Was this before or after you found the heads?

Colin: No, this all came to light after we found those heads, as I recall.

Paul: Right, I think we've just about, er... you've no idea where the heads are now...

Colin: No.

Paul: You wouldn't like them back, but you'd like to... take on the ownership, shall we say?

Colin: I would like to know where they are. I would like to know who's got them for the simple reason that I don't believe they're theirs to have. That's the truth of the matter. I'm not saying I want them. If, y'kna... in my opinion I own the heads and I should be able to say, "Put them in a museum", if they want them in a museum. I should make that choice. It shouldn't be whoever's got them now, because whoever's got them has the heads illegally because they were never ever given to anybody. They were passed from pillar to post. From a personal point of view, this has been going on since I was eleven year old. I'm 52 years old. Isn't it about time some more tests were done on it or something like that? To find out [if] this story about Mr Craigie making them, did he make them? I don't believe he did make them, but wouldn't it be nice to have a proper test done to find out if he did make them? Why is all this stuff still carrying on? I don't know.

Paul: Nigel Craigie reckons they're his property, because his father made them.

Colin: Well, this just proves what I said earlier. When he made them, which I don't believe he did, personally I believe he thought something'd come out of it. He was always going to say they were his property if he made them.

Paul: Do you think they'll ever be found?

Colin: I'm beginning to think they won't. I just... like I say, it's been a lot of years and they've been passed around, and you hear all these tales of where they are and where they were – you find out where they were, briefly, but you never find out where they are now. I don't know what can be done about it to find them, where they are, to be honest. All you can do is ask, and there's never any answers, is there?

This Herculean transcription by Graham has already been condensed and paraphrased by half from almost 12,000 words, but forms an essential document despite the challenges to previous material with its insights and corrections.

CHAPTER 21
WHEREABOUTS OF THE HEXHAM HEADS?

No reader will by this stage be surprised to learn that my best efforts and those of many fellow researchers have failed completely to discover the current whereabouts of the Hexham Heads. Their location is as mysterious as that of the Ark of the Covenant or the gold plates which spawned the Church of Latter Day Saints. A more secular but equally strange missing object fell from the sky on Silpho Moor in 1957, and similarly to the script which inspired Mormon founder Joseph Smith, when decoded the hieroglyphs in the flying saucer-shaped object which dropped from the North Yorkshire sky also had a message, warning mankind to mend its ways. [1] I became fascinated by this tale and began the task of tracking down this object, supposedly of extraterrestrial provenance (the writers of the hieroglyphics deliberately chose not to reveal their origin), although mindful it was almost certainly a hoax, but a very expensive and elaborate one to carry off. My efforts were quickly hampered when viewing microfilm of the *Yorkshire Post* and *Leeds Mercury* at Leeds Central Library and finding the relevant 'very good coverage', as writer David Tansley described it, from the edition of 9 December 1957 absent. My inquiries produced three separate leads - an unidentified solicitor's office safe, and unnamed Scarborough fish and chip shop and an anonymous Hull scrap metal dealer – all of which proved dead ends. Similarly, Dave Clarke told me those locations sounded familiar to the time when he also tried to follow the Silpho Moor spoor without success.

From misty, boggy Silpho Moor and its mystery, the Hexham Heads were last heard of in multicultural Kilburn, an area of N.-W. London bisected by the Celtic route which became Watling Street and is now the A5. Presuming Frank Hyde (see Chapter Eight), then the Heads custodian and a Kilburn resident, to have died and wishing to contact his closest relations, I wrote to the Kilburn Times requesting it print an appeal and outlining the lurid story. As there has been no response, I presume my efforts were spiked.

So, as with the Silpho Moor object, the Heads seem to have gone the way of many a fortean artefact – missing, presumed lost. Over the years I have heard and come across many fanciful suggestions as to the Heads whereabouts, ranging from the plausible to the ludicrous or banal. All have been followed up to no avail. Here are the candidates and the realities:

- **Don Robins** would seem as noted earlier to have washed his hand of the affair following Frank Hyde's 'intervention and subsequent disappearance'.
- **Paul Devereux** photographed the Heads at Robins' home (echoes of Des Craigie at the sink, this was in the kitchen!). A postcard dated 29 April 1997 offering encouragement for my brave self-employment move included this, 'I don't know where the heads are now (though last I heard

they were <u>back home up North</u>). Ross hasn't got them and is very touchy about it all'.

- **Dr David Clarke** was involved with Paul Devereux on a couple of projects and I jokingly asked during the filmed interview if he had the Heads. "Not that I've noticed, no!", he replied, adding, "Although I do have several other stone heads". He also mentioned Robins and Ross: "... I do remember what she said about the Hexham heads, that she claimed – I'm pretty sure about this – that she had no idea about where they were at that time, when we were talking in 1994, because I was pressing her on that. I was like you, I wanted to know where they are now. And she was very, very clear that she didn't know. The last person that had any contact with them from what she could remember was Don Robins'.

- **David Sutton**, editor of *Fortean Times*, publishes columns by both Devereux and Clarke and occasional articles by Mike Hallowell, who in conversation tipped me off that he had heard that someone at *F.T.* had the Heads, specifically mentioning both Sutton and contributor Ian Simmons, a professional exhibitions curator (founding editor Bob Rickard having launched an abortive bid to set up a fortean museum some years ago, which could have had some bearing on the rumour). Sutton eventually responded with, 'No, we haven't got them I'm afraid – good to let you stew for a bit though'.

- **Nick Redfern**, another regular *F.T.* contributor, told me he had heard from someone (probably from a shadowy Midlands character who had compiled a Hexham Heads file brimming with misinformation called Paul Slattery) that they were definitely in the hands of a collector.

- **Chris Wild(e)** was a collector who visited Anne Ross with carved examples in his car and is the only serious private individual amassing them known to me, but others may well exist.

- **Richard Charles Feachem** described his as "wild by name, Wild(e) by nature" and suspected the Heads could have appeared anonymously on eBay.

- **Frank Hyde**'s executors might well have though the Hexham Heads worth a punt on eBay or they have more likely end up in a skip and as you read this are creating mischief and mayhem at some landfill site.

- **Peter Moth** grilled Dr Ross back in 1972 and in Graham's 2011 filmed interview commented, "I'd definitely like to know if they turn up, but I suspect they're either in Anne Ross's effects or in the depths of Southampton University".

- **Lindsay Allason-Jones** was filmed earlier the same day but I was the interviewer, plus she worked for a university and ran a museum. You don't need to be Poirot to note that the previous people were all connected and I had thought the network of which I am a part – most are personal friends – would have produced some solid lead, but the heads seem to have (so far) evaded the six degrees of separation notion (highlighted in the 1993 film of that name starring Will Smith). A Milan University study of 721 million users like myself of Facebook found that 92% were even four acquaintances away from knowing each other. [2] Yet I have appealed several times for anyone with the Hexham Heads or knowledge of their whereabouts to come forward without success. Asking Lindsay if she could give me a clue as to where I should be seeking, I was following in the footsteps of many other journalists:

> "I have no idea. If [Professor Hodson] was sent the heads again, or sent other heads, they were not sent through the museum. We have quite clear indications that they were sent back to the Robson family... But I think what is interesting is that over the thirty years I was in the museum there was a regular correspondence, either phone, letter or later e-mail from journalists wanting to know "where are the Hexham heads?" And it was usually under the title of "Unsolved Mysteries" or something like that. And I used to say, "We don't have the heads, but we do have the analysis of the heads which shows they were made of con-

crete". And at that point they usually put the phone down, because they didn't want to know that! But I have never seen the heads – nobody ever brought the heads in to me again, nobody ever called me and said they'd found them, or if you're looking for them you'll find them in such-and-such a place".' [3]

Finders, keepers?

Whereabouts is one thing, but if the Heads ever do resurface, the next stage could be a battle over ownership. The Robson boys Colin and Leslie dug them up and earlier this year Colin told me:

Paul: You've no idea where the heads are now...

Colin: No.

---

                                       great s

   HEXHAM HEADS : I have been interested in this whole story for a long while and have collated a series of study notes initially dating from 20th Feb. 1976 when Nationwide covered the bones of the story. The psychological aspects were intriguing, the potential break-up of the marriage etc. (not for quoting) – last May I spoke to Anne Ross on the telephone, I had previously received some help on Celtic dragons you see. I was naturally interested in your short 'Heads & Tales' article in L.H. 77 but is it likely that a foremost Celtic scholar could be taken in by Craigie's home-made head. (Let me quickly add that psychologically this seems to be a 'natural' thing to do. I have such a head that I made out of Portland stone in 1964, mine is more of a skull in fact. Frazer and others have written much on the subject. I understood that Don Robins was going to subject the originals to laser and other tests if and when he can track the originals. This is a very strange story for it not only originates from an authoritative source (A.R.) but contains psycho-physical aspects with singularly incongruous element of non-Celtic origin – what is one to believe? Anne Ross has been 'psychic' since child-hood, but then she is not the only one to have seen the man/animal . I could discuss the parapsychological theories, but after all they are still theories however cleverly constructed. What then? Nigel Neal's Stone-Tape theory, but that was fiction wasn't it, or was it? The stone-tape theory is an interesting cop-out. Do you think the psycho-physical results could be reproduced in a physics lab ? No, we appear to be dealing with something deeper than image storage, I think you will agree. I wonder if you found anything of significance at Hexham as a place, for as you will know Hexe is the German root for witch. Sir Walter Scott in "Letters on Demonology & Witchcraft" 1830 writes " It was no unusual thing to see females,from respect to their supposed views into futurity, and the degree of divine inspiration which was vouchsafed to them, arise to the degree of HAXA, or chief priestess, from which comes the word Hexe, now universally used for witch. It may be worthwhile to notice the word Haxa is still used in Scotland in its sense of a druidess,or chief priestess, to distinguish the places where such females exercised their ritual......." The church at Hexham as you may have seen, contains a St. George & Dragon made by local masons and housed in Prior Leschman's 15th C. chantry. Whatever the Hexham heads are, with such accounts given of the man/animal which so disturbed Anne Ross , her daughter and others (incidentally the the husband never saw it), we are left with a lot of explaining to do , especially when the 'manifestations' continued after the heads had been removed. Anne Ross seemed to think that her other Celtic heads had been activated and as you know after she had had the exorcists in,the collection was removed. The whole thing would seem to be a variation on a theme of haunting but there is a glaringly obvious link in all this which I admit was not discovered by me but also is something perhaps too important to be left.

Paul: You wouldn't like them back, but you'd like to take on the ownership, shall we say?

Colin: I would like to know where they are. I would like to know who's got them, because... for the simple reason that I don't believe they're theirs to have. That's the truth of the matter. I'm not saying I want them. If, y'kna... in my opinion I own the heads and I should be able to say, "Put them in a museum", if they want them in a museum. I should make that choice. It shouldn't be whoever's got them now, because whoever's got them now has the heads illegally because they were never ever given to anybody. They were passed from pillar to post. But it's not just that. Personally, from a personal point of view, this has been going on since I was eleven year old. I'm 52 years old. Isn't it about time some more tests were done on it or something like that? You know what I mean? To find out... you know, this story about Mr. Craigie making them, did he make them? Did he make them personally – you've heard my point of view, that I don't believe he did make them, but wouldn't it be nice to have a proper test done to find out if he did make them? If he did make them, why is all this stuff still carrying on? I don't know.

Paul: Nigel Craigie reckons they're his property, because his father made them.

Colin: Well, this is just... this proves what I said earlier. When he made them, which I don't believe he did, personally I believe he thought something'd come out of it. He was always going to say they were his property if he made them.

Paul: Do you think they'll ever be found?

Colin: I'm beginning to think they won't. I just... like I say, it's been a lot of years and they've been passed around, and you hear all these tales of where they are and where they were – you find out where they were, briefly, but you never find out where they are now. I don't know what can be done about it to find them to be honest. All you can do is ask, and there's never any answers, is there?

Paul: Nope! It's one of these facts, anything which is supernatural, which is paranormal, even which is controversial, they tend to disappear. [4]

When I interviewed his sister Judith in 2011 she was equally adamant, telling me in no uncertain terms, "They're our property. They were leant, not given".

But **if** they were made by Des Craigie might not the family have a legitimate interest? Son Nigel thinks so, "My sister has the claim". So that puts Nancy in the equation.

But perhaps as they were found on Tynedale District Council property they would rightly belong to the council? One thing's for sure, only m'learned friends are the sure-fire winners **if** the Heads ever turn up!

CHAPTER TWENTY-TWO
TEMORARY LIKE ACHILLES
(A SUMMING-UP)

'There is a fictional coloration to everybody's account of an "actual occurrence", and there is at least the lurk somewhere of what is called the "actual" in everybody's yarn'. – Charles Fort

Having first become aware of the Hexham Heads mystery forty years ago and becoming personally involved from 1977 onwards it is still a **mystery** to me. Countless hours of research, contemplation and discussion with experts, witnesses and my close associates – Stu, Graham and Olly – have led to some tentative conclusions. In fact, with the same shared information even the latter trio have different opinions on the events and evaluation. My own deliberations have always been transitory and to quote the character Horselover Fats in the brilliant *VALIS* by Philip K Dick, 'Every day he developed a new one [theory], more cunning, more exciting, more fucked'.

So, reader, doubtless you have your own opinions after reading what I trust is a fulsome digest of the available facts in this 'cold case'. In true fortean fashion I present my thoughts , for what they're worth.

The Heads themselves. My dilemma here has been a conflict between myself as the antiquarian who espoused leys (aka ley-lines) and wants to see the Hexham Heads vindicated as Romano-British era artefacts and on the other the folklorist who loves to see an archaeologist squirm and geologists arguing over a rampant example of ostension, whereby a cult from another age impinges on the modern day to create an anachronistic replica which creates such amusing division and diversion. The Heads could be ancient; they could be modern. My own opinion has swung like a pendulum and there's no shame in admitting caution. I have provided plenty of Celtic background for consideration, but equally I have allowed rein for those with a preference for a modernist creation. Yet there's no denying those artefacts' provenance was essentially irrelevant to the mayhem and mystery they caused. Essentially they belong to **myth**.

Genius loci / shrine? Anne Ross posited a likely shrine where the Heads were (re?)discovered. I concur. That's one weird location.

Anne Ross. Personal experience has taught me to be wary of 'experts', but Doctor Ross believed the Heads were ancient and there could be evidence of a shrine. Under pressure and some dodgy petrological analyses she wavered and conceded doubt. All to her credit. I may have been guilty of prying into her personal life, but it was not for vicarious reasons but an attempt to get a rounded picture and see if her personality and family life had any significant bearing on the events. Hence I have concluded she has suffered psychic backlash.

Desmond Craigie. By devoting a whole chapter to consider prankster Des as also performing the role of trickster, it can be assumed I prefer the Romano-British (Celtic) origination for the Heads. Logically his claim appears plausible, but his hoaxing antics make me sceptical. Having met the man and liking him, I take no pleasure in casting doubts on his veracity.

Weresheep and werewolf. If the creation of the Heads lies essentially in the realms of myth and dating is essentially irrelevant, I've also proven to my own satisfaction the resulting weirdness lies not in by whom or when they were created but what the human mind projects into the mystery and reacts to what is reflected. Consequently the zooform element also responds to this personal input with a rural woman witnessing a man-headed sheep and an urban family surrounded by Celtiana haunted by a wolf-headed man, thus endorsing the deck of cards theory for paraphysical entities.

Nor should the bizarre thread regarding sheep stealing be ignored. Whether Nellie Dodd was psychologically influenced by seeing a man carrying a carcass on his back in the middle of the night, I found flimsy circumstantial evidence of a creature or haunting by a weresheep in the nearby slaughterhouse and to cap it all a 500-year-old wood carving of a sheep-stealer in Hexham Abbey. More than coincidence? Oh, and my family's mythology includes a Yorkshire long-deceased ancestor from Castle Bolton who was hanged – as a sheep-stealer.

Whereabouts? Essentially this has been the **Quest for the Hexham Heads**. My personal quest has been to solve the mystery and the finding of the Heads would have been a bonus. Stu, Graham, Olly and I still have a few leads to follow so all is not lost on either count, and hopefully publication of this book will bring forth further information and informed speculation.

As for the gruesome twosome themselves, some think it preferable they are now in some placeless void of their own making. I agree. But the journalist in me needs to know just where. If you know…

---/---

It's human to rationalise, but maybe that's our Achilles' heel. We fail to see the larger picture. For every inclusionist like me there's a thousand separatists/specialists. Yet, I suspect, even I have failed to see the full and true picture.

As Bob Dylan sang:

And the princess and the prince
Discuss what's real and what is not'.

There are no answers outside the Gates of Eden.

CHAPTER TWENTY-THREE
POSTSCRIPT / APPENDIX

Following my telephone conversation with Richard Charley Feachem, son of Dr Anne Ross and Richard 'Dick' Feachem, we had a brief correspondence between 21 and 23 April 2011. I have appended it here as a tribute to his mother in her declining years. It is basically a question and answer affair with me beginning by asking:

Paul: Regarding Hexham Heads, I'm particularly interested in <u>the nature and behaviour of the creature</u>. * The red eyes: did they 'glow' and perhaps bulge? * Any colour to it? Dr Don Robins mentioned black.* Did you see it just the once? * Was there ever any detectable smell associated with the creature? Either, perhaps,'earthy' or 'pungent/sulphuric'? * Were there any physical traces? Scratch marks, soil on carpet, excrement? * Was there an aura of evil when it appeared?

Richard: Hi Paul, I'll answer what questions I can. The eyes of the wolf-type thing glowed red. It was black in colour. I saw it once. That's all I remember!

Paul: Which leads me to the <u>exorcism</u>. * In 1977, I was in Hexham and met both lads who found the Heads and Des Craigie who claimed to have made them before a scheduled meeting in Wall with leading exorcist Dom Robert Petitpierre. Your mother mentions a Father Harrison, also a deliverance expert who came to your house with your local vicar (do you recall his name). Was the exorcism effective?

Richard: As for the Exorcism I have no memory at all of any of that.

Paul: Should I assume your mother only studied paganism in a Celtic context and was not a practising pagan?

Richard: Yes, my mother only studied paganism, she did not practise it ever.

Paul: I have a transcript of an interview your mother gave to David Clarke when he was researching *Twilight of the Celtic Gods* where she mentions 'the two children,' yet Peter Underwood, in his autobiography refers to a younger daughter than Berenice (correct spelling? Jenny Randles writes Bernice in *Mind Monsters*), who saw the creature and dropped a tray on the stairs as both had been to collect it together from your sick father. What's her name, sister or step-sister, birthdate and could I contact her? As for Berenice was she from a previous marriage of your mother or father? It's inherited psychism I'm wondering about. If it's not to personal might I inquire how she died and whether it could have any connection, however tenuous?

Richard: The only childen were me and my step sister Berenice, there are no other children. Berenice was from a previous marriage of my mother. Berenice died of a blood clot on her brain after a heavy fall.

Paul: Your mother also told David Clarke the family normally didn't talk about the experience, but that you "told us things which we had totally forgotten." Does anything strike you as valid which might be relevant to my inquiry? Some small detail, perhaps, which might be a vital clue?

Richard: The only thing I remember is what I have already told you about, waking to see this thing standing with the hall light behind it in the doorway of my bedroom. It was stooped, a humanoid shape, pointed ears and glowing, *narrow* red eyes, I screamed and it turned and jumped over the landing banisters and that is all the memory I have of that experience, although out of the 23 years I lived in Southampton that is the most vivid of my memories. I can not remember any other detail at all, as far as smell etc, I was young, terrified and until your friend contacted my mum via letter I had not thought about it since then.

Paul: An intriguing gem from her interview revealed - "I've had experiences with supernatural wolves myself when I was a child, so whether that's valid I don't know." Sounds so to me - a vital factor, perhaps - at least more than coincidental. Did she ever elucidate further on this?

Richard: My mother has never mentioned anything to do with wolves as a child but then I know very little of my mothers' childhood as I never asked her, too late now as the memories would not be accurate anymore.

Paul: Your mother mentioned the "Hexham thing" and presumed it was the same. Actually, it wasn't. I spent three hours interviewing two of the children of Nellie Dodd (the one witness in Hexham), one of whom was awake but hid under the bedclothes and they were insistent what their mother described was half-man/half-sheep. The Press seem to have baulked quickly at this hybrid and switched the description to werewolf (weresheep just doesn't fit any mental stereotype!) for dramatic artistic licence's effect. That's an observation not a question, though I assume there was nothing sheeplike whatever about what was going on in Southampton?

Richard: WereSheep, that's a good one! No, this thing did not resemble any kind of sheep I've ever seen, even if a sheep stood on its hind legs it could not look like the thing I saw!

Paul: Almost finished! Out of interest, may I ask what your profession is? Can in have your birthdate?

Richard: Before caring for my mum full time I was a gardener, my birthdate is 1966.

Paul: And I hope this doesn't sound presumptuous or impudent, but to illustrate my book, would it be possible to borrow a photo of your mother - one taken preferably in the 1970s - perhaps with her and some archaic heads?

Richard: I'll see if I can find a picture of mum from those years but I might not have one, I will look and if I find one I'll scan it and email it to you.

Paul: As you can see, I'm passionate about and committed to this authorial investigation and a consummate professional. I'm a stickler for leaving no stone unturned and achieving 100% accuracy if possible. Also I want to put the record straight, particularly as so much nonsense has been published about the Hexham Heads. Your co-operation is greatly appreciated and it is a shame your mother cannot answer the questions herself or be able to enjoy a celebration of her scholarship and role in this modern mystery.

Richard: Not much help I'm sorry to say but apart from the werewolf experience I have little memory of my years in Southampton and absolutely no other memories to do with the Hexham Heads and I have sat and cast my mind back to those years but nothing comes to mind.

Have a nice weekend.

Regards, Richard

I thanked Richard and mentioned that *Fortean Times* had published a cartoon strip of the Hexham Heads mystery. [1] His reply was warm but left me with the impression that he wanted to draw a line under our correspondence. I only hope that my style of investigative journalism has not offended Richard nor any others, particularly second generation family members, who have featured in this book. Richard wrote:

Richard: Hello Paul, Whenever I think of a cartoon strip I always remember the wonderful Giles and the old grandma asleep in her deck chair and the little boy lighting a fire underneath it or some other such fun that Giles could imagine! I hope the cartoon was fair to my mum but her natural hair colour is red. It is odd that P. Underwood wrote of two sisters, I can not imagine where he got that idea from.

The problem in our modern society is making people understand that strange, unexplainable things do happen. I expect, at the time, and even perhaps now that many would believe I awoke to see an intruder standing in my doorway that night but if an intruder had jumped over the banister he/she would have fallen at least 25-30 feet and would have broken something! Memories of sound are hard to recall but I can't remember the thing making any, even when it jumped and landed somewhere downstairs there was no sound. I do, however, remember the sound of my scream!

Book jackets are probably your best bet for a good picture of mum, I did look through my collection but have none from that time.

I look forward to reading your book as I believe you will write the account of the Hexham Heads that needs to be written and hopefully many will enjoy and appreciate your hard work and the fascinating mystery of the Hexham Heads!

Best regards,

Richard

REFERENCES

CHAPTER ONE: THE FINDERS

1. Don Robins, *The Secret Language of Stone*, Rider, 1988
2. 'Eerie tale of the two idol heads', *The Journal*, 3 March 1972
3. 'Terror from the Celtic mists…', *The Evening Chronicle*, 3 March 1972
4. Nerys Dee, 'The Head Cult', *Prediction*, September, 1977
5. Myles Hodnett, 'Haunted Heads brought wolfman to the door', *Tynedale Life*, September, 2008
6. Myles Hodnett, 'Heads brought terror from the distant past', *Tynedale Life*, December, 2008

CHAPTER TWO: THE NEIGHBOURS

1. Bob Rickard, 'A Celtic Werewolf', *Fortean Times*, No. 15, 1976 (Partial *Nationwide* broadcast transcript)
2. Myles Hodnett, 'Heads brought terror from the ancient past', *Tynedale Life*, December 2008
3. 'Eerie tale of the two idol heads', *The Journal*, 3 March 1972
4. Sadie Holland, pers. comm. to David Clarke, early 1994
5. Myles Hodnett, 'Haunted Heads brought wolfman to the door', *Tyne dale Life*, September 2008
6. Don Robins, 'Images in Stone', *The Ley Hunter*, No. 76, 1976
7. Don Robins, 'The Hexham Heads', *Alpha*, No. 8, 1980

CHAPTER THREE: THE ARCHAEOLOGIST

1. 'Eerie tale of the two "idol heads"', *The Journal*, 3 March 1974
2. 'Terror from the Celtic mists…', *Evening Chronicle*, 3 March 1972
3. Kenneth Rayner Johnson, introduction, *Folklore, Myth and Legends of Britain*, Reader's Digest, 1973
4. Don Robins, 'The Hexham Heads', *Alpha*, Issue 8, 1980
5. Peter Underwood, *No Common Task: The Autobiography of a Ghost Hunter*, Harrap, 1983
6. Anne Ross, pers. comm. to Ian Wilson, 3 December 1994
7. Mary Ackroyd, 'Crossbow fiend kills kitten', *Southern Daily Echo*, 18 February 1986

CHAPTER FOUR: THE CLAIMANT

1. 'Out of the mists of 1956 . . .', *Evening Chronicle*, 6 March 1972

2. 'Heading into "grave error"', *The Journal*, 7 March 1972
3. Sydney Foxcroft, 'Myth of the "evil" heads', *Sunday People*, 13 January 1974
4. 'New twist to head puzzzle', *The Journal*, 20 March 1974
5. 'Heads – and tales – of doom', *The Journal*, 15 January 1974
6. '"Celtic" idols will be buried', *The Journal*?, n.d. 1975?

CHAPTER FIVE: THE BROADCASTER

1. Peter Moth, filmed interview with Graham Williamson, 2 December 2011
2. Peter Moth, pers. comm. to Paul Screeton, 28 November 2011

CHAPTER SIX: THE GEOLOGISTS

1. F. Hodson, 'Two Celtic (? Romano British) Stone Heads from Hexham, Northumberland. Ex Hancock Museum, Newcastle', *pers. comm.* Dr A Ross, 10 March 1972
2. Professor Frank Hodson, Appendix to 'Some New Thoughts on Old Heads', by Anne Ross, *Archaeologia Aeliana*, 5th series, Volume 1, 1972
3. 'Relics that spooked a boffin', *The Journal*, 14 January 1974
4. Anne Ross, pers. comm. to Dr David Smith, 17 February 1974
5. D A Robson, 'Report on Heads 4 and 5, from Hexham', 8 May 1974
6. 'Professor's stone heads mistake . . .', *The Journal*, n.d., but believed to be January 1975
7. 'New twist in the head puzzle', *The Journal*, 20 March 1974
8. Roger Miket, pers. comm. to Anne Ross, 29 October 1971, with cryptic addition in longhand at foot of page 'Heads sent off 25/11/71. Packed by R Miket'.
9. Jenny Robson, pers. comm. to Dr David Smith, n.d.
10. Dr David Smith, pers. comm. to Dr D A Robson, 24 May 1974
11. D J Smith, pers. comm. to Mr Craigie, 3 June 1974
12. D J Smith, pers. comm. to Mr and Mrs Robson, 25 February 1975
13. Dr D A Robson, memorandum to Dr D J Smith, 16 January 1975
14. D J Smith, pers. comm. to Mr and Mrs Robson, 25 February 1975
15. Jenny Robson, pers. comm. to D J Smith, 24 March 1975
16. D J Smith, pers. comm. to D A Robson, 7 April 1975

CHAPTER SEVEN: THE SCIENTIST

1. Anne Ross and Don Robins, *The Life and Death of a Druid Prince: The Story of Lindow Man, an Archaeological Sensation*, Rider, 1989
2. Don Robins, *Circles of Silence*, Souvenir Press, 1985
3. Don Robins, *The Secret Language of Stone*, Rider, 1988
4. Don Robins, 'The Emperor's old clothes', *Alpha*, No. 6, 1980
5. 'The Hexham Heads', *Alpha*, No. 8, 1980
6. Don Robins, 'Images in Stone', *The Ley Hunter*, Nos. 76 and 77, 1976 and 1977

CHAPTER EIGHT: THE EXPERIMENTER

1. w1.1564.telia.com/~u156400111/asmusdoc/historytimeline7.htm

2. Peter Underwood pers. comm. to David Taylor, 28 July 2011

CHAPTER NINE: THE BRAINS TRUST

1. Lindsay Allason-Jones, interviewed by Paul Screeton, Great North Museum, 2 December 2011

INTERLUDE ONE: WEREWOLVES, WULVERS & WERESHEEP

1. Jonathan Downes and Richard Freeman,'Shug Monkey and Werewolves', *Fortean Studies*, Vol. 5, 1998
2. Patrick Harpur, Daimonic Reality: A Field Guide to the Otherworld, Viking Arkana, 1994
3. Lionel Fanthorpe, *Fringe Weird Report*, www.lionel-fanthorpe.com/forum/thread505364/pg/
4. *The Paranormal Database*, various vampire and werewolf reports, www.paranormaldatabase.com
5. Sunday Mirror online, 13 January 2010
6. Tim Weinberg, 'The Specimens of Alex C.F.', *Fortean Times*, No. 283, 2012; www.alexcf.com
7. '"Werewolf" case still baffles detectives', *The Journal*, 14 February 1991
8. Jesse Saxby, *Shetland Traditional Lore*, Grant & Murray, 1932
9. Bernhardt J Hurwood, *Terror By Night*, Lancer Books (US), 1963
10. Graham McEwan, *Mysterious Animals of Britain and Ireland*, Robert Hale, 1986
11. Nick Redfern, *Three Men Seeking Monsters*, Paraview, 2004
12. My account has been adapted partly from the original collected by Montague Summers,
    The Werewolf, Kegan Paul, Trench, Trubner & Co., 1933
13. Nerys Dee, *The Head Cult*, Prediction, September, 1977
14. Nerys Dee, pers. comm. to David Clarke, 18 February 1991
15. *Unknown Creatures*, 'Unknown Creatures – Maryland Goatman',
    www.unknown-creatures.com/maryland-goatman.html
16. *Essortment*, 'The Goatman Legend of Prince George's County',
    www.essortment.com/goatman-legend-prince-georges-county-64862.html
17. Robert Curran, pers. comm., 18 March 2011
18. Austin Whitall, *Guide to Patagonia's Monsters & Mysterious Beings*, h
    http://patagoniamonsters.blogspot.com/html
19. Jonathan Downes and Richard Freeman, 'Shug Monkey and Werewolves', *Fortean Studies*, Vol. 5, 1998

CHAPTER TEN: PAGAN CELTIC
(OR ROMANO-BRITISH) TRADITIONS

1. The Call of the Celts, BBC 2, 31 October 1986
2. Jeremy Harte, 'How old is that old yew?', *At the Edge*, No. 4, n.d.;
   www.forestry.gov.uk/forestry/INFO-6UFC5F
3. *The Sunday Post*, 9 September 2007
4. Paul Devereux, 'Moot 91 – The Best Ever?', *The Ley Hunter*, No. 115, 1991
5. 'Significance of those shieling stones', *Dundee Courier*, 14 April 2000; *Folklore Frontiers*, No. 41, 2002
6. *The Scotsman*, 19 April 2011
7. David Clarke, 'Twilight of the Celtic Gods', *Northern Earth*, No. 126, 2011
8. Stan Beckensall, phone interview with Paul Screeton
9. Dr David Clarke, interview with Paul Screeton, 17 ay 2011
10. John Billingsley, interview with Graham Williamson, 2011
11. Lindsay Allason-Jones, interview with Paul Screeton, 2 December 2011

12. Paul Screeton, *Folklore Frontiers* Facebook forum, Ref. 100, 2012
13. *Private Eye*, No. 648, 17 October 1986
14. Paul Screeton, 'Catcote "dig" inspires some thoughts on the Roman occupation', *Mail*, Hartlepool, 6 April 1964; reprinted *I Fort The Lore*, CFZ Press, 2011
15. Miles Russell and Stuart Laycock, *UnRoman Britain: Exposing the Great Myth of Britannia*, The History Press, 2010
16. Anne Ross, 'Some New Thoughts on Old Stones', *Archaeologia Aeliana*, 5th Series, Vol. 1, 1973
17. Aubrey Burl, *Rites of the Gods*, J M Dent & Sons, 1981
18. Stuart Qualtrough, 'Pub Ghoul's Nasty Habit', *Daily Sport*, 21 October 1993
19. Paul Devereux, *Haunted Land*, Judy Piatkus, 2001
20. Anne Ross, 'The Divine Hag of the Pagan Celts', *The Witch Figure*, ed.: V Newall, Routledge & Kegan Paul, 1979
21. Anne Ross, *Pagan Celtic Britain*, 1967
22. I M Stead, 'The body in the bog', *The Independent*, 4 July 1989
23. Richard Morrison, 'Mud brother', *The Knowledge* (*The Times*), 12 April 2008
24. 'Ethel makes no bones about it', *Hartlepool Mail*, 9 October 1985
25. Susan Critchley, 'Skeletons reveal lovers' sad story', *Hartlepool Mail*, 5 February 1986
26. William Hunter, 'A 400AD mystery "whodunit"', *The Daily Telegraph*, 22 August 1986
27. D H Haigh, *The Anglo-Saxon Sagas*, J R Smith; internet archive, anglosaxonsagase00haighquoft

CHAPTER ELEVEN:
PSEUDO-CONTINUITY & THE ARCHAIC HEAD

1. Sidney Jackson, *Celtic and Other Stone Heads*, privately published, 1973
2, Guy Ragland Phillips, *Brigantia: A Mysteriography*, Routledge & Kegan Paul, 1976
3. John Billingsley, interviewed by Graham Williamson, 2011
4. John Billingsley, 'Celtic Survivals', *The Dalesman*, February, 1980
5. Jo Knowsley, 'Bloody trail of head hunters carved in stone', *The Sunday Telegraph*, 11 May 1997
6. Anne Ross, 'New Thoughts on Old Stones', *Archaeologia Aeliana*, Series 5, Volume 1, 1973
7. John Billingsley, *Stony Gaze*, Capall Bann, 1998
8. *Northern Earth*, No. 112, 2007
9. Judi Alston, *pers. comm.* to Paul Screeton, 1 April 2012
10. Judi Alston, *pers. comm.* to Paul Screeton, 4 April 2012
11. Paul Screeton, 'Strange Seaton Carew', *Folklore Frontiers*, No. 14, 1991; almost identical, *Northern Earth Mysteries*, No. 50, 1992
13. Marie-Louise McKay, *The Lion Roars and the Monkey Bites*, Printability Publishing, 2011
14. Paul Screeton, *Who Hung the Monkey? A Local Legend*, Printability Publishing, 1991
15. Paul Screeton, 'Strange Seaton Carew', *Folklore Frontiers*, No. 14, 1991; slightly amended, *Northern Earth Mysteries*, No. 50, 1992
16. Paul Devereux, précis of Anne Ross, 'Moot 91 – The Best Ever?', *The Ley Hunter*, No. 115, 1991
17. Jon Whitfield, pers. comm., 3 May 2011
18. Felicity Hunter, 'Gran injured in freak accident', *Hartlepool Mail*, 31 January 2012
19. John Whitley, 'Artist on the site of the angels?', *The Northern Echo*, 14 September 1996
20. 'Green Goddess or an eyesore?', *The Sunday Post*, 2 October 2011
21. chainletterauthor.blogspot.com/2010/02/interview-with-hexham-heads.html
22 *The Sun*, 21 October 2010
23. 'The Head Cult', *Prediction*, September 1977

24 'A head start for fun', *Daily Mirror*, 7 August 1993
25. *The Last Wolf*, CD, 1997
26. Charles Shepherd, 'The Significance of the Celtic Speaking Head – and Neck', *Quest*, No. 33, 1978

CHAPTER TWELVE:
CHRISTIAN CONVERSION & PAGAN SUBVERSION

1. Paul Screeton, *Quicksilver Heritage: The Mystic Leys – Their Legacy of Ancient* Wisdom, Thorsons, 1974; Abacus, 1977
2. Paul Screeton, *Mars Bar & Mushy Peas: Urban legend and the cult of celebrity*, Heart of Albion Press, 2008
3. Guy Ragland Phillips, 'The Pattern of Sockburn', *Folklore Frontiers*, No. 7, 1988
4. Guy Ragland Phillips, *Brigantia: A Mysteriography*, Routledge & Kegan Paul, 1976
5. Stan Beckensall, *Hexham: history beneath our feet*, Priv. Pub., 1991
6. Paul Screeton, 'Hunting Dragons and Leys in North Yorkshire', *Northern Earth Mysteries*, No. 5, 1980
7. John Billingsley, post to *Northern Earth* Readers forum (NERf), 16 February 2011
8. Adam Funk, post to *NE*Rf, 17 February 2011
9. Barry Teague, post to *NE*Rf, 17 February 2011
10. http://brit.arch.ac.uk/ba/ba60/feat2.shtml
11. Alby Stone, post to *NE*Rf, 17 February 2011
12. John Billingsley, post to *NE*Rf, 12 November 2011
13 Carol, post to *NE*Rf, 12 November 2011
14 David Taylor, post to *NE*Rf, 15 November 2011

CHAPTER THIRTEEN:
MEETING AN EXORCIST & DELIVERANCE APLENTY

1. www.theanglocatholic.com/2010/01nashdom-abbey
2. Dom Robert Petitpierre, *Exorcism: The Findings of a Commission Convened by the Bishop of Exeter*, Society for Promoting Christian Knowledge, 1972
3. Richard Deutch, *Exorcism: Possession or Obsession?*, Bachman & Turner, 1975
4. Russell Miller, 'The Ghost Hunters', *Daily Mirror Magazine*, n.d.
5. Paul Screeton, *Tales of the Hexham Heads*, private, 1980
6. Paul Screeton, 'The Long Man of Wilmington' column, *The Ley Hunter*, No. 89, 1980
7. Journalists, 'Who is pulling the strings?', 7 January 2011, operation-mockingbird.blogspot.bcom/2011/01,who-is-pulling-the-strings
8. Mark Newton, interviewed by Paul Screeton, 22 June 2011
9. Brian Tilley, 'Catholic community mourn death of beloved priest', *Hexham Courant*, 17 June 2011
10. Anne Ross, interviewed by David Clarke, 2 July 1994

INTERLUDE TWO:
A PHENOMENOLOGICAL CORNUCOPIA (or, weird shit happens)

1.   Paul Screeton, 'Coming Up Heads', *Fortean Times*, No. 59, 1991
       2. Paul Screeton, 'Alan Garner and the Shamanic Process', *Common Ground*, No. 6, 1982;

anthologised in *I Fort The Lore*, CFZ Press, 2011
3. Don Robins, *The Secret Language of Stone*, Rider, 1988
4. Paul Screeton, 'The Hexham Heads', letter, *Fortean Times*, No. 220, 2007
5. Alan Murdie, pers. comm. to David Taylor, 12 August 2011
6 BBC, *Unfair Exchanges*, 20 January 1985
7. Harry Thompson, Viewing Review column, *The Journal*, 26 January 1985
8. John Wade, 'Quatermass and his creator', *Best of British*, March, 20129.
9. Jill Eyers, pers. comm. to Paul Screeton, 2 April 2012
10. Sylvia Ritson interviewed by Paul Screeton, 18 March 2011
11. Don Robins, 'The Hexham Heads', *Alpha*, No. 8, 1980
12. David Clarke with Andy Roberts, *Twilight of the Celtic Gods*, Blandford, 1996
13. Sonia Smith, *Hampshire & The New Forest: Stories of the Supernatural*, Countryside Books, 2011
14. Paul Screeton, 'Priscilla, Cleaner of the Uni', *Folklore Frontiers*, No. 66, 2011
15. Lindsay Allason-Jones, interviewed by Paul Screeton, 2 December 2011

CHAPTER FOURTEEN: GENIUS LOCI & PLACES OF POWER

1. Nigel Pennick, *Earth Harmony*, Century, 1987
2. Nigel Pennick, *Anima Loci*, The Library of European Tradition, 1999
3. John Michell, *The Earth Spirit*, Thames & Hudson, 1975
4. Rudolf Otto, *The Idea of the Holy*, Oxford University Press, 1933
5. Paul Screeton, 'Folklore of the Settle-Carlisle Line', *The Labyrinth*, Issue 3, 2000; *Folklore Frontiers*, No. 39, 2001; *Northern Earth*, No. 102, 2005
6. Roger Luckhurst, 'The Contemporary London Gothic and the limits of the "spectral turn"', *Textual Practice*, Vol. 16, 2002
7. Colin Wison, *Poltergeist! A Study in Destructive Haunting*, New English Library, 1981
8. Nigel Craigie, interview by Paul Screeton, 30 September 2011
9. Mark Newton, talking to Paul Screeton, 22 and 26 June 2011
10. Stu Ferrol, pers. comm., 9 April 2012
11. 'Skeletons of bodies unlock secrets of an ancient villa', *The Times*, 3 December 2011; via *Current Archaeology*, issues 260 and 261
12. http://www.bbc.uk/news/science-environment-14401305
13. Jill Eyers, pers. comm., 2012
14. David Hambling, 'Absolutely True. Honest!', *Flipside*, No. 37, 2009
15. Barry Scott, pers. comm., 14 March 2011
16. Representative pieces on the GaGa costume story as it unfolded: *The Sun*, 9 and 14 September 2010, 23 July 2010 and 13 August 2011
17. Stuart Ferrol, 'The Hexham Wolf', *Fortean Times*, No. 192, 2005
18. Charles Fort, *Lo!*, John Brown Publishing, 1996

CHAPTER 15: 'CURSED' HEADS: ASPECTS OF MISFORTUNE

1. David Clarke, doctoral thesis draft, 1998
2. Keith Ludden, 'There's no flies on Little Mannie', *The Sun*, 2 July 1991
3. David Clarke, doctoral thesis draft, 1998
4. Ian Macgill, 'Cursed Head goes under the Hammer', *Yorkshire Evening Post*, 13 November 1990
5. Sandro Monetti, 'Family Cursed by Humpty Dumpty', *Daily Star*, 14 November 1990
6. 'Curse of the Druid's Head', *Today*, 14 November 1990; Kevin O'Bierne, no title,

Wear Wolf, Number One, 1991
7. Andy Roberts, letter, *Wear Wolf*, 2nd Issue, 1991
8. Steven Teale, 'Changes of fortune for cursed couple', *Bradford Telegraph & Argus*, 28 December 1991
9. Andy Roberts, pers. comm., 24 January 1992
10. David Clarke, pers. comm., 14 December 2011
11. Steve Jones, fortean Yahoo forum, 13 November 2011
12. David Clarke, doctoral thesis draft 1998
13. David Clarke, interviewed by Graham Williamson, on 17 May 2011
14. Lindsay Allason-Jones, interviewed by Paul Screeton, 2 December 2011

CHAPTER SIXTEEN: THE PARANORMAL & PSYCHOLOGY

1. David Taylor, 'The Stone Tape Theory: An examination of the historical origins', *Folklore Frontiers*, No. 68, 2011
2. Dr David Clarke, interviewed by Paul Screeton, 17 May 2011
3. Dominic Brayne, '*Nationwide* and the Celtic heads', *Fortean Times* forum, 22 September 2003
4. Patrick Harpur, *Daimonic Reality*, Viking, 1994
5. Paul Screeton, *Daimonic Reality* review, *Folklore Frontiers*, No. 23, 1994
6. Steve Jones, 'Shuffling the Deck: Hooded Entities and Shapeshifters', *Folklore Frontiers*, No. 67, 2011
7. Tom Graves, *Needles of Stone*, Turnstone Books, 1978
8. Paul Devereux, *Haunted Land: Investigations into Ancient Mysteries and Modern Day Phenomena*, Piatkus, 2001
9. Michael Persinger & Gyslaine Lafreniere, *Space-Time Transients and Unusual Events*, Nelson-Hall, 1977
10. Alexandra David-Neel, *With Mystics & Magicians in Tibet*, Penguin, 1931; republished as *Magic and Mystery in Tibet*, Crown, 1937
11. Kevin McClure, 'Tulpas', *Common Ground*, No. 1, 1981
12. Richard Freeman, *Explore Dragons*, Heart of Albion Press, 2006
13. Jonathan Downes, *The Owlman and Others*, CFZ Press, 4th edition, 2006
14. John Michell, 'Satanic curses: Bogus social workers and demonic abductors', *Folklore Frontiers*, No. 12, 1991.
15. Stuart Bell, *When Salem Came to the Boro: The True Story of the Cleveland Child Abuse Crisis*, Pan, 1988
16. Paul Screeton, 'Suffer the little children', *Folklore Frontiers*, No. 12, 1991

CHAPTER SEVENTEEN:
SUBURBAN SHAMAN, er, DES CRAIGIE?

1. Nigel Craigie, pers. comm., 1 April 2011
2. Harry Ferrol, interviewed by Stu Ferrol, 31 May 2011

CHAPTER EIGHTEEN:
BEDROOM INVADERS

1. Adam Douglas, *The Beast Within*, Orion, 1992
2. Carol K. Mack & Dinah Mack, *A Field Guide to Demons, Vampires, Fallen Angels and other*

subversive spirits, Profile Books, 2010
3. John A. Keel, *Strange Creatures from Time and Space*, Sphere, 1976

CHAPTER NINETEEN:
PSYCHIC BACKLASH?

1. Tony 'Doc' Shiels, *Monstrum! A Wizard's Tale*, Fortean Tomes, 1990
2. Doc Shiels and Paul Screeton, 'Shielsian Shamanism', *The Shaman*, No. 5, 1984; reprinted Paul Screeton, *I Fort The Lore*, CFZ Press, 2011
3. Ronald Sheridan and Anne Ross, *Grotesques and Gargoyles*, David & Charles, 1975
4. Doc Shiels, pers. comm. to Paul Screeton, 4 May 1982
5. Anne Ross, interviewed by David Clarke on 2 July 1994
6. George P Hansen, *The Trickster and the Paranormal*, Xlibris, 2001
7. Keith Hardiman, pers. comm. to Paul Screeton, excerpts 9 December 2011 and 14 May 2012 combined
8. David Clarke, doctoral thesis draft, 1998

CHAPTER TWENTY:
COLIN ROBSON AT 52 (TALES OF THE UNEXPLAINED)

1. Colin Robson, interviewed by Paul Screeton, 17 April 2012

CHAPTER TWENTY-ONE:
WHEREABOUTS OF THE HEXHAM HEADS?

1. David Tansley, *Omens of Awareness*, Nevill Spearman, 1977; Sphere, 1977
2. Jane Hamilton, 'We're all just 4 mates apart', *The Sun*, 23 November 2011
3. Lindsay Allason-Jones, interviewed by Paul Screeton, 2 December 2011
4. Colin Robson, interviewed by Paul Screeton, 17 April 2012

CHAPTER TWENTY-THREE:
POSTSCRIPT / APPENDIX

1. Martin Gately and Quique Alcatena, 'The Cryptid Kid', *Fortean Times*, No. 268, 2010

THE WORLD'S WEIRDEST PUBLISHING COMPANY

HOW TO START A PUBLISHING EMPIRE

Unlike most mainstream publishers, we have a non-commercial remit, and our mission statement claims that "we publish books because they deserve to be published, not because we think that we can make money out of them". Our motto is the Latin Tag *Pro bona causa facimus* (we do it for good reason), a slogan taken from a children's book *The Case of the Silver Egg* by the late Desmond Skirrow.

WIKIPEDIA: "The first book published was in 1988. *Take this Brother may it Serve you Well* was a guide to *Beatles* bootlegs by Jonathan Downes. It sold quite well, but was hampered by very poor production values, being photocopied, and held together by a plastic clip binder. In 1988 A5 clip binders were hard to get hold of, so the publishers took A4 binders and cut them in half with a hacksaw. It now reaches surprisingly high prices second hand.

The production quality improved slightly over the years, and after 1999 all the books produced were ringbound with laminated colour covers. In 2004, however, they signed an agreement with Lightning Source, and all books are now produced perfect bound, with full colour covers."

Until 2010 all our books, the majority of which are/were on the subject of mystery animals and allied disciplines, were published by `CFZ Press`, the publishing arm of the Centre for Fortean Zoology (CFZ), and we urged our readers and followers to draw a discreet veil over the books that we published that were completely off topic to the CFZ.

However, in 2010 we decided that enough was enough and launched a second imprint, `Fortean Words` which aims to cover a wide range of non animal-related esoteric subjects. Other imprints will be launched as and when we feel like it, however the basic ethos of the company remains the same: Our job is to publish books and magazines that we feel are worth publishing, whether or not they are going to sell. Money is, after all - as my dear old Mama once told me - a rather vulgar subject, and she would be rolling in her grave if she thought that her eldest son was somehow in `trade`.

Luckily, so far our tastes have turned out not to be that rarified after all, and we have sold far more books than anyone ever thought that we would, so there is a moral in there somewhere…

Jon Downes,
Woolsery, North Devon
July 2010

CFZ PRESS

Other Books in Print

Sea Serpent Carcasses: Scotland *by Glen Vaudrey*
Headhunters of the Amazon *by W. Up de Graaf*
The Grail by Ronan Coghlan
CFZ Yearbook 2012 edited by Jon and Corinna Downes
ORANG PENDEK: Sumatra's Forgotten Ape by Richard Freeman
THE MYSTERY ANIMALS OF THE BRITISH ISLES: London by Neil Arnold
CFZ EXPEDITION REPORT: India 2010 by Richard Freeman *et al*
The Cryptid Creatures of Florida by Scott Marlow
Dead of Night by Lee Walker
The Mystery Animals of the British Isles: The Northern Isles by Glen Vaudrey
THE MYSTERY ANIMALS OF THE BRTISH ISLES: Gloucestershire and Worcestershire
by Paul Williams
When Bigfoot Attacks by Michael Newton
Weird Waters – The Mystery Animals of Scandinavia: Lake and Sea Monsters by Lars Thomas
The Inhumanoids by Barton Nunnelly
Monstrum! A Wizard's Tale by Tony "Doc" Shiels
CFZ Yearbook 2011 edited by Jonathan Downes
Karl Shuker's Alien Zoo by Shuker, Dr Karl P.N
Tetrapod Zoology Book One by Naish, Dr Darren
The Mystery Animals of Ireland by Gary Cunningham and Ronan Coghlan
Monsters of Texas by Gerhard, Ken
The Great Yokai Encyclopaedia by Freeman, Richard
NEW HORIZONS: Animals & Men *issues 16-20 Collected Editions Vol. 4* by Downes, Jonathan
A Daintree Diary -
Tales from Travels to the Daintree Rainforest in tropical north Queensland, Australia by Portman, Carl
Strangely Strange but Oddly Normal by Roberts, Andy
Centre for Fortean Zoology Yearbook 2010 by Downes, Jonathan
Predator Deathmatch by Molloy, Nick
Star Steeds and other Dreams by Shuker, Karl
CHINA: A Yellow Peril? by Muirhead, Richard
Mystery Animals of the British Isles: The Western Isles by Vaudrey, Glen
Giant Snakes - Unravelling the coils of mystery by Newton, Michael

Mystery Animals of the British Isles: Kent by Arnold, Neil
Centre for Fortean Zoology Yearbook 2009 by Downes, Jonathan
CFZ EXPEDITION REPORT: Russia 2008 by Richard Freeman *et al*, Shuker, Karl (fwd)
Dinosaurs and other Prehistoric Animals on Stamps - A Worldwide catalogue by Shuker, Karl P. N
Dr Shuker's Casebook by Shuker, Karl P.N
The Island of Paradise - chupacabra UFO crash retrievals,
and accelerated evolution on the island of Puerto Rico by Downes, Jonathan
The Mystery Animals of the British Isles: Northumberland and Tyneside by Hallowell, Michael J
Centre for Fortean Zoology Yearbook 1997 by Downes, Jonathan (Ed)
Centre for Fortean Zoology Yearbook 2002 by Downes, Jonathan (Ed)
Centre for Fortean Zoology Yearbook 2000/1 by Downes, Jonathan (Ed)
Centre for Fortean Zoology Yearbook 1998 by Downes, Jonathan (Ed)
Centre for Fortean Zoology Yearbook 2003 by Downes, Jonathan (Ed)
In the wake of Bernard Heuvelmans by Woodley, Michael A
CFZ EXPEDITION REPORT: Guyana 2007 by Richard Freeman *et al*, Shuker, Karl (fwd)
Centre for Fortean Zoology Yearbook 1999 by Downes, Jonathan (Ed)
Big Cats in Britain Yearbook 2008 by Fraser, Mark (Ed)
Centre for Fortean Zoology Yearbook 1996 by Downes, Jonathan (Ed)
THE CALL OF THE WILD - Animals & Men issues 11-15
Collected Editions Vol. 3 by Downes, Jonathan (ed)
Ethna's Journal by Downes, C N
Centre for Fortean Zoology Yearbook 2008 by Downes, J (Ed)
DARK DORSET -Calendar Custome by Newland, Robert J
Extraordinary Animals Revisited by Shuker, Karl
MAN-MONKEY - In Search of the British Bigfoot by Redfern, Nick
Dark Dorset Tales of Mystery, Wonder and Terror by Newland, Robert J and Mark North
Big Cats Loose in Britain by Matthews, Marcus
MONSTER! - The A-Z of Zooform Phenomena by Arnold, Neil
The Centre for Fortean Zoology 2004 Yearbook by Downes, Jonathan (Ed)
The Centre for Fortean Zoology 2007 Yearbook by Downes, Jonathan (Ed)
CAT FLAPS! Northern Mystery Cats by Roberts, Andy
Big Cats in Britain Yearbook 2007 by Fraser, Mark (Ed)
BIG BIRD! - Modern sightings of Flying Monsters by Gerhard, Ken
THE NUMBER OF THE BEAST - Animals & Men issues 6-10
Collected Editions Vol. 1 by Downes, Jonathan (Ed)
IN THE BEGINNING - Animals & Men issues 1-5 Collected Editions Vol. 1 by Downes, Jonathan
STRENGTH THROUGH KOI - They saved Hitler's Koi and other stories by Downes, Jonathan
The Smaller Mystery Carnivores of the Westcountry by Downes, Jonathan
CFZ EXPEDITION REPORT: Gambia 2006 by Richard Freeman *et al*, Shuker, Karl (fwd)
The Owlman and Others by Jonathan Downes
The Blackdown Mystery by Downes, Jonathan
Big Cats in Britain Yearbook 2006 by Fraser, Mark (Ed)
Fragrant Harbours - Distant Rivers by Downes, John T
Only Fools and Goatsuckers by Downes, Jonathan
Monster of the Mere by Jonathan Downes
Dragons:More than a Myth by Freeman, Richard Alan
Granfer's Bible Stories by Downes, John Tweddell
Monster Hunter by Downes, Jonathan

Fortean Words

T he Centre for Fortean Zoology has for several years led the field in Fortean publishing. CFZ Press is the only publishing company specialising in books on monsters and mystery animals. CFZ Press has published more books on this subject than any other company in history and has attracted such well known authors as Andy Roberts, Nick Redfern, Michael Newton, Dr Karl Shuker, Neil Arnold, Dr Darren Naish, Jon Downes, Ken Gerhard and Richard Freeman.

Now CFZ Press are launching a new imprint. Fortean Words is a new line of books dealing with Fortean subjects other than cryptozoology, which is - after all - the subject the CFZ are best known for. Fortean Words is being launched with a spectacular multi-volume series called *Haunted Skies* which covers British UFO sightings between 1940 and 2010. Former policeman John Hanson and his long-suffering partner Dawn Holloway have compiled a peerless library of sighting reports, many that have not been made public before.

Other forthcoming books include a look at the Berwyn Mountains UFO case by renowned Fortean Andy Roberts and a series of books by transatlantic researcher Nick Redfern.

CFZ Press are dedicated to maintaining the fine quality of their works with Fortean Words. New authors tackling new subjects will always be encouraged, and we hope that our books will continue to be as ground breaking and popular as ever.

Haunted Skies Volume One 1940-1959 by John Hanson and Dawn Holloway
Haunted Skies Volume Two 1960-1965 by John Hanson and Dawn Holloway
Haunted Skies Volume Three 1965-1967 by John Hanson and Dawn Holloway
Haunted Skies Volume Four 1968-1971 by John Hanson and Dawn Holloway
Haunted Skies Volume Five 1972-1974 by John Hanson and Dawn Holloway
Haunted Skies Volume Six 1975-1977 by John Hanson and Dawn Holloway
Grave Concerns by Kai Roberts

Police and the Paranormal by Andy Owens
Dead of Night by Lee Walker
Space Girl Dead on Spaghetti Junction - an anthology by Nick Redfern
I Fort the Lore - an anthology by Paul Screeton
UFO Down - the Berwyn Mountains UFO Crash by Andy Roberts
Warminster: Cradle of Contact by Kevin Goodman

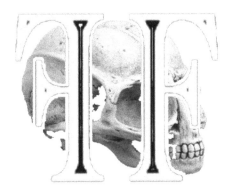

Fortean Fiction

J ust before Christmas 2011, we launched our third imprint, this time dedicated to - let's see if you guessed it from the title - fictional books with a Fortean or cryptozoological theme. We have published a few fictional books in the past, but now think that because of our rising reputation as publishers of quality Forteana, that a dedicated fiction imprint was the order of the day.

We launched with four titles:

Green Unpleasant Land by Richard Freeman
Left Behind by Harriet Wadham
Dark Ness by Tabitca Cope
Snap! By Steven Bredice

Lightning Source UK Ltd.
Milton Keynes UK
UKHW031443111120
373209UK00011B/1011